Cambridge Studies in Cultural Systems

Clifford Geertz, editor

1   The anthropological romance of Bali 1597–1972: dynamic perspectives in
    marriage and caste, politics and religion
    James A. Boon

2   Sherpas through their rituals
    Sherry B. Ortner

Sherpas through their rituals

SHERRY B. ORTNER

Associate Professor of Anthropology
University of Michigan

CAMBRIDGE UNIVERSITY PRESS

Cambridge
London   New York   Melbourne

Published by the Syndics of the Cambridge University Press
The Pitt Building, Trumpington Street, Cambridge CB2 1RP
Bentley House, 200 Euston Road, London NW1 2DB
32 East 57th Street, New York, NY 10022, USA
296 Beaconsfield Parade, Middle Park, Melbourne 3206, Australia

© Cambridge University Press 1978

First published 1978

Printed in the United States of America
Typeset by Robert Bush, Colchester, Essex, England
Printed and bound by the Murray Printing Company,
Westford, Massachusetts

Library of Congress Cataloging in Publication Data
Ortner, Sherry B   1941–
Sherpas through their rituals.
(Cambridge studies in cultural systems; 2)
Bibliography: p.
1. Sherpas–Religion. 2. Buddhist doctrines–
Himalaya region. I. Title. II. Series.
BL2032.S45O77   294.3'4'3   76–62582
ISBN 0 521 21536 6 hard cover
ISBN 0 521 29216 6 paperback

In gratitude to Samuel Ortner

In memory of Gertrude Ortner and Ida Panitch

Contents

Preface   *page* ix

1   Introduction: some notes on ritual   1

2   The surface contours of the Sherpa world   10
    Economy   14
    Social organization   18
    Religion   30

3   Nyungne: problems of marriage, family, and asceticism   33
    The ritual   34
    The problems of the ritual   36
      Merit making and social atomism   36
      Gods, parents, and social sentiments   41
      Ascetic ideology and the crisis of the children's marriages   43
    The solutions of the ritual   48
      The fostering of altruism   48
      Nyungne as passage to postparenthood   52
      Ascetic ideology and family structure   55

4   Hospitality: problems of exchange, status, and authority   61
    The party   61
    The problems of hospitality   65
      The problem of giving and receiving   65
      The power of food   68
      Problems of status, power, and authority   74
    The solutions of hospitality   78
      The "empty mouth" principle and the etiquette of giving and
        receiving   78
      Seating and joking: the party as politics   82
      "Civilized" coercion and the reproduction of hosts   85

vii

5   Exorcisms: problems of wealth, pollution, and reincarnation   91
         The rituals   92
             The do dzongup   93
             The gyepshi   95
         The problems of the rituals   98
             Demons, greed, and social predation   98
             Pollution, disintegration of self, and subversion of the social order   103
             Reincarnation theory and the social order   110
         The solutions of the rituals   113
             Exorcisms as purifications: reconstituting the psychic hierarchy   114
             Rich and poor: resynthesizing the social hierarchy   120
             Self and social order: dilemma   125

6   Offering rituals: problems of religion, anger, and social cooperation   128
         The ritual calendar and the rite of offerings   129
         The problems of the ritual   132
             Torma and the body problem   132
             Gods, demons, and the problem of moods   137
             Hospitality, anger, and body   141
         The solutions of the ritual   144
             Bodying the gods   147
             The molding of anger   149
             Hospitality: mediating religion and the social order   152

7   Conclusions: Buddhism and society   157
         The ritual mechanism   163

     Notes   171

     Bibliography   187

     Index   191

Preface

The field research upon which this book is based was carried out between September 1966 and February 1968. It was made possible by a National Institutes of Mental Health Predoctoral Fellowship and a National Science Foundation Field Research Grant. To both NIMH and NSF I extend my appreciation and thanks, and my hope that their programs, so valuable to scholarship in anthropology, will soon again attain the scope they had at the time I was fortunate to be in graduate school.

The research was first written up as a dissertation for the Department of Anthropology, University of Chicago. For their encouragement and criticism of my work on the dissertation, I would like to thank the members of the department, particularly Professors Clifford Geertz (now at the Institute for Advanced Study, Princeton, New Jersey), Nur Yalman (now at Harvard University), McKim Marriott, David M. Schneider, and Melford E. Spiro (now at the University of California at San Diego).

But this book is not in any direct sense a revision of the dissertation. Basically, I went back to the field notes and started again from scratch. The dissertation contains important data not included here, and I have indicated some of it in notes to the present text. The overall thrust of the book, as well as most of the specific discussions and analyses, are not in the dissertation.

In Nepal, many people were helpful in facilitating my work. The people of the Foreign Ministry of His Majesty's Government assisted me in securing my original permission to live and work in the Sherpa area, and were able to arrange things so that I was allowed to renew this permission through intermediaries, saving me twenty days of trekking every three months.

The people at the Swiss Association for Technical Assistance (SATA) were also very helpful — they received my mail and conveyed it to me by an incredibly complex method for the entire period of my stay, and extended many other kindnesses as well. I would particularly like to mention Regula Rutishauser (now Regula Roth), who was conducting a school for Tibetan immigrant children at the SATA center at Chialsa, and N. B. Chhetri, who was associated with the SATA agricultural project at Jiri.

Dr. and Mrs. John McKinnon of New Zealand, who were in charge of what was then the only hospital in the Sherpa area, at Kunde, also extended their kind hospitality (including several hot showers) to me. In addition, they supplied medical advice and supplies for me to convey to the people of "Dzemu," as well as information based on their own observations of the Sherpas of their area.

I would also like to mention Mr. and Mrs. Tom Mendies, proprietors of the Snow View Hotel, whose many small favors made my three separate stays in Kathmandu genuinely relaxing and productive.

Of the Sherpas themselves, I must single out my cook, translator (in the initial phases), and all-around assistant, Mingma Tenzing of Thami, for a major citation. (Mingma was sent to me by Col. James Roberts, who thus gets a vote of thanks as well.) Mingma's unfailing consideration, good humor, and fundamental decency contributed to an extent that I cannot begin to measure to the success of the field project from beginning to end. My debt to him is enormous, and my gratitude in equal measure.

It is impossible for me to mention by name all the other Sherpas (as well as many Tibetans, especially monks) who cooperated with me in what to them must have often appeared strange and useless endeavors, who submitted patiently to my questions and gave serious and thoughtful answers, invited me to their homes and temples, tolerated my intrusion at essentially private events, and in general — needless to say — made the whole undertaking an actuality. To the villagers of "Dzemu," and of all the other Sherpa villages I visited, and to the lamas and monks of the various Sherpa and (immigrant) Tibetan monasteries where I was so kindly and openly received, I must express my great gratitude.

My close friend and colleague, Robert A. Paul, was with me in the field, doing his own research on Sherpa monasticism. It is impossible to estimate his contribution to the success of the fieldwork and the dissertation, but I wish formally to thank him here in this small way.

The writing of this book has had other support, both financial and personal. It was launched by a grant (#2680) from the Wenner-Gren Foundation for Anthropological Research. And it was sustained in a major way by a year at the Institute for Advanced Study in Princeton, New Jersey, underwritten by National Science Foundation funds (GS–31730 X 2).

Many friends have read all or parts of this book, and offered extremely useful criticism and encouragement: Robert Brenner, Clifford Geertz, Robert Paul, Paul Rabinow, Michelle Rosaldo, Renato Rosaldo, Terence Turner, and Harriet Whitehead. In addition, the "Chicago Seminar" in New York City discussed parts of the book at some of our meetings. Its members included, in addition to Rabinow, Paul, and myself, Steve Barnett, Karen Blu, Jean-Paul Dumont, Kevin Dwyer, Nancy Foner, Judith Friedlander, and Edward Schieffelin.

Some final notes on the book: I have changed the name of the village in which I worked to "Dzemu," which means "beautiful" in the Sherpa language. I have also given pseudonyms to all individuals, most monasteries and most other villages mentioned in the text. The Sherpas' position in Nepal, geographically as well as politically, has certain sensitive aspects. The pseudonyms are by way of protection of privacy, between neighbor and neighbor, village and village, and for the Sherpas as a whole vis-à-vis governmental agencies and even foreign political interests. I have tried throughout the book to provide the information necessary to situate socio-logically an informant's statement, or to generalize about a village or a monastery. I see no need to specify people and places further, and some potential harm in doing so.

The spelling of native terms is neither phonetic nor based on some standard set of conventions. The terms have been rendered in writing so as to evoke from the English-speaking reader the sounds as I heard them. Probably the major distortion wrought by this tactic is the loss of the distinction between the long *a* (usually trans-literated as *ā*, and pronounced as in the English *calm*), and the short *a* (usually trans-literated as *a*, and pronounced as in the English *cut*). I have rendered both simply by *a*.

After completing the manuscript and turning it in to the publisher, I revisited the Sherpas for the first time since the original fieldwork. I spent four months among them, in Kathmandu, in "Dzemu," and in a village in Khumbu, making a film for Granada television of England. Restraining my temptation to write an essay on the powerful experience of returning to one's original field area after a long time, I will simply say the following. First, I felt strongly reassured that the overall argument of the book is essentially correct; indeed, I came to wonder what took me so long to see it. And second, the visit provided me with some new data relevant to particular discussions in the book. In some cases I have incorporated them into the text, in others I have put them in notes, indicating that they were obtained in 1976 rather than in the "ethnographic present" of the text, which is 1966–1968. I have also indicated, where relevant, whether they were obtained in Solu or in Khumbu.

Finally, I must say that there is always a sense in which an anthropological analysis (or even a description) does some sort of violence to the people and the culture being discussed. Readers who have had contact with Sherpas, and who have found them to be warm, friendly, hospitable, and generous (as I did), will find it peculiar that I talk about antisocial tendencies in Sherpa society. To this I can only respond, first, that I think the Sherpas often find it easier to be generous to out-siders than to one another, and second, that my discussions of "the closed family," of the difficulties of exchange, and so forth, are *analytical* discussions. Often the Sherpas are successful in achieving solidarity and mutual support, but often too they are not. My argument is that when they are not successful, when sociality fails and relations are strained, this is not a matter of individual "deviance," but arises out of structures that systematically constrain people's behavior in this not-unexpected direction.

Similarly, the discussions about demons and exorcisms may lead the reader to imagine that Sherpa religion is a religion of fear. There is indeed some nervousness about demonic infiltration, as well as about retaliation from guardian gods and spirits who have been offended in some way. But the Sherpas do not walk around in a state of religious anxiety, and I wish here to correct any such impression that might be conveyed by my discussion. The Sherpas perform most of their rituals because, although this might sound pedestrian, it is *traditional* to perform those rituals, and because disorder might ensue if they don't. The world is not a continuously threatening place; the point is to insure that it doesn't become so.

S. B. O.

New York
February 1977

1. Introduction: some notes on ritual

One may envision the task of an ethnography as opening a culture to readers, un-
folding it, revealing it, providing not only a sense of surface form and rhythm, but
also a sense of inner connections and interactions. If this is one's vision of the task,
certain ways of launching upon it will be more powerful and effective than others.
One could of course begin with the standard categories — kinship, economy, politics, religion — yet this approach is problematic, not only because the categories
are externally imposed but because they are undynamic. They do not carry one
into an experience of the interconnections that must be at the heart of the discussion.

One could also proceed by way of, to borrow a phrase from Kenneth Burke, "the
representative anecdote," the little vignette of social life actually observed, that was
for the field-ethnographer, and will ideally be for the reader, especially revealing
of important cultural dynamics. One recalls, for example, the incident of the dis-
turbed Javanese funeral described by Geertz (1957b), where the corpse could not
get buried for the politics of the situation. The episode raised problems of religious
and political interpretation for all present, Javanese and ethnographer alike. As in
this example, the incidents that are used as representative anecdotes in ethnography
generally involve breakdown or conflict, moments where the rules are called into
question, or contradictory rules are invoked, where "reality bargaining" (Rosen)
is called into play. The very uncertainty of the situation, the very unpredictability
of the outcome, serve to bring to the foreground cultural "stuff" that is normally so
taken for granted as to be almost inarticulable.

One could also approach the presentation through what Singer has called
"cultural performances," rituals or other culturally formalized events that the people
themselves see as embodying in some way the essence of their culture, as dramatizing the basic myths and visions of reality, the basic values and moral truths, upon
which they feel their world rests. One recalls here Warner's superb account of the
Yankee City tercentenary celebration where, in something like an anthropologist's
dream, the natives constructed a parade of floats dramatizing forty-two carefully
selected (and highly interpreted) events in the town's history. In this event, as
Warner says, "the citizens of Yankee City collectively state what they believe themselves to be" (89). Less spectacularly, every society has some major ritual events,

1

Mingma Tenzing, his wife Pasang Hlamu, and their son Ang Tsultim

activated by culturally defined life crises, or geared to the rhythms of the calendar, that are for its members deeply meaningful, and that can reveal to us the sources and forces of meaning in its culture.[1]

Both approaches — through representative anecdotes and cultural performances — can provide powerful entrée into the workings of a particular society. The choice may ultimately reflect more the intellectual style of the ethnographer than the intrinsic superiority of one or the other approach, although one could argue that cultural performances have the advantage of being selected, as it were, by the culture rather than by the observer. In any case, this book in fact works through cultural performances, utilizing three Sherpa religious rituals and one recurrent formal secular event to "open" Sherpa culture to the reader. Such an approach to a culture through what may be called its formal statements, its moments of greatest self-display, thus requires further comment.·

To say, as I did above, that such performances — generally rituals — dramatize basic assumptions of fact and value in the culture is to summarize what is actually a far more complex point. More specifically and accurately, such "fundamental assumptions" are actually constructed, or reconstructed, and their fundamentality reestablished, in the course of the rituals themselves. Rituals do not begin with the eternal verities, but arrive at them. They begin with some cultural problem (or several at once), stated or unstated, and then work various operations upon it, arriving at "solutions" — reorganizations and reinterpretations of the elements that produce a newly meaningful whole. The solutions (and the means of arriving at them) embody the fundamental cultural assumptions and orientations with which we are partly concerned.

Equally important, however, are the problems from which the ritual departs. By this I do not mean the problem of curing illness, or turning boys into men, or whatever the stated purpose may be. Rather I mean the conflicts and contradictions of social experience and cultural meaning that are encoded in, and alluded to by, the ritual symbolism. Such issues are of course linked, perhaps arbitrarily, perhaps not, to the stated concern of the ritual. The Sherpa rite of atonement, for example, utilizes symbols of the family, and we must ask why a sense of sin is culturally tied to, and takes meaning from, family organization (and vice versa). The Sherpa rites of exorcism utilize symbols of wealth and poverty, and we must ask why the demons that are exorcised, and the defilements that are cleansed, derive meaning from inequities in the economic and political structure (and vice versa). The symbols of the rituals, in other words, lead us toward discovery of structural conflict, contradiction, and stress in the wider social and cultural world.

These points determine the organization of this book. After a general ethnographic chapter, each subsequent chapter begins with a brief description of a cultural performance. Following the description, the rite (or in one case secular event) is then dissected, and some of its symbolic elements are used as leads or guides into exploring problematic structures, relationships, and ideas of the culture. The first half of each chapter, in other words, consists of ethnographic description, but description constrained by the ritual context in which the problematic phenomena were signaled. Thus, for example, the issue of status ranking is highlighted at secular parties, since everyone must sit in rank order. In this context (Chapter 4) I thus explore a range of problems posed by the status hierarchy in secular social relations. When in the following chapter I consider exorcisms, on the other hand, the issue of status arises again, signaled by the symbols of wealth and poverty in the ritual. In this context, then, I explore the relationship between the status hierarchy on the one hand, and religious ideology and institutions on the other. The use of multiple ritual "lenses" is thus not only a device for getting at different problems in the culture, but also serves — Rashomon-like — as a perspective shifter, a way of seeing different aspects of any given institution, which may be problematic in different ways in different contexts, or for individuals in different social locations or at different stages of life.

If the first half of each chapter is a ritual-guided ethnographic account, the second half returns to the action of the ritual and asks what sorts of solutions to the problems, what sorts of experience of them are systematically constructed over the course of the event. Here we are in the realm of symbolic analysis as such, analysis of the semantic mechanisms by which the symbols and meanings are interrelated and moved toward the conclusions and resolution of the rite. If, loosely, the first half of each chapter is paradigmatic, a description of the universe of elements upon which the ritual will operate, the second half is, again loosely, syntagmatic, an analysis of the narrative or discursive organization of these elements constituting the movement of the ritual from formulation of problem to experience of solution.

This dimension of the analysis in turn raises the question of what ritual does, not as a heuristic device for us, but as a certain sort of event and experience for the society and the people. The traditional answer to this question for anthropology has been in functionalist terms, stressing the ways in which ritual shores up and stabilizes existing structures, reinforces norms, and contributes to the reproduction of the system. The very concept of ritual, within this view, embodies notions of accommodation, reconciliation, mediation. Ritual generates or regenerates a given view of the world, and engenders commitment to existing institutional structures and modes of social relationship. Ritual restores equilibrium, however unstable or antagonistic it may be. A ritual that shatters one's world view and one's social relations is either not a ritual as the term is normally used, or else is in the service of some other system of meaning and relationships to which it delivers one.

Certainly such assertions are not "wrong," and certainly ritual plays an important role in keeping the system together. But the functionalist perspective, as has by now been well explored, has a number of problems. One of the most troublesome is that it is so broadly applicable that it tells one virtually nothing. Any element of social process can be shown, through ingenious argumentation, to play a role in the restoration of equilibrium and the validation of the status quo. This is particularly the case when the analysis is confined to a body of synchronic data, where long-range trends of change are not visible, and where it is never clear whether even the most apparently "contradictory" elements may not be working to the advantage of, rather than tending to undermine, existing structures. It is always possible to show, and it has always been a standard functionalist line of analysis to show, how apparently "dysfunctional" elements of the social process really serve the system by providing outlets for pressures and resentments built up within existing structures.

More modern varieties of functionalism, careful to avoid this particular analytic cliché, but still concerned to understand how the status quo is sustained despite evident inequities and contradictions, focus upon the ways in which various elements of the system — especially "ideology" and ritual — mediate contradictions or in other ways function to 'mystify' the workings of the system to actors embedded in it. I do not actually deny the (limited) validity of these neofunctionalist orientations, and some of my interpretations will arrive at points consistent with such a perspective.

Yet however subtly, insidiously, and pervasively Sherpa religion and ritual may serve to "mystify," and hence perpetuate, contradictory and oppressive social structures, this perception cannot be the starting point of an analysis of these phenomena. Whatever latent functions religion may perform for the system and the status quo, it is first and foremost a system of meanings — goals, values, concerns, visions, world constructions — and we cannot know in any nontrivial way what it does — or how it does it — until we know what it says. Precisely the same may be said of ritual. Within ritual, by definition a situation removed from the normal processes of social life, what we find is primarily manipulation of consciousness, of, by, and for actors, through symbolic objects, constructions, and arrangements. These objects and arrangements embody cultural, and especially religious, meaning, conveyed to actors over the course of their participation, and realized by actors as they achieve appropriate structures of consciousness. The ritual process is in the first instance a matter of meaning creation for actors, whatever latent functions it may perform for the system at large.

Now of course most meaning arrived at by actors in ritual is already "there," the historically developed and socially rooted body of conceptions and orderings of consciousness that we call "culture." The ritual process, then, is a matter of shaping actors in such a way that they wind up appropriating cultural meaning as personally held orientations. At the same time, however, because cultural orientations are, at the abstract level, diffuse, general, somewhat unsystematic, and often mutually contradictory, it is in ritual that they receive the shaping and systematization that render them more directly relevant to and reflective of the realities of actual social life. Ritual, then, is a sort of two-way transformer, shaping consciousness in conformity with culture, but at the same time shaping culture in conformity with the more immediate social-action and social-structural determinants of consciousness in everyday life.

I am, however, primarily concerned with the first aspect of the process, the shaping of consciousness that takes place in ritual, what Godfrey Lienhardt called "the control of experience." The terms "consciousness" and "experience" pose some difficulty for anthropologists, implying as they do some sort of access to actors' psychological states. It seems incontrovertible that the ritual intent is to affect psychological states, facilitated by a variety of well-established dissociation-inducing mechanisms — music, dance, rhythmic chant, verbal repetition, incense, and the like. Yet to be on the safe side of this question of psychological imputation, I could simply say (and can easily show) that there is a restructuring of *meaning* in ritual, leaving aside the question of whether all or some or none of the participants actually experience this as a genuine reorganization of seeing and feeling. I shall, however, maintain the position of assuming a more permeable boundary between what happens "out there" in the public process of the ritual, and what the participants actually experience in going through it, or more accurately, in going through hundreds of performances of it over the course of a lifetime. Ritual may be, to adapt a phrase from Geertz, "a story they tell themselves about themselves" (1972: 26), but it is rarely "just a story"; assuming any degree of engagement in the symbolic process on the part of the participants, it is also a felt experience they undergo. I would argue further that any ritual worth its salt makes nonengagement difficult, at least for the duration. People of course need not attend, and when they do, it may be for reasons (sheer custom, keeping up social standing, lack of anything better to do, etc.) quite extraneous to the intent of the rite. Yet once they get in the door, as it were, I shall assume that the process is powerful enough to engage them and draw them through the transformations of meaning/consciousness that the ritual embodies.

This particular view of ritual, as restructuring actors' perceptions, feelings, and interpretations of their world through various processes of symbolic/semantic manipulation, is assumed in a number of important anthropological studies.[2] One, however, both describes and demonstrates the process with particular clarity, and parallels most closely the approach I shall be taking in this book: Godfrey Lienhardt's monograph, *Divinity and Experience.* As a way of both contextualizing and forecasting my own analytic intentions, then, I shall summarize his discussion here.

Lienhardt provides detailed analysis both of the particular symbolic elements and the overall narrative progression of a series of Dinka rituals, showing the symbolically manipulated movement from defined problematic states to subtle resolutions. The resolutions in turn are realized, as he says, as reorganized subjective *experiences* of the problematic elements, reorganized relationships between self and situation. Lienhardt shows, in other words, how ritual creates a transformation of subjective *orientation* to the "facts" of the situation. I shall quote him at some length, for at the time I read these passages, many years ago, they were a sort of revelation to me, a powerful reorganization of my own (intellectual) experience of ritual:

The practice called *thuic* involves knotting a tuft of grass to indicate that the one who makes the knot hopes and intends to contrive some sort of constriction or delay. . . . No Dinka thinks that by performing such an action he has actually assured the result he hopes for. . . . This "mystical" action is not a substitute for practical or technical action, but a complement to it and preparation for it. The man who ties such a knot has made an external, physical representation of a well-formed mental intention. He has produced a model of his desires and hopes, upon which to base renewed practical endeavor. (283)

As Lienhardt says, the action of *thuic* is relatively trivial, yet

the principle involved . . . is similar to that which obtains in symbolic action in situations which, by their very nature, preclude the possibility of technical or practical action as a complete alternative. (ibid.)

Lienhardt thus applies the same principle to the analysis of a series of other rituals, culminating in the analysis of the mortuary ceremonies of the masters of the fishing spear, who are buried alive lest they die a natural death and take the vitality of the society with them.

. . . the ceremonies described in no way prevent the ultimate recognition of the ageing and physical death of those for whom they are performed. This death is recognized; but it is the public experience of it, for the survivors, which is deliberately modified by the performance of these ceremonies. It is clear also that this is the Dinka intention in performing the rites. They do not think that they have made their masters of the fishing-spear personally immortal by burying them before they have become corpses, or, in some accounts, by anticipating their deaths by ritual killing. (313–14)

Or again:

The Dinka know, as we have said, that the master dies. What they represent in contriving the death which they give him is the conservation of the "life" which they themselves think they receive from him, and not the conservation of his own personal life. The latter, indeed, is finally taken away from him by his people so that they may seem to divide it from the public "life" which is in his keeping, and which must not depart from them with his death. . . . The human symbolic action involved in the "artificial" burial must be seen to transform the experience of a leader's death into a concentrated public experience of vitality . . . (316–17)

And as a summary statement:

The symbolic actions . . . thus re-create, and even dramatize, situations which they aim to control, and the experience of which they effectively modulate. If they do not change actual historical or physical events – as the Dinka in some cases believe them to do – they do change and regulate the Dinka's experience of those events. (291)

Lienhardt's discussion implicitly embodies an approach to ritual (and other aspects of cultural process) later articulated more explicitly by Clifford Geertz. And while Geertz tends to be less interested in analysis of narrative sequence – in movement "from problem to solution" – then Lienhardt was or than I will be, he provides both an overall view and a number of specific concepts that lead us more systematically into the process of cultural analysis. It will be useful, then, to sketch the outlines of his approach here.[3]

The fundamental assumption running through Geertz's work is that human beings constantly generate models of their own situation, in order to orient themselves and hence function in an effective and satisfying manner within it. A "culture" is the system of such publicly and collectively subscribed-to models operating for a given group at a given period of time – the terms, forms, categories, images, and the like that function to interpret a people's own situation to themselves.

The shape and content of any particular symbolic complex may be said to be a product of two distinct factors, and it is thus in terms of these factors that it must be analyzed and understood. These are, *first,* the actual social, historical, natural, and psychological realities operating in the society at the time; and *second*, the (conscious or unconscious) strategic (what some would call "ideological") orientations encoded in the ways in which the symbols select and interpret those realities. An example of a relatively conscious source of "strategic bias" in a particular symbolic construct might be the "interests" of the subgroup putting forth that particular construct; an example of a relatively unconscious source of bias might be the tendency of a group to define its reality in contradistinction to that of a neighboring group. In general, it is at least fair to say that the "ethos" of a culture, its particular style and bias in construing reality, is the product of complex historical development and is only partly amenable to synchronic explanation.

Geertz's "model of/model for" distinction (1966) refers to the two dimensions of analysis noted above. The "model of" aspect refers to how cultural symbols "catch up" and attempt to render intelligible the immediate problems of social structure, economic structure, kinship, ecology, and the like — not to mention the more existential dilemmas of suffering, evil, and bafflement — in a given society. And the same symbolic models that "represent" the complex realities of the group also cast them in a certain light, interpret them, in ways that — the "model for" aspect — shape attitude and even action toward "evidently" reasonable congruence with the definitions of the situation. As Kenneth Burke, discussing poetry and other "critical and imaginative works," succinctly put it: "[They] size up the situation, name their structures and outstanding ingredients, and name them in a way that contains an attitude toward them" (1957: 3).

The important thing to understand is that any given cultural/symbolic complex is both a "model of" and a "model for" — these are two aspects of a single process. As a group represents its situation to itself and to the outside world, it uses terms and images that select and emphasize some aspects of that situation, that distort or ignore others, and that, in the process, permeate the entire structure with certain moral and affective orientations. As actors participate in or employ such constructs, their attitudes and actions become oriented in the directions embodied in the form and content of the construction itself; the construct — the model, if you will — makes it difficult for them to "see" and respond to the situation in a different way. Such cultural models, further, are a priori neither conservative nor radical — they may be anything from templates for simply regenerating the system as it is presently constituted, to revolutionary programs that depict the situation in such a way as to reveal its evils and exhort people to destroy it. Culture is *always* biased — selected, partial, interpreted — but both the source and the direction of bias are precisely among the key, if not *the* key — problems of cultural analysis.

From this general view of the cultural process, then, a series of analytic questions flow. First, and definitely first: What are the problematic realities of the culture to which the symbolic construction under analysis is addressing itself (i.e., what is it a model of)? Second, what strategic orientations toward those realities are embodied in the construct (i.e., what is it a model for)? (An adequate account on the first question should provide clues to the *sources* of the biases revealed in answering the second.) And third, very simply: How does it work? How, in its peculiar construction, does the symbolic construct accomplish its task in a powerful and convincing way, so that its respondents in fact accept it as an accurate rendering of "reality," and adopt its implied orientation of attitude and/or action? It is the third question that actually demands the execution of symbolic analysis as such, an analysis of semantic structure and process that seeks to reveal how the problematic phenomena have been portrayed and interrelated, by means of various semantic devices, so as to have cast the situation in the light in which it in fact emerges.

These analytic questions are, I think, clear enough, and they provide an overall framework for the approach I shall be taking. There is, however, no simple recipe for analytic procedure. The actual details of method, as will be seen, vary from case to case. The rituals I will be analyzing themselves use a variety of symbolic mechanisms in formulating problems and fashioning solutions, and my analyses will follow their contours as closely as possible. No single interpretive scheme is used, no attempt is made to reduce all ritual process to Freudian psychodrama, structuralist mediations, or any other totalizing approach one might name, although elements of many are drawn upon.

One final point. The reshaping of consciousness or experience that takes place in ritual is by definition a reorganization of the *relationship* between the subject and what may for convenience be called reality. Ritual symbolism always operates on both elements, reorganizing (representations of) "reality," and at the same time reorganizing (representations of) self. The experience of each dimension depends upon the experience of the other: A certain view of reality emerges from a certain experience of self; a certain sense of self emerges from a certain experience of reality. In the case of Sherpa Buddhist rituals, much of the symbolic action consists of attempts to translate external "reality" — social and natural conditions — into "self," subjective psychological states. Quite faithful to Buddhist orthodoxy in this respect, many Sherpa rituals manifest this psychologizing movement or progression, and it is to this point that I shall return in the conclusions.

2. The surface contours of the Sherpa world

Nepal is certainly one of the more romanticized places on earth, with its towering Himalayas, its abominable snowmen, and its musically named capital, Kathmandu, a symbol of all those faraway places the imperial imagination dreamt about. And the Sherpa people, the subject of this book, are perhaps one of the more romanticized people of the world, renowned for their mountaineering feats, and found congenial by Westerners for their warm, friendly, strong, self-confident style.

What there is about the Sherpa world that conduces to such a style is probably impossible to isolate, although it has variously been attributed to their glorious mountain environment, their Buddhist religion, or, by the Sherpas themselves, to the especially pure water found exclusively in the Sherpa region. In any case, in buoyant, outgoing social style as well as in robust physical type, they resemble their own racial, cultural, linguistic, and religious cousins the Tibetans, and differ substantially in both style and physique from the South Asians and the Chinese, the two major groups that bracket the greater Tibetan culture area.

It has been fairly well established that the Sherpas migrated into their present location in Nepal from the Khams region of eastern Tibet about 450 years ago.[1] It is not clear why they left; harrassment by marauding Mongol tribes, or religious persecution by the reformed Tibetan Buddhist sect have been suggested, although it seems equally plausible that there was some local upheaval in the feudal social structure. In any event, they made their way, a journey of some 1,250 miles, to northeastern Nepal, where they settled in the then uninhabited region in the general environs of Mount Everest.

Nepal at that time was not the unified polity it is today. The Sherpas were left to their own devices, and they spread over the area they now inhabit. Although gradually they came to have an ethnic identity separate from the Tibetans, and to develop a dialect not mutually intelligible with the Tibetan spoken just over the border ("just over the border" meaning a seven-day trek over a 19,000-foot pass), they continued to be oriented toward Tibet as a source of social, economic, and religious influence. A second influx of immigrants apparently came into the Sherpa area from the immediately adjacent part of Tibet about 150 years ago, and became incorporated as Sherpas. Tibetan immigrants who did not come to be considered Sherpas also continued to settle in the Sherpa area, and now form a substantial pro-

A Solu valley

portion of the population of the region. Before the Chinese takeover of Tibet, the
Sherpas went on frequent trading expeditions over the border, and acted as middlemen in Nepal for trade between Tibet and India. (Both trade and immigration still
go on, though much more infrequently and on a much smaller scale than before
the fall of Tibet in 1959. See von Fürer-Haimendorf, 1975.) Further, Sherpa religious specialists went to Tibet for training; the monastery in the adjacent Tibetan
region played a large role in the development of Sherpa religion, and its refugee
monks, now living in the Sherpa area, are playing an important role in Sherpa
religion today. The religion of the Sherpas, though it has no doubt undergone much
change, is still essentially that unique and exotic form of Buddhism that developed
in Tibet, a school within the broad Mahayana tradition known variously as Lamaism,
Tantrayana, Vajrayana, or simply Tibetan Buddhism.

But while Tibet was (and still is, symbolically) the spiritual focus for the Sherpas,
Nepal was and is the concrete reality with which they had, and have, to cope. The
country as a whole is one of extreme ecological variation. Its southern border, with
India, is at sea level, but in the space of only about 100 miles the country rises to
the crest of the Himalayas, peaking at over 29,000 feet with Mount Everest. North
of the strip of dense, swampy, malarial jungle, known as the Terai, which runs

along much of the southern border, the terrain of Nepal is composed of a series of high ridges, running north and south, divided by deep canyons down which flow the rivers — relatively shallow, rocky, and extremely fast-running — that drain the Himalayas.

Before 1952, at which time Nepal was opened to the world, there were no roads capable of carrying vehicles in the country beyond the Kathmandu valley. Subsequently, the government of India built a road from the Indian border to Kathmandu, and during the time of my fieldwork the Chinese completed a very well-engineered road (capable, it was whispered, of carrying four tanks abreast) from Lhasa, the capital of Tibet, over the Himalayas and into Kathmandu from the north. These are still the only major vehicle roads in Nepal,[2] and since they run for the most part from north to south, crossing the narrow dimension of the country, while Nepal is 500 miles long from east to west, it is still fair to say that there are no roads in most of Nepal.

The trails throughout the country, along which people travel, are so steep and precipitous, and the bridges over the rivers so narrow and tenuous, that it is rarely practical to use animals either for riding or for carrying loads. Most travel must thus be effected on foot, and most goods must be transported on people's backs. From Kathmandu to Dzemu, where I lived and worked from December 1966 to February 1968, one must walk eastward for ten days over this extremely rugged terrain, although I gather that public buses on a segment of the Chinese road (as everyone calls it) have now cut this time to six days.

The area inhabited by the Sherpas lies partly among the mountains subsidiary to Mount Everest, partly along the Dudh Khosi (Milk River) which drains Mount Everest, and partly in a lower valley about 50 miles south of the upper villages. The upper area is known as Khumbu, the area along the river is called Pharak, and the lower valley is called Solu. The inhabited Khumbu comprises altitudes of from 12,000 to 14,000 feet, with grazing stations as high as 16,000 feet; the inhabited Solu comprises altitudes of from 8,500 to 10,500 feet, with grazing stations up to about 14,000 feet. The entire area is known, to both Nepalese and Sherpas, as Solu-Khumbu, although the native Sherpa term for Solu is Shorung.

While it is difficult to get exact population figures, the number of Sherpas in Solu-Khumbu was put at over 14,000 in 1965 (Oppitz: 109); about another 7,000 Sherpas were reported in the Darjeeling area of India (ibid., following a 1965 British report) and, while I have seen no figures on the number of Sherpas in Kathmandu, I would guess something like 3,000 or 4,000. Thus the total number of Sherpas may be 24,000 or 25,000, although many of those in Kathmandu or Darjeeling may also have been counted in the Solu-Khumbu census.[3]

The village of Dzemu is located in a protected side valley of Solu, at about 9,600 feet. The climate is temperate, with winter temperatures rising as high as the 50s at noon, and rarely dropping below the teens. Snow in Dzemu is light and infrequent, being precipitated by the high ridges that surround the valley and rarely reaching the valley floor. In the summer, from the middle of May to the middle of

A Khumbu village

October, the entire Solu-Khumbu is subject to the Indian monsoon, with rain virtually continuous but of variable intensity, in Solu, and only coming for part of the day in Khumbu. The normal temperature during monsoon in Dzemu is a damp, chilly 60 or so degrees, although it goes up into the 70s and perhaps to 80 when the sun comes out. The range of temperature, in short, at least where I was situated, is quite moderate, although up in Khumbu the winters are far more severe.

The Solu valley, being further south than Khumbu, lower in altitude, and having a more moderate climate, is relatively fertile, and devotes most of its economic energy to agriculture. Solu villages are located where possible on the relatively gentler slopes, so that there is a minimum of terracing, compared with the spectacular terraced hills in other parts of Nepal.[4] Higher up on the slopes surrounding the villages are the grazing pastures, and much of the rest of the terrain is covered with evergreen forest, composed predominantly of conifers and rhododendrons, the latter flowering gloriously in the spring. There are some deciduous trees in these forests, and some slopes of the Solu area are more deciduous than evergreen. The Sherpas say that the evergreen forests are secondary growths, and that the whole of the Dzemu valley, at least, was once covered by deciduous trees. In much of Khumbu, on the other hand, the vegetation is primarily scrub, and the land very poor.

The typical Solu village is composed of fifteen to twenty houses dispersed over a relatively large area, with fields in between. In Khumbu, the villages are often larger — up to 200 houses — and the houses are clustered together. Dzemu is somewhat large and atypical for a Solu village, having approximately thirty houses (depending on how one counts) clustered together, surrounded by fields. About ten more houses up to a mile or so in all directions from the central village are also considered part of Dzemu. In addition to the houses, fields, and pastures, the village has a fine temple and a school, one of a number in Solu-Khumbu built and supported by Sir Edmund Hillary in gratitude for Sherpa aid in his conquest of Everest.[5]

If one walks for three and a half hours southeast from Dzemu, one reaches Dorphu, the site of one of the best weekly bazaars in eastern Nepal. At Dorphu one can buy any of the local products, as well as a wide range of things not produced in the village. High-country Sherpas bring down salt, which they obtain on trading missions in Tibet, and wool from their yaks. From the south, other tribes bring up a whole range of warm-weather, low-altitude products — rice, oranges, bananas, pineapples, "chinese" pears, coconuts, cucumbers (the size of watermelons), tomatoes, peanuts, tea, spices. From Kathmandu, professional traders bring cloth, trinkets, candy, cookies, kerosene, pots, dishes, and even window glass. Nepalese butchers slaughter two or three buffalo just before the bazaar opens each week, and sell the meat. Most important, for the Sherpas, is the rice. Rice cannot be grown in their villages because of the altitude, but though expensive and a luxury, it is essential to the ideal production of hospitality.

Within this environment, then, the Sherpas live their Sherpa lives. In the remainder of this chapter, I shall outline as briefly as possible some basic facts of their economy, social organization, political structure, and religious practices. These will provide some sense of the outer shape of ordinary Sherpa existence. The remainder of the book will be devoted to getting beyond the kind of knowledge provided by such "facts," and understanding the significance and interpenetration of those facts for those who live within them.

Economy

The Sherpa economy may be characterized as one of mixed agriculture and animal husbandry, supplemented by cash from labor and trading ventures. Given the differences of land and climate between Solu and Khumbu, their economic emphases are correspondingly different. Khumbu has only one short growing season, and relies to a much greater extent on herds, trade, and labor as guides and porters for trekkers and mountaineers. Solu is predominantly agricultural, although pastoralism and trading continue to play important roles in the economy.

The people of Dzemu grow potatoes, wheat, barley, and corn as staples; in garden patches they grow beans, peas, radishes, squash, and greens, as well as garlic and chili as spices.[6] Barley and wheat seem to be the original crops brought from Tibet. The potato was introduced only about 100 years ago; legend has it that the first seeds came from the British ambassador's garden in Sikkim. Corn was introduced within the last thirty years or so, with great success, although it will not grow above 10,000 feet. Dzemu is the last village of the valley to be able to grow it; in Phungmo, about 2 miles further north, and a few hundred feet higher, corn cannot be raised. Squash too was very recently introduced; I believe an American trekker gave some seeds to one of the Dzemu women. The Sherpas, having contact with so many exotic nationalities, are rather adventurous about growing new foods, although in the manner of preparing them they all tend to boil down (as it were) to the same thing.

Spring and fall are the busy times of the agricultural calendar, although there is work to be done virtually throughout the year. In the May–June–July period, the barley and wheat are harvested, and corn and garden vegetables are planted. Potato plants must be coddled throughout the summer – the soil around the base of each plant is broken up, then mounded up to support the plants as they grow heavy – and one sees the people crouching in the fields at this back-breaking labor during the rains of the monsoon. Potatoes are gathered in toward the end of the summer, a process that involves going through the fields plant by plant, collecting each potato as it reaches optimum size and ripeness, but before it rots. The sheaves of grain are stored through the summer and threshed in the fall, when they provide seed for the new planting and the stalks provide straw for the animals in the winter months. From late August into December, wheat and barley fields are prepared – plowed, composted, replowed – and then planted. Garden vegetables, and, toward the end of the period, corn must be harvested during this time. And then it is time to prepare the fields for the potatoes, which are planted in late December and January. The major breathing period of the year occurs from mid-January, after the potatoes are planted, into March, when they must begin to be nursed. There is also a relatively slack month in the middle of the summer, after the last of the cereals have been harvested and before potato gathering begins.

All the ground of the Sherpa region is rocky and must be cleared for planting. The fields of Dzemu are of somewhat better quality than most, being relatively level and quite fertile, but the opening of a new field still involves a great deal of rock-clearing work. While occasionally a family will obtain some virgin land and create a new field for agricultural use, the arable land is, for the most part, treated as being in fixed supply.

The land inheritance pattern is such that a father's land is divided equally among his sons, and theirs among their sons, theoretically ad infinitum. This policy, as one would imagine, tends to create postage-stamp fields. In the old days this problem could be solved by the practice of fraternal polyandry, in which all the sons, or several of them, married a single wife. The sons collectively held the land inherited from their father, and all the sons of their wife inherited the same undivided body of property. But the Nepalese government has outlawed polyandry (although there are still a few cases), and the problem is now handled in a variety of ways. A father may enlarge his holding by buying land from someone who, for whatever reason, wants or needs to sell. Alternatively — and this is the most common practice today a son may sell his small share to one of his brothers and go off to seek his fortune elsewhere: trading, working on mountaineering and trekking expeditions, working for Westerners in Kathmandu, working on road crews for the Indian government. Sometimes he never comes back, but just as often he returns to his native village with his money and tries to buy a better stake of property than the one he would have inherited. This pattern is especially popular in cases in which a father has not been able to provide all his sons with houses, for the money made in the outside world can be used to buy or build a house, in addition to buying land.

There is also some alleviation of the land-distribution problem in young men going off and becoming monks, but this does not work as well for the Sherpas as it did in Tibet. In Tibet the monasteries fully supported their monks. A monk would not retain a stake in his father's property, and his brothers thus would each get larger holdings. Among the Sherpas, however, the monasteries are not self-supporting, and a monk must be given at least a partial inheritance, to be worked by his family, for his support.

Each nuclear family owns its own land and handles its own economic affairs. The economy is geared toward subsistence — the ideal state is one in which a family can support itself entirely from its own harvests and then have a bit left over that can be sold for cash. This ideal is of course not attained for every family every year. There are wealthy families with so much land that they hire tenant farmers (usually non-Sherpas) to work it, keeping half the crop; there are middling families, not-rich-not-poor, as the Sherpas say, who get by — a potato or wheat blight will make the difference — from year to year; and there are poor families that must supplement their incomes however they can. Dzemu is one of the more well-to-do Sherpa villages, with six or eight very wealthy families, only three or four very poor ones, and the rest just carrying on. More will be said below about wealth, poverty, and status.

But land, as I said, is only part of the economic picture. Also important to the Sherpa economy — very important in Solu, paramount in much of Khumbu — are the herds of animals: cows, yaks, and cow–yak crossbreeds known as *zom* (f.; *zopkio,* m.). While only the wealthier families can afford to keep yak and zom, almost every family has at least one or two cows, and the more well-to-do may have fifteen, twenty, or more. The cows are valued for their milk and butter, and the oxen are used for plowing. Cows are kept in the village, on the ground floors of houses, all year round, while zom and yak are kept up in dairy stations in high pastures. They, too, are valued primarily for their dairy products, and the yaks also yield wool. In keeping with Buddhist law, the Sherpas never slaughter animals. However, when an animal dies of old age or as the result of falling down a mountain (a not-improbable occurrence, although some of the accidents are a bit suspicious), or by some other mischance, some of the meat will be eaten, some sold, some dried for later consumption. Cows are driven to the pastures outside the village every day and brought back in the evening. Cow tending is generally done by the young servants, children, or old people of the household, who cannot do heavy agricultural work. The cows are milked every evening, and the milk may be used or sold, or turned into yoghurt or butter. Butter is highly prized by the Sherpas, both for its good taste (zom butter being considered the best), and for the high prices it fetches when sold.

The crossbreeds and yaks (the latter being relatively rare in Solu, where the altitude is not quite rarified enough for their taste) are kept at high grazing stations and tended by various adolescent and adult members of the family who take turns, each spending about a month at a time up at the station. The high pastures are technically owned by clans, and grazing stations may be set up anywhere on one's own clan's land. Those tending the herds lodge in flimsy temporary structures which may be abandoned or moved as a grazing area is exhausted. Families with small landholdings may place greater emphasis on their herds, and spend proportionally more time at the grazing stations. The animals in the stations are milked every night. While some of the milk is drunk, most is turned into butter, and some into curds, yoghurt, and a type of dry, crumbly cheese. Because butter can always be sold at good prices throughout the area, people with large herds may become very wealthy in cash, even if they own little or no land.

Indeed, producing and selling butter is probably the most lucrative venture in which the average Sherpa can engage. Even within the village, where almost everyone has a few cows, there is always a demand for it. The really ambitious fellow, however, will carry 50 to 100 pounds of butter to Kathmandu, where it sells for one-and-a-half to three times as much as in the Sherpa area. Even if a man has no milk-giving animals, he may buy butter at the local price in Solu-Khumbu and realize a tidy profit from its sale in the capital. Butter is the Sherpas' primary market commodity, and its high price even within the village reflects its commodity status.

There are a number of other ways in which a villager can earn cash. He can work for other households (though only the poorest will do this); he can make and sell beer and liquor to villagers and travelers; he can do portering work for trekkers and wealthy Sherpas during slack periods of the agricultural cycle. In Khumbu, working on mountaineering expeditions has been an important source of cash (as well as killing not a few Khumbu men in the prime of life), but Solu men have not been very much involved in this work.[7] In Khumbu many men still engage in trade across the Tibetan border, and most Sherpas also engage in local petty trade, buying up odds and ends, and selling them for whatever profit they can make. However, only the wealthiest men, who have tenant farmers, servants, and/or a large family to work their land, or the poorest, who have little or no land to work, can afford to go into full-time trading.

Social organization

The Sherpas are estimated, on the basis of clan-history texts, to have left the Khams region of eastern Tibet at the end of the fifteenth century. It would be extremely valuable to know the particulars of the social structure of the region at the time, and the place of the emigrating families within that structure. Tibet developed, over centuries, an exceedingly complex, centralized, theocratic feudal structure,[8] but the situation in Khams at the end of the fifteenth century is unclear. It seems unlikely that the migrating families were of royal or noble status, or they would surely have made much of this in their clan histories. There is evidence, however, that they were wealthy, for the texts speak of their converting large amounts of land and livestock into gold and silver for the purposes of emigration, of their being well received at various monasteries, and sponsoring lavish ceremonies, along their way (Oppitz: 73–6).

While it is possible that there were class differences among the emigrant families, which were subsequently obscured by intermarriage because of the small size of the group, it is equally plausible that all the families were of more or less equivalent status. Whatever the historical facts, however, the significant point for the present is that nothing remotely resembling the feudal hierarchical structure of Tibet was (re-)constructed by the Sherpas in their new environment. And they represent themselves, in their documents, as having migrated by clans (*ru*), or rather by individual families that produced clans over time.

The whole of Sherpa society today is divided into named, exogamous patrilineal clans. Every person inherits a clan affiliation from his or her father and must marry someone of a different clan affiliation. Ninety percent of the present Sherpa population belongs to one or another of the clans descended from the original immigrant families. These true Sherpa clans now number fifteen, derived by fission from an original set of four "protoclans," two of which have remained conceptually intact under single clan names, thirteen of which are divisions from the two other original clans. These thirteen now function as full-fledged clans with distinct names and exogamy rules, but they form two sets (of eight and five clans, respectively), each set retaining a tradition of its common descent from a protoclan and thus not intermarrying among themselves (Oppitz: passim).

The system has been represented concentrically in the literature (von Fürer-Haimendorf, 1964; Oppitz), with the clans descended from the original immigrants at the core. In the first ring around the core are the clans that migrated into the Sherpa area from the adjacent region of southwest Tibet about 150 years ago, and that are by now considered full-fledged Sherpa clans in every respect. In the second ring are clans that were created by intermarriage with other ethnic groups in Nepal,

but which nonetheless styled themselves as Sherpas, formed themselves into exogamous clan units, and established continuous marriage relationships with other
Sherpa clans. Finally, around the fringes are the so-called Khambas, immigrants
from Tibet who are not organized into exogamous patrilineal units, and are not
considered Sherpas, though they form a substantial segment of the population in
Khumbu. And beyond the fringe, as it were, are the Yemba, who were a sort of
untouchable caste in Tibet, and whom even the Khambas will not marry.

In a general way, the units are ranked from highest at the core to lowest at the
fringes. Within the core (which, again, comprises 90 percent of the population considered truly Sherpa) there is also by now something of an informal hierarchy. The
Lama clan, one of the two original clans remaining unsubdivided, is explicitly considered highest, especially by its own members. And the Gordza clan seems to have
a taint of lowness; they were formerly a blacksmith (and possibly "untouchable")
caste-like group. But all of this is informal and, except for the undisputed economic
and political dominance of the Lama clan in certain parts of Solu, and some teasing
of Gordza clan children, the clans which form the core of the system are on a fairly
equal footing.

Marriage between members of core clans and members of first-ring Sherpa clans
seems to be relatively unproblematic. In any case, it is largely an academic question
in Solu, where noncore clans are virtually unrepresented. Marriage between members of full Sherpa clans and members of clans deriving from mixture with other
ethnic groups is frowned upon but not forbidden. I would guess the mixed clans
primarily marry with other mixed clans, and secondarily with first-ring rather than
core Sherpa clans. Marriage between Sherpas and Khambas is supposedly a serious
offense (phrased in terms of polluting the Sherpa individual and his or her clan),
involving loss of one's status and rights in the Sherpa community.[9] Marriage with
Yembas is more or less unthinkable.

As might be guessed from all this, the primary function of the clans, in modern
times, is to regulate marriage. The clans are not now corporate groups, although the
division of grazing lands and forest into clan-owned units indicates that probably
originally they were. It also seems likely that originally the clans were fully localized in exclusive territories and villages. In Solu most of the villages are still clan-
exclusive (Dzemu being a Lama-clan village), although in Khumbu this pattern does
not hold, and most Khumbu villages contain male members of several different
clans.

In addition to not marrying a fellow clan member, one should not theoretically
marry a member of one's mother's or grandmother's lineage. Although this is not
strictly adhered to, it is part of the rationale that rules out matrilateral cross-cousin
marriage, that is, marriage with one's mother's brother's daughter, even though she
does not belong to one's clan. Patrilateral cross-cousin marriage, that is, marriage
with one's father's sister's daughter (who also does not belong to one's own clan) is
also considered repugnant, though the Sherpas are aware of cross-cousin marriage
practices in Tibet and among neighboring tribes in Nepal.[10]

Internally, the clans are divided into lineages, the members of which trace their relationship to a common remembered ancestor, usually no further back than the great-grandfather of the living adult males of the lineage. In lineages in which a particular ancestor was well-known and prestigious, the lineage may remain conceptually intact beyond the usual four generations, but in others, in which the ancestor is not remembered, segments will split and become separate lineages after four or even three generations.

In Dzemu, the most important lineage is composed of the descendants of the oldest brother of T., a man who became very wealthy in the latter part of the nineteenth century through various dealings with the Nepalese government, and who then devoted large portions of his wealth to the encouragement and support of religion. The men of this lineage constituted most of the "big people" of the village, although they have no official power or authority and cannot be considered in any way leaders or rulers.

The lineages, though localized, are not necessarily corporate units, although they come closer to this status than the clans. The only true corporate group is the mutual-aid group that crystallizes around each nuclear family; the family's lineage is usually the core of this group. Yet when a lineage is squabbling among itself, or is simply on the verge of splitting as a result of old age and social drift, only part of one's lineage may be in one's mutual-aid group, and the group generally contains nonlineage members — neighbors, friends, perhaps some relatives by marriage — as well. More on these groups below.

Descending further in scope from the lineages, we reach the nuclear family — parents and unmarried children — the smallest but in many ways the most important unit of Sherpa social organization: It is the economic unit, as well as the unit of participation in all public, social, and religious projects. Each nuclear family ideally has a separate residence. In the course of a man's active working years, he should build or buy a house for each of his sons except the youngest. As each son gets married, he is given a house and his share — equal to that of his brothers' — of the father's land and herds. The youngest son will inherit the parents' house and he must therefore live there, even after he has a wife and children. He must support the parents in their old age, and he is responsible for making their funerals when they die. Thus a significant percentage of households in a Sherpa village are composed of three generations — old parents, youngest son and his wife, and their children. However, many parents are explicitly sensitive to the potential for friction in such an arrangement and they often build or buy a small house or hut to which they move when the youngest son gets married, taking only a few essential domestic items and leaving everything else in the house. Old people continue to work as long as they can, retaining one or two fields to support themselves, or, if they have turned over all their remaining property to the youngest son, they will work in his fields and receive food from him.

Daughters are given dowries of money and movable goods, and they retain no rights to the parents' immovable property. After marriage they must live at their husband's residence, generally in another village, often quite far away. Thus, once married, daughters are no longer of importance to their natal family, although parents and married daughters visit each other from time to time. (In Khumbu, with multiclan villages, there is more local endogamy.)

A father with no sons may leave his property to his younger brother, or to the younger brother's sons, or he may resort to taking a son-in-law who is willing to move into his home with his daughter. Such a son-in-law (*maksu*) inherits all of his wife's father's property, although there is no fictional change of his clan affiliation, and his children belong to his own clan rather than that of his wife and father-in-law. In Dzemu, taking a resident son-in-law has been strongly frowned upon, because the village likes to maintain its Lama-clan exclusiveness and not see Lama-clan land lost to an intrusive other clan.[11]

Traditionally, marriages are arranged by mutual consent of the parents of the boy and girl, although the veto of either child is often respected. Naturally, parents try to make advantageous matches, in terms of money and status, for their children. Yet there have always been ways around arranged marriages, and frequently the negotiations between two sets of parents are by way of validating a relationship that has already been established. In Solu where, given single-clan villages, there are no prospective mates within the village, it is nonetheless possible to see marriageable opposite numbers at the bazaar, at weddings, funerals, or in a number of other contexts, and thus to begin a courtship. In Khumbu, where co-villagers are not necessarily co-clan members, the possibilities for young people to initiate their own courtships are even greater. Besides the standard monogamous marriages, there is a small amount of polygyny, usually undertaken after the first wife has been established as barren, and a slightly greater amount of polyandry, generally hushed up because of its illegality. There is some preference for a younger brother to marry his older brother's widow, but even if this does not take place the widow, if she has sons, usually remains in her marital village because her sons have property rights there. If she wishes to remarry with someone other than a brother of her husband, she must make a token payment to the husband's family. The divorce rate is rather high – 30 percent by one recent estimate (Oppitz: 124) – and many powerful personalities, male and female, have gone through three or four spouses.

Marriage proceeds in stages over a period of years, each stage having a specific name. After the first several stages, in which agreement between all concerned is established, dowry is fixed, horoscopes are consulted, and plans for the wedding are made, the first of the actual wedding events (the *demchang*) takes place. Following this event, the couple is considered to be formally married such that children subsequently born are legitimate, and if either party wishes to be divorced from the other, he or she must make a payment to the other's family. The amounts of these payments vary, but the sums are quite substantial by Sherpa standards.

Even after this stage of the proceedings, the husband and wife commonly continue to live with their respective families, with the husband paying visits to his wife in her parents' house. There is some tradition of groom service during this time — the husband will generally do some labor for his in-laws when he comes to visit his wife — but there is no hard and fast rule for this.[12]

The final stage of the proceedings, at which the husband goes to collect his wife and her dowry and bring it all back home, may not take place for a number of years. The period of postponement depends primarily on economic factors — whether the bride's family has been able to put together her dowry, whether they can spare her labor, whether the groom has a house to which he can bring back his bride. If the bride's family has not been able to raise her dowry but if the other two factors have been satisfactorily arranged, the couple may live together for many years and have several children before the final stage takes place. In this case, bringing back the bride from her parents' home is symbolically reenacted.

The nuclear family unit of husband, wife, and children is the effective unit of day-to-day life in the village, owning its own property and handling its own economic affairs. Beyond this, the wider social organization of the village incorporates families, in various ways, into relatively stable relationships with their fellow villagers. There are, of course, informal ties of friendship and neighborliness. Every family is also involved, as noted earlier, in an enduring mutual-aid group (*tsenga tsali*), the core of which is made up of other families of its lineage but which also includes some nonlineage members. All families standing in a mutual-aid relationship to one another are obligated to give each other gifts of foodstuffs and small sums of money, as well as personal labor, at certain established times of festivity or need. They contribute labor to one another at times of house building or repairing, at various times in the agricultural cycle, and in the preparation and serving of large-scale hospitality; they give money and foodstuffs as contributions to each other's hospitality expenses at times of birth, marriage, and death; and they give each other money gifts toward the future of a new baby and a newly married couple, and toward the dowry of an engaged daughter. They may also be called upon for help or contributions in unusual situations of need, although not to help defray such purely personal expenditures as for new clothes, jewelry, or a trip to Kathmandu. Contributions of gifts and labor are seen as investments and are always fully reciprocal over time. One gets back what one gives; one gives because one has received and because one can count on receiving in the future. Because this type of reciprocity operates between families rather than individuals, the obligations of the parents become those of the sons, gradually taken over by them as the parents get old and fully inherited by them when the parents die.

It is worth noting the special place of these mutual-aid groups, tsenga tsali, in the system. Because they are based in the first instance on lineage relationships, it is within their context that lineage, and kinship in general, receive greatest attention. Although any individual's network of relatives may be quite large, it is also quite vague, and kin really come into their own as special people when they can help one in concrete ways. The "natural" kinship basis of mutual-aid group formation may be what lends an expectation of great reliability to these groups, but the real help these groups provide in turn contributes to the sense that kin are special people who can be counted on. Along these same lines, it seems probable that lineage segmentation follows mutual-aid group segmentation (for whatever reason — growth beyond practical size, friction within the group), rather than vice versa.

Note too that tsenga tsali relationships somewhat contradict the ideal of the economically autonomous nuclear family. Although families hold property privately, they do not in fact produce from that property privately. Production has an important collective dimension, involving the labors of tsenga tsali members.

Beyond this immediate exchange group, each family is involved in reciprocity relationships with a wider group called "village people," in the specific sense of co-villagers with whom one has obligations of token exchange. Participation in this wider network, as well as in the smaller groups, is basic to full membership in the community, and villagers will see to it that new residents, if they have any sort of respectable status at all (e.g., the anthropologist), are incorporated as quickly as possible. Virtually everyone in the village is invited to weddings and funerals, the two biggest hospitality events any family has the opportunity to host. And every family that attends such an event should give a small gift of money and foodstuffs to the host family. Such a gift must, of course, be reciprocated at the next opportunity, and thus one stands in this more limited reciprocity relationship with virtually the whole village. (But because this is not completely universal, even within the village, people generally keep records of their obligations in this wider sphere, so that they will know precisely who is owed what and how much.) "Village people" do not give personal labor to one another on a reciprocity basis, and it is this, more than anything else, that distinguishes the closer, more intensive tsenga tsali ties from this larger reciprocity network. If one needs labor beyond that supplied by one's smaller mutual-aid group, one will pay wages to any "village people" who do such work, generally people from the poorer families of the village. The boundaries of the village effectively mark the limits of one's reciprocal-aid relationships.[13]

Mutual-aid groups, and reciprocity relationships in the wider sphere of "village people," operate through direct interaction between individual families on a one-to-one basis. In addition, each family contributes money and labor to the public enterprises and institutions of the village that operate for the general welfare. Thus, every family that uses a particular water mill must contribute whatever is necessary to keep up that mill. In Dzemu there are two mills, and several times a year groups of men, representing the participating families, get together to make repairs on their respective mills, generally concluding their labors with an extended drinking party. The families using the larger of the two mills in town also collect money among themselves to pay a small wage to a caretaker.

Similarly, when a new addition to the Dzemu school was built through the generosity of Sir Edmund Hillary, every family in the seven villages that use the school contributed several days of labor to the enterprise, most people contributing their personal labors, the wealthy sending their servants.

Finally, each family must support the ceremonial life of the village temple. For any given temple event, two or three people, representing their families, volunteer to be sponsors. They each provide a portion of the money, food, and labor needed to support the event from beginning to end: They feed the lamas throughout their work on the services; they contribute all the materials for the altar; they provide the food for ritual distribution to the laymen at the end of the services; they pay the lamas; and, in some cases, they provide a feast for the entire village. All temple sponsor work is, with one exception, voluntary. Some families do it more frequently than others, but every family does some every year or two. The one exception is the annual Dumji festival, for which sponsorship contributions and chores are compulsorily assigned to families on a rotating basis. The expense of being a Dumji sponsor is very high — several thousand rupees, or at least that is how much it seems from the sponsor's point of view — but in Dzemu the responsibility for being a Dumji sponsor only falls on a household every fifteen years or so.

The various sorts of obligations just described — to one's aid group, to "village people," and to the public institutions of the village — are the primary forces that connect the family units of the village into larger networks of relationships with one another in very concrete, on-the-ground ways. This, of course, is part of what we mean when we talk about social organization. But the village (and ultimately, if anyone bothered to figure it out, the whole of the Sherpa people) is structured in terms of another, more abstract, sort of organization — a status hierarchy. And while status is built, in part, on such concrete things as wealth, and while it may engender, in part, such concrete things as more wealth, as well as a marginal amount of political leverage, it is nonetheless largely a symbolic statement about people's "place" vis-à-vis other people. It orders people, but it does not, in itself, necessarily create relationships between them. Yet, given the Sherpa way of seeing the world, in which everything, wherever possible, is arranged from high to low, the social hierarchy is at least as important, and as real, as the concrete contributions and reciprocations of day-to-day interaction.

The effective unit of the hierarchy, especially in a one-clan village, is the lineage, although within each lineage every single individual could be (and is, when status is marked in seating orders at parties and in the temple) ranked down to the very last one. A particular lineage becomes established as highest by virtue of having had an illustrious or influential founder. Within that lineage, descendants of the founder's oldest son are highest, descendants of the second son are next, and so forth. The statuses of other lineages in the village may then be calculated on the basis of genealogical nearness to the founder of the highest lineage — descendants of his older brothers are higher than those of his younger; both are higher than descendants of his father's brothers, and so forth.

All of this sounds rigid, but it is not. Many of the lineages of Dzemu cannot calculate with any precision their genealogical relationship to the dominant lineage, and it is clear that status depends on a number of other factors that always tacitly play a role in such calculations. Wealth is certainly one such factor. It can raise the status of a family and, if they keep it long enough, and play the status game hard enough, it will raise the status of their entire lineage within a generation or two. But the really unbeatable combination is wealth and piety; a wealthy family that devotes much of its money to the support of religion is on the way to the top. In addition, an individual's force of character may sometimes, and his advancing age will always, raise his personal status. While the high status of an elderly individual would not affect the overall ordering of the lineages, descendants of a highly respected, beloved, or admired personage might inherit his status, thus actually re-ordering the hierarchy to some extent.

Status jockeying, then, is a vital part of Sherpa village life. The Sherpas, as noted, like to arrange things from high to low; it is one of the basic ordering principles of their universe. Yet the hierarchy is always fluid. Family and lineage fortunes and reputations rise and fall, although at any moment in time people, especially those at the top and the bottom, tend to see the hierarchy as being fairly fixed and find it difficult to imagine being anywhere near the place of the other. On the other hand, as in many places, the *nouveaux riches* have a very lively sense of mobility. They see that their wealth begins to open a number of doors, and they devote a great deal of energy to getting across the threshold.

The political structure of the village tends to follow the status hierarchy, but it does not amount to very much in terms of real politics. There is no official head man (such an office may once have existed but it doesn't any more), but should some problematic situation arise that affects the community as a whole, a group of five or six men may get together to discuss it. (This would not happen in the case of private disputes.) Such a group will always contain some of the "big people," as well as some community-minded and/or upwardly mobile men of middling status. These ad hoc committees have no official powers or responsibilities and no means of enforcing compliance with anything, beyond playing upon the concern of others to stay in the generalized good graces of the big people. One member or other of this category always winds up being the village representative to the district council, the political body that ties the local region into the larger national political system.

In Dzemu, members of the dominant lineage also pack the two committees of the village concerned with its public institutions, the school and the temple. These committees hold and handle the funds for the two institutions, they hire and pay the school masters (mainly their own relatives),[14] and are responsible for the whereabouts of temple and school property (religious paraphernalia, school books and supplies, the school's first aid kit, the temple's pressure lanterns, and so forth). I might note that there were always disputes concerning the amounts and whereabouts of the treasuries (not to mention the whereabouts of the pressure lantern); they were some of the ongoing sources of friction in the village.

All of this — ad hoc meetings and membership on the school and temple committees — does not add up to much in the way of real power, although it does add up to some deference, enjoyed very much for its own sake. But it should be stressed that in no way could these people, singly or collectively, be said to "run" the village and that, basically, the political structure of a Sherpa village is highly amorphous. No one has final authority, there are no *formal* mechanisms of social control, and individuals almost never build groups of followers, or form alliances or factions, that would develop effective (even short-term) dominance over other elements or over the village as a whole.

But if no one has any real power, if there is no ultimate authority, what keeps things in order? What prevents crime, what settles disputes? Essentially, the Sherpas depend on internalized constraints for prevention. This works, on the whole, rather well, no doubt because of the small sizes of the communities. And when inner constraints fail and some unfortunate event occurs (as such things tend to do), the villagers resort to ad hoc measures, or sometimes do nothing at all.

Inner constraints, as the Sherpas conceive of them, include first of all the desire to avoid shame, which comes when people know and gossip about things one has done, ranging from the foolish or embarrassing to the criminal. Second, there is the desire to avoid personal pollution, which affects one as the result of certain types of acts, and which corrupts one's inner being — often leading to illness — whether people know about one's acts or not. While many sorts of polluting acts are not social and do not have social consequences, such things as fighting, killing, and improper sexual liaisons are both social crimes and personal pollutants. Thus the desire to avoid the very heavy pollution resulting from such acts may at least partially constrain people from committing them.[15] And, finally, there is the desire to avoid sin, out of concern for one's ultimate salvation. All of the major social crimes — theft, violence, murder, adultery — as well as, theoretically, angry thoughts and words, which is to say, disputes — are considered highly sinful. And while no one would claim that these crimes never occur, nor that the relative infrequency of crime if not of disputes is entirely due to Buddhist piety, the avoidance of sin and of a consequent miserable rebirth is considered by the Sherpas themselves an important restraint on human passions and failings.

Unfortunately, of course, the inner constraints do not always constrain. Disputes develop with great regularity, and crime occurs from time to time. In the case of disputes, I was told that a well-respected individual might informally play the role of middleman in trying to settle them, but I never saw anyone play this role while I was in Dzemu, and disputes just more or less smoldered along. Occasionally they would erupt into serious public arguments, and even more occasionally into physical fights. Relatives and friends will try to calm an argument only when it seems to be verging on violence, and they will shepherd the combatants off in separate directions if a fight actually breaks out.

As for the Sherpas' ways of handling really serious crimes, their general tendency, somewhat to the bafflement of their ethnographers, is to do nothing at all. If the offender — say, a thief — is unknown, there will be no systematic efforts to discover who it is, although in a town of 200 inhabitants the people will have a pretty good idea of the probable culprit. Even if the offender is known, the injured party may do no more than gossip and complain to others; rarely will he instigate a confron-

tation. In one of the more famous events of Sherpa history on this point, a man
in one of the major Khumbu villages stabbed and killed another man in a gambling
argument. (Murder is virtually nonexistent among the Sherpas, who take the Buddhist injunction against killing very seriously.) The man retired to his house for two
weeks while the people, stymied, did nothing. He ultimately ran away to Tibet.

The rather remarkable deficiency of Sherpa political and judicial mechanisms
illustrated by this story, and often observed in less dramatic circumstances, has been
attributed to their Buddhism. Because the Sherpas believe that a person will receive
just retribution for his evil deeds in his next incarnation, so the argument goes, they
do not take it upon themselves to judge or punish one another in their present lives.
There is probably truth to this argument, but it is certainly not the whole story.
A full explanation would have to be historically based, and my own view is that
Sherpa politics have been in a prolonged state of transition. I suspect that originally
the clans had considerable collective political authority, but that this has broken
down as the private property system has become consolidated, and as the Nepalese
state has increasingly made claims of providing independent juridical mechanisms.

Indeed, the end of the Khumbu murder story, as it was told to me, is that the
villagers, horrified post facto at their ineffectuality in dealing with the situation,
actually requested the government of Nepal to set up district courts in their area.
Whether this is true or not, the fact is that the Sherpas now have recourse to these
courts for settling their disputes and for seeing that criminal offenses are prosecuted.
It should be stressed, however, that most Sherpas mistrust and even fear the courts,
and are extremely reluctant to make use of them. They do not believe that the
courts would give a fair hearing to "small people."

The intrusion of Nepalese courts into what has perhaps sounded thus far like an
hermetically sealed Sherpa world, but which is not, of course, any such thing, raises
the subject of relations between the Sherpas and the wider social universe in which
they live. Nepal is an official Hindu state and a caste society. The highest Nepalese
castes are the Brahmins (called *Bahun*) and the Chhetris; the lowest are the untouchable metalworkers, tailors, and leather workers. The Sherpas, as a non-Hindu
ethnic group living in the country, are fitted into the system in the ranks above the
untouchables. They accept, in a general way, the validity of the Hindu caste system
— they respect Brahmins and Chhetris (mostly in the abstract, since they rarely see
them), and avoid certain specified kinds of contacts with untouchables. Beyond
this, however, they in no way conceive of themselves as lowly people, and in fact,
in the matter of religion they feel themselves superior to all non-Buddhists. But they
do not place themselves in opposition to greater Nepal — although there is quite a
bit of grumbling about land reform, which I will discuss in a moment — and they
are well-behaved as a group in relation to the larger Nepalese system.[16]

Within the past 20 years or so (it must be recalled that Nepal was only opened
to the world in 1952), the government has been trying to institute a certain amount
of political and economic reform, and to weld the country into a unified political
system with a common national consciousness. The Panchayat system of district

councils throughout the country, each composed of local representatives and headed by governors from Kathmandu, has been touted as a way of giving the people a voice in the government, but mainly operates at present to hand down government policies to the people. One of the primary policies is land reform, which would limit large landholdings and, in a complicated way, spread the wealth. The government is also in the process of establishing the district court network, in an effort to create a uniform system of justice throughout the country, as well as a network of schools, with obligatory attendance up to a minimum age, conducted in the Nepali language and imparting such basic knowledge of national culture as how to recognize pictures of Nepal's map, flag, and king.

How successful all these institutions — economic, legal, educational — will be in achieving their stated goals is a moot point. But that they will have — and are having — substantial impact on the Sherpas is beyond a doubt. Here are some points of impact: (1) The Nepalese courts, as we have just seen, are slowly entering the Sherpa legal system. (2) A number of talented Sherpa youths, who did well in the village schools, and whose previous natural option would probably have been the monastery, have gone on instead to the district high school, and a few of them have gone on to university in Kathmandu. (3) The principle of democratic election of representatives to the Panchayat council (especially in the form of the secret ballot) seemed, in a tiny way, to titillate the Sherpas with the possibility of achieving leadership by virtue of personal qualities independent of inherited status. While force of character has always played an important role in Sherpa society, it was always constrained by kinship affiliations in its effect upon village social hierarchies. Democratic ideas could invert the importance of these two principles, but that seems still to be very far in the future. (4) The land reform policy had not yet, when I was there, had any discernible effects on the distribution of Sherpa land-holdings, but (a rather nebulous) awareness of the policy did provoke quite a bit of consternation among those who had much to lose, and one Sherpa is even said to have suggested that the Sherpas move back to Tibet. (He was squelched, I was told, by reminders of current Chinese policies in Tibet.) But this last point suggests that one of the effects on the Sherpas (and perhaps on the many other non-Nepalese ethnic groups in the country) of the government's increasing presence in their lives, may be a rise in ethnic consciousness. Indeed, one Dzemu man proposed, and was taken much more seriously than the exodus-to-Tibet fellow, that the village school should start teaching "our Sherpa religion," to balance the heavy dose of modern notions to which the children are being exposed.

While Kathmandu increasingly comes to the villages, in the form of government edicts and agencies, the villagers increasingly go off to the cities, whether to make their fortunes, escape difficult personal situations, or simply to be where the action is. There has probably always been, for as long as the Sherpas have been Sherpas, a fairly constant trickle of people away to the cities, although it has no doubt intensified in recent years. The traditional urban focus for the Sherpas has been Darjeeling, in India, about as far east of Solu-Khumbu as Kathmandu is west. Many Sherpas who go to Darjeeling, it is my impression, are people who for one reason or another have a problematic personal situation at home — a bad marriage, a poor inheritance, an uncomfortable status. Indeed, Darjeeling has traditionally been the refuge for the disaffected, or disinherited, or deviant Sherpa. Incestuous couples, fallen monks and nuns, and assorted criminals seem to gravitate there, to avoid the consequences of their acts. But many of the emigrants are no doubt ordinary people, who simply go off to make a better living than they could have made at home. They become full-time traders, or laborers on Indian crews building roads in far-flung places like Bhutan and Assam. Some have become successful road-building contractors, hiring other Sherpas and contracting jobs from the Indian government.

More recently, Kathmandu has become a second urban focus on the Sherpa map. It seems that it has become so largely within the last twenty-five years, since the opening of Nepal and the beginning of the major era of mountain climbing. Kathmandu seems to attract a rather different lot of Sherpas. On the one hand, there are the Brahminizing types who hobnob with members of His Majesty's Government; on the other hand, there are the young men attracted by the bright lights, who aspire to be "modern," and who generally work for Westerners in one capacity or another.

But the impact of the urban centers, as the government comes to the provinces and the people go off to the cities, is not the whole of the Sherpas' experience with other ways of life. The histories of Solu and Khumbu are somewhat different on this point, but both have had continuous interaction with non-Sherpas for centuries. In both areas there are settlements of blacksmith-caste Nepalese; Nepalese tailors come through on a regular basis to make clothes for the Sherpas; Nepalese butchers and traders, as well as representatives of other hill tribes, can always be seen at bazaar. Sherpas of both areas go on pilgrimages, visits, and trading trips that take them through other tribal villages and areas. All Sherpas are bilingual in their own language and Nepali.

Both Solu and Khumbu, since the opening of Nepal, have also seen a steady stream of exotic nationalities coming through on treks and mountaineering expeditions, and many Sherpas have served as guides and porters for these people. But Khumbu has had more sustained contact with the mountaineers — mainly British, Germans, Swiss, New Zealanders, Americans, and Japanese — and it also has a large population of Tibetan immigrants not present in Solu. In Solu, on the other hand, there are many settlements of other Nepalese hill tribes. In fact, there are quite a few "Solu" villages in what are essentially other tribes' territories, and a few wealthy Solu Sherpas have become landlords in these territories with the members of resident ethnic groups as tenant farmers. As a generalization, it might be said that Solu has come under more South Asian culture influence, while Khumbu has had both more Tibetan and more Western influence. In many ways, because of their remoteness from the South Asian groups and their continuous infusion with Tibetan culture, via immigrants, Khumbu appears to be more traditionally Sherpa than Solu, but it is noteworthy that Solu has within the past twenty years or so been the center of much more vital growth and expansion of traditional religion.

The point of all this is that the Sherpas have lived with cultural pluralism for centuries. It has no doubt continuously changed their culture, but it has also given them a lively sense of cultural diversity and quite a solid ethnic identity.

Religion

I have saved for last, in this general sketch of Sherpa life and institutions, a discussion of what the Sherpas would certainly place first — their religion, which as far as they are concerned is the sine qua non of all the rest. Much of this book will be devoted to religion, and here I will simply outline very briefly its main institutions and practices. (See also Paul, 1970; and Funke.)

The Sherpas, as noted above, are Tibetan Buddhists. As good Buddhists, they believe in — "assume" is probably more accurate — the basic Buddhist principles of sin and merit, and of reincarnation to various states of being, exalted or miserable, depending on the amounts of sin and merit accumulated in the course of a lifetime. As good *Tibetan* Buddhists, they also believe in a vast array of gods and spirits who must be propitiated if things are to go well with man. The sect they adhere to is the Nyingmawa, the unreformed, oldest sect of Tibetan Buddhism, which places great emphasis on coercive rites, many of which were dropped or cleaned up in the later reformed sects. Specifically, they stress the so-called Sang-ngak texts, which emphasize fierce rites of exorcising and destroying demons. Among the Sherpas, as throughout Tibetan Buddhism, the execution of religion is in the hands of trained specialists, known in the popular literature as lamas, although technically this term was reserved for heads of monasteries and is now mainly used by the Sherpas to refer to village priests (as opposed to monks).

The first great wave of religious reform in Tibet, late in the fourteenth century, created the institution of celibate monasticism, which was to become so popular and widespread that by the twentieth century it was estimated that a fifth of the men of Tibet were monks. The Nyingmawa sect, however, continued to permit its lamas to marry, although it also developed, much later, a monastic tradition of its own. To this day, among all groups adhering to the Nyingmawa tradition, one finds both married lamas in villages and celibate monks (*tawa*) in monasteries. (In fact, the Sherpas also used to have "married monasteries" as well as celibate monasteries. A reform movement to make monasteries completely celibate has not yet been completed.) Dzemu had four resident married lamas while I was there and a number of its sons and brothers were off in monasteries, although not, I was told, as many as in earlier times.

Probably no more than 2 or 3 percent of Sherpa men are actually under monastic vows, although many, if not the majority, of men have had some instruction in monasteries, whether as novices who did not complete the full set of vows, or as full-fledged monks who broke the vows, or simply as lay students who took instruction in reading, writing, and fundamentals of religion from a lama. Most Sherpa men can thus at least chant a few basic Tibetan religious texts, and many can use the Tibetan script to write a simple letter or message.

The first Sherpa monastery to be established was Tengboche, in Khumbu. There are now five major Sherpa monasteries — Tengboche and Thami in Khumbu, Chiwong, Takshindo, and Tsodukpa in Solu — as well as a number of minor ones. Tengboche, Thami, and Chiwong are the largest and most influential; Tsodukpa is the newest and smallest, but its head lama is very learned and is attracting some serious disciples. In addition, there is the refugee Tibetan monastery now called Tupden Chöling, founded in Solu by the head lama and monks of Rumbu monastery of the adjacent region of Tibet, who fled to Nepal during the Chinese invasion. This monastery, under the extraordinarily vigorous leadership of its highly respected, indeed revered, reincarnate lama, the Tushi Rimpoche, is currently having a great impact on Sherpa monasticism. And, finally, there are several Sherpa nunneries, with resident populations of celibate female monastics. Unfortunately, very little is known about these institutions. All are linked in some way with a monastery, although they are usually geographically separated.[17]

In Tibetan Buddhism, in contrast to much of Southeast Asian Buddhism, taking the monastic vows is meant to be, and is for the majority of those who take them, a lifetime commitment. The world of the monastery is meant to be, and to a great extent is, wholly separate from village lay life and village religion. Monks neither officiate at nor attend village ceremonies with the exception of funerals, when it is considered essential to have monks as well as village lamas reading the texts. And villagers rarely attend monastery ceremonies, with the exception of the big annual monastery festival of Mani Rimdu.

I will give here only the briefest notes on village religious practices, because I will deal with them at length further on.

There are, first of all, frequent services in the village temple, conducted by the local lamas on a variety of ritual occasions at specified times throughout the year. Such services entail the construction of complex and beautiful altar arrangements (destroyed at the end of the service), and the reading of texts appropriate to the occasion. Few laymen attend the reading of the texts, but every service culminates with a distribution of food, for which all the villagers rather magically (to me) know exactly when to appear. Once a year there is a big festival, *Dumji,* celebrated in most of the larger village temples. At Dumji the lamas not only read the texts, but dress up in impressive costumes and dance the roles of the appropriate gods. All the villagers attend the entire Dumji cycle, which goes on for four festive days.

In addition to public temple events, village religion also consists of privately sponsored services, usually held in the sponsor's home, on the occasions of birth, marriage, illness, and death. A household may also sponsor the performance of ceremonies in the absence of any life crisis, simply for the purpose of gaining merit, luck, protection, or all three, for the household. All religious services have a broadly common structure, centering on offerings and petitions to the gods, and offerings and threats to the demons, and closing with a distribution of ritual foods to all present.

And finally, village religion includes the primordial tradition of shamanism. The shaman's primary function is to cure illness. He goes into a trance, and communicates with spirits in order to discover why they have afflicted the patient with illness and what they require as the price of their allowing the patient to get well. What they require is food, just like every other natural and supernatural being in the Sherpa world, and the shaman, when he comes out of his trance, supervises the patient's family in assembling the proper offerings and conveying them in the proper manner to the spirits.

Shamanism in the greater Tibetan culture area has a long and complex history in its relationship with the intrusive Buddhist institutions and ideas. Many of its distinctive ritual forms and basic assumptions were appropriated long ago, over a period of centuries, as Buddhism in Tibet became Tibetan Buddhism, and most of its functions continue to be appropriated by lamas, whenever they can manage it, in Tibetan Buddhist communities today. Over the same period of centuries shamanism itself also underwent much change, but it has recognizably survived into the present, among Sherpas and Tibetans, as a marginal but tenacious institution. However, with the recent invigoration of Sherpa Buddhism, and the Sherpas' first glimpses of the marvels of Western medicine, it seems to have gone into rather serious decline and may finally be on its way out (Ortner, n.d.b).

In this chapter I have sketched in the broadest strokes the general outlines of Sherpa society — history, economy, social and political organization, and religion. Virtually every institution touched upon here will receive more detailed treatment within the context of the analyses of rituals that form the core of this book. In those contexts, however, we shall see these institutions not as objective "things," which I would argue have very little significance in themselves, but rather as interacting with — articulating with and mutually enforcing, or conflicting with and mutually contradicting — one another within the totality that is Sherpa society and culture. We shall see them as it were from the inside, in terms of the significance they have (or create) one for another, and in terms of the significance they have (or create) for Sherpa actors made by and making their society. We shall begin with the most orthodox of the Sherpa rituals, *Nyungne*, the holiday of merit making, faith avowing, and atonement.

3. Nyungne: problems of marriage, family, and asceticism

The most striking aspect of orthodox Buddhism is its ascetic ideology, and the monastic tradition built around this ideology. Among the Sherpas, only about 2 percent of the men are under active monastic vows, and the entire lay population is by definition failing to live up to the highest ascetic ideal of celibacy. But these points give no indication of the degree to which the ascetic ideal nonetheless weaves through the lives and institutions of the Sherpa people. For much of life takes place as it were in counterpoint to this ideal, and occasionally in direct conflict with it.

There are, however, opportunities to enact (a version of) the ascetic ideal within lay life. Once a year, in the late spring, there is a four-day holiday called Nyungne, during which individuals may practice certain acts and renunciations, becoming "like monks" for the period of the holiday. There is a second, less stressed observance of a similar nature about six months later. And pious lay people may also spend a day fasting and performing religious actions on the full-moon and no-moon days of each month. In all cases the point is to approximate the ideal of asceticism and to gain religious merit toward a good rebirth.

The key vow of Buddhist asceticism, and the symbol of all the other renunciations of "the world," is celibacy, abstention from sexual relations. On this point alone, we are immediately cued to the fact that much of the religious ideology strikes particularly at the institutions of marriage and family, or more precisely, insofar as the religion attacks all aspects of worldly existence, it does so *through* an attack on marriage and family. And very astutely too, for these institutions are the loci of reproduction for the entire system. Marriage is one of the critical transformation points of the social process: It embodies the intersection of alliance (in the loose sense meaning simply horizontal exchange relationships between groups) and descent (vertical transmission relationships over time); it causes the breakup of old and the formation of new property units; and it launches the reproduction, both biologically and sociopsychologically, of persons who, if properly socialized, will in turn reproduce Sherpa society and culture.

We begin our entry into the workings of Sherpa society, then, with an analysis of the Nyungne ritual, which we shall consider in relation to some issues of marriage and family, and in relation to the counterpoint between the ascetic ideal and the normal practices of secular Sherpa life.

Cherenzi

The ritual

Nyungne is a period of atonement, the observance of which brings a high and powerful sort of merit to the participants. It involves fasting and other abstentions, together with acts of humility and contrition, and is the major occasion on which the lay people may systematically enact and experience the ascetic ethic.

Participation in Nyungne, as in all other Sherpa rituals, is strictly voluntary, and on a purely individual basis. Some people observe it annually, while others decide to do so on an ad hoc basis, often because of some recent disturbing event in their lives. The year I was in the field only eight village people, and a few mendicant religious widows, *genchu*, observed the holiday in the temple, although no one in the village worked on that day. The small number of participants was a matter of much head shaking, for it was said that the previous year twenty-five people had observed the holiday. In any case, although Nyungne is open to all, the majority of participants are normally late-adult and old persons, and this is culturally recognized.

The complete celebration extends over four days.[1] On the first day there is a *sang* ceremony, involving offerings to the local gods in order to mobilize their crusade against the demons and hence, by way of a complex logic, to purify the area for the performance of the main ritual.[2] The participating lamas then spend the rest of the day making ritual objects for the Nyungne altar, and that evening they and the lay people who intend to observe the fast are given a big meal in the temple by volunteer sponsors.

On the second day, the penitents spend the day in the temple, with the lamas leading them in simple prayers and recitations. Three times on that day and three times on the next they recite a long prayer begging for forgiveness from sin, release from suffering, and achievement of enlightenment. The remainder of the time they chant the formula of taking refuge in the religion, various mantras, and other simple prayers. During each recitation of the prayer of expiation, the worshipers perform repeated prostrations. One observer counted 90 prostrations each time the prayer of expiation was recited, three times on each of the two main days of the holiday, or 540 prostrations, give or take a few (von Fürer-Haimendorf, 1964: 183). My most learned lama informant said that there should be approximately 100 prostrations each time the prayer is repeated and that it should be repeated twenty-one times. Whatever the precise count, it is clear that performing prostrations is central to the observance of Nyungne.

The penitents are served one large meal at midday of the second day, by the sponsor-volunteers. Following this meal, there is a complete fast through the third day, until the dawn of the fourth, at which time the participants are given a big meal. During this period, too, there is to be absolutely no conversation.

On the fourth day, following the breaking of the fast, the lamas make altar items for a *tso*, to be held that evening. Most of the village shows up for the tso ceremony, a party of high gods and human congregation in celebration of the merit accrued and good effects wrought by the Nyungne observance. Following the tso, people volunteer for the various contributions for next year's Nyungne.

From the point of view of the Sherpas, the point of observing Nyungne is to accrue merit, and hence to negate sin, by observing the various rules of renunciation. The two primary rules are absention from food and drink, and from conversation. Others variously mentioned were: no sex, no work, and no wearing of metal or leather.[3] During the period of full observance, no musical instruments are played in the temple, although instruments play their normal role in the services preceding and following the big fast. Also during the period of full observance, children are barred from the temple, on the explanation that they will not be able to keep quiet.

On all other occasions they are not only not barred from the temple, but are not even castigated for making disturbances.

The rite is directed to the god Pawa Cherenzi (Skt., Avalokiteśvara),[4] who is identified with mercy and compassion. The lay notion seems to be that he can, in his merciful compassion, absolve one of one's sins, and that one apologizes to him for those sins and asks for his absolution. But Sherpas also know, though they probably do not fully emotionally accept, that the gods cannot help one attain salvation, either by dispensing merit or wiping out sins. The correct — that is, orthodox — dynamic of the observance, which is also widely understood and often held simultaneously with the incorrect one, is that one *identifies* with Pawa Cherenzi, making oneself all-compassionate like him, and it is this transformation of the self that brings merit and ultimately salvation. It should be noted that Pawa Cherenzi is a *shiwa* god, a deity whose basic disposition is benign and peaceful, as opposed to *takbu*, fierce and violent. The Nyungne altar items, correspondingly, are decorated with flower and rainbow designs, and the entire effect of the altar is one of calmness and radiant beauty. This is the only ritual to a shiwa god in the official village ritual calendar.[5]

Nyungne is a relatively simple ritual, although it poses a particular problem for analysis: In the rituals to be examined in later chapters, the symbolism carries us into diverse realms of social life and experience; in Nyungne all avenues of symbolism lead us back to a single institution, the family. Yet, as we shall now see, it forces us to look at the family from several different perspectives — from the outside, from the bottom up (children vis-à-vis parents), and from the top down (parents vis-à-vis children). And while there is inevitably some redundancy in the discussion, in general when a point is repeated it is in the context of a different perspective, and has different significance in that context. We now turn to the ritual symbolism of Nyungne and the various ways in which it opens the Sherpa family to us.

The problems of the ritual

Merit making and social atomism

Beginning at the most orthodox level, there is one and only one answer for why one observes Nyungne: to make merit, *payin.* There are many ways of making merit, but Nyungne is considered to be among the most powerful and effective of them.

Merit is an abstract tally or record of the virtuous deeds performed by the individual in the course of his or her lifetime. It contrasts with demerit or sin (*dikpa*), the tally of one's bad deeds. One's relative amounts of merit and sin determine one's fate in one's next life: The more merit and the less demerit one has when one dies, the better the state one will be reborn to.

While demerit cannot be wiped out once it has been recorded, it can be counterbalanced and hence neutralized by an equivalent amount of merit. But it is not enough to do virtuous deeds only when one knows one has sinned. The basic conditions of life are such that one is sinning almost all the time, whether one knows it or not. Thus one should perform virtuous deeds whenever one has the opportunity, in order to keep ahead of the game. Further, most sinful acts entail more demerit than virtuous acts entail merit. That is, one generally needs to do more virtuous acts to gain enough merit to nullify the demerit gained from only a few sinful ones. Thus once again it is important to do as much merit-work as one possibly can, for one never knows how one's score actually stands at any given time.

Theoretically, this entire moral system operates of its own natural force, and cannot be interfered with in any way. In particular it is said that the gods have nothing to do with payin and dikpa. They are not affected one way or the other when one sins, and cannot do anything to help one achieve a better rebirth than the one deserved on the basis of one's accumulated merit and demerit.

The cultural category of virtuous deeds, as of sinful deeds, is quite large, but it can for convenience be broken down into a few major subcategories. The most familiar of these, for a Westerner, includes a wide variety of what we would call acts of charity (*gyewa-zhinba*). Second, in no particular order, any sort of act which in any way supports the religion is meritorious. Third, and most relevant for the analysis of Nyungne, is any act of conscious and active abstention from sin. And fourth, and least meaningful to Westerners although rather notorious in the literature on Tibetan religion, is a category of mechanical actions and processes — spinning prayer wheels, circumambulating religious monuments, having a cloth printed with prayers or mantra waving in the wind — the operations of which automatically accrue merit for the doer or, in the case of a mechanism worked by wind or water, "for the whole world."

While space forbids a complete analysis of the corpus of meritorious deeds in Sherpa culture, all of them could, one way or another, be related to the ultimate Buddhist aim of eradicating a sense of ego or self in the subject. Eradication of the self could, logically, proceed in two possible directions. On the one hand the self may be reduced, limited, minimized to the point of its disappearance. On the other hand, the self may be enlarged, expanded beyond its original boundaries, eradicated in the sense that it becomes identified not with the private "me" but with the whole world. Broadly, the first two categories of meritorious action — charity and support of the religion — work on the second principle: The self identifies with larger, universalistic interests. And the second two categories — abstention from sin and performance of mechanical actions — work on the first principle: The self's demands are systematically denied and invalidated, and/or replaced by acts that involve no conscious agency at all.

In nonreligious terms, the basis of merit may be stated more starkly — absolute impersonality. Leaving aside the category of charity acts for a moment, what is striking about the whole set is how little it has to do with positive social deeds for specific social others. For example, within the general meritorious class of abstention from or counteraction of sin, the act that seems to play the greatest role in the

Sherpa imagination is saving the life of an animal destined for slaughter.[6] The mechanical acts of turning prayer wheels and the like are merely the logical extreme of the principle of nonpersonalism implicit in the whole system.

The category of charity seems an exception to this point. Charity at least involves interaction between two actors; it seems a social act. But the significant point about charity, I would suggest, is that it entails no reciprocation, nor indeed any relationship of any sort between donor and recipient. Further, although in theory it is meritorious to give to people who are economically needy, in practice this probably ranks as the least popular mode of charitable giving. Highest in popularity and merit is to give to very sacred individuals (i.e., reincarnate lamas), and thus this type of charity has more to do with supporting the religion than with actually helping anyone who needs help. Second in popularity and merit seem to be the various modes or occasions of indiscriminate giving: One distributes largess to all who come within purview of the giver, as at *gyowa*, funeral feasts. Helping individuals in need ranks very low. This might be rationalized in religious terms by assuming that these people are suffering because of evil deeds in past lives and therefore do not warrant much consideration. But analytically the point seems to be that these acts are too personalistic and approach the possibility of implicating the donor in some sort of relationship, precisely counter to the antipersonal tendency of the whole merit system.

The point cannot be stressed too strongly: The basis of merit, and of other modes of seeking salvation as well, is antirelational. Even where apparently social, as in giving charity, the point is precisely that the donor gives with no expectation or demand of return. Thus charitable giving does not contain its own mechanisms for creating or sustaining relationship between giver and recipient, does not contain, in other words, a tendency toward social bonding but rather tends in the opposite direction. It is clear from these points that the solitary asocial individual, who gives nothing and owes nothing, is simply the outer limiting case of the tendency contained within the logic of even the most social of meritorious actions, the charity act. And in fact this limiting case is idealized in Buddhism in the image of the fasting hermit, with minimal physical needs and no social relations — precisely the role we see dramatized in the observance of Nyungne, as people fast and do not speak to one another.

Now, the orthodox point of all this, for the actor, is to lose one's sense of ego and hence to lose all those distinctions and categories that mire one in the false appearances of the world. The final transcendence of those false appearances is salvation, which in turn, in this Mahayana tradition, is the condition for helping others achieve salvation. The ultimate aim, in other words, theoretically becomes social again, but only at the end of a long train of development through personal autonomy and social isolation.

This religious bias toward autonomy and antirelationalism resonates strongly with the basic structures of Sherpa society. In orthodox religious contexts — in monasticism, in Nyungne, and in any act of merit making — the individual is the locus of this idealized autonomy. Only the individual can save him- or herself, and the best way to do so is to isolate oneself *as* an individual, in order not to be distracted by worldly concerns from one's single-minded quest for salvation. Within the structures of secular society, however, the unit that most closely approximates the Buddhist ideal of unsocial self-sufficiency is not the individual but the family, which we must now examine.

The private-property-owning, highly independent nuclear family is the "atom" of Sherpa social structure. While of course every family has a network of kin that may be activated on a variety of occasions, and although families also depend upon long-term mutual-aid relationships for various forms of vital material assistance, nonetheless a whole range of cultural and structural factors emphasize the ideal autonomy and self-sufficiency of the nuclear family unit.

Ensconsed in its own house and operating as a self-sufficient enterprise, the nuclear family is both the normatively valued institution and the statistically prevalent form.[7] As described in the preceding chapter, it is the unit of economic life. Ideally, a family owns its own agricultural land, and is free to buy and sell its land, although in some cases not to members of other clans. It also owns its own house and, if it can afford them, herds of dairy animals, and again, it is free to buy and sell at will. The family as a team also works its own land, ideally sustaining itself from its own produce, and having enough left over to fulfill its hospitality and other reciprocity obligations, and to contribute to collective events. In theory, at the economic level, if everything were working properly, no family would need anyone or anything else.

The image of the Sherpa family as a clearly bounded unit, even a "closed" unit opposed to the rest of society, is engendered, reproduced, and reinforced by a wide variety of beliefs and practices beyond the purely economic. One source of reinforcement is the internal structure of the family itself — strong emotional bonds between parents and children are culturally stressed and subjectively experienced. Further, there is a relaxed intimacy within the household that contrasts with the experience of many "outside" social occasions. Children do not use honorific forms of grammar to their parents within the house. Family meals are warm and relaxed affairs, and etiquette rules do not apply. Pollution constraints are not operative either: Family members pass cups of beer around from mouth to mouth. And often there is relaxed and informal joking, not the nasty ragging to be heard at parties, but rather, significantly enough, occasional parodies of customs of formal etiquette of the social world "outside."

The notion of the family as a sort of "refuge" from the world "outside" is suggested by a Sherpa proverb that links mother and father with *konjok* ("Father konjok lowest, mother konjok higher, lama konjok highest"). "Konjok" is thought of by the Sherpas as a god with parental connotations of both generativeness and protection, but the term more importantly refers to the religion as a whole: The *konjok sum* is the "triple gem" of Buddhism (Buddha, doctrine, and community) within which, every time one avows one's faith, one "takes refuge."[8] Thus the proverb, by linking parents to Konjok as sources of aid, suggests that mother and father are lower-order "refuges," as the religion ("lama") is the highest.[9] The real intimacy and relaxation of life within the household supports this sense of family as refuge, as does the fact that, by and large, one's family will stick by one through thick and thin against assaults of any sort from outside. Internally of course there is often much conflict, and occasionally even violence — between husbands and wives, between fathers and sons, between brothers — as well as certain sorts of callous neglect to be discussed below. But these do not undercut the sense of family as a relaxed and up to a point reliable haven from the larger social world.

In addition to these points, there are a variety of beliefs and practices that further emphasize the "closure" of the family against society. There are first what might be called antipenetration symbols: Sherpa houses are all locked with enormous, complicated padlocks when no one is home, and bolted and barred heavily from the inside when the family goes to sleep. Many Sherpa families also keep ferocious guard dogs, legendary among trekkers and travelers, but also feared by members of the local community. And while no doubt there is some objective basis for fearing theft, the lock-and-dog syndrome seems to exceed by far the objective need, and would both express and regenerate the image of the closed household.

Along with antipenetration symbolism, there is what might be called anti-drainage symbolism. Thus the family is imputed with a sort of vital essence, the luck (*yang*) of the household, which must be contained and prevented from draining away. Many households have a day, discovered through horoscopic divining, on which the members must not sell, pay, or give anything past the portals of the house.[10] They will not even give their neighbors a few embers with which to get a fire started. Should anything be given out on such a day, it is said, misfortune will fall upon the household.[11]

There are also a number of ceremonies specifically directed toward investing a family, beginning at marriage, with luck, and then for shoring up or preventing this family luck from draining away. At weddings a scarf in which money and grain are tied is swung over the heads of the bride and groom to insure the yang of their new family/household. At funerals, after the corpse is taken out, a little ceremony is done to prevent it from taking the yang of the household with it. And any family may at any time commission the performance of a *yang-guup* ceremony by the lamas, to regain or shore up the luck of the house.

The concern with holding in and shoring up the family yang, while "symbolic," suggests not inaccurately a more general resistance of families toward exchange. The point applies not only to the exchange of goods, but to the "exchange" of children in marriage, and we shall see below that there is good evidence for familial resistance at this level as well.[12]

Finally, it should be noted that there are real historical and contemporary precedents for families being very closed and self-contained, and not participating in the social life of the community. They are, of course, the focus of disapproval and gossip, but it is by no means unknown that some families follow this course anyway. And given the absence of coercive processes and coercive will in Sherpa society, nothing can or will be done about it.[13]

Thus the image of the tight and even introverted Sherpa family is generated and sustained by at least the following factors: (1) far-reaching economic independence of the unit, and economic interdependence of the members; (2) strong emotional ties between parents and children; (3) real internal intimacy of domestic life; (4) symbolic beliefs and practices that impute a sort of vital essence to the family, an essence that must be hoarded and shored up; (5) actual historical and contemporary examples of families that isolate themselves from village social life. In light of this barrage of factors, it is not surprising that the image of the Sherpa family as closed and self-sufficient is heavily projected:

The Sherpa family consisting of husband, wife, and their unmarried children . . . constitutes a social and economic unit of great independence . . . the Sherpa family is not permanently embedded in a web of close kinsfolk. From the moment of its establishment as a separate unit . . . a married couple stands by itself, responsible to no one and relying on no one's support. (von Fürer-Haimendorf, 1964: 39)

It is important, however, to be clear about the relationship between image and reality. Sherpa families *are*, at least implicitly, embedded in social networks, *are* responsive to the obligations entailed by those relationships, and will often speak in terms of the importance of those networks as potential sources of aid and support. At the same time, subsistence production and consumption is almost entirely conducted within the confines of the family, occasions for the activation of the larger network are infrequent, and families may move about (to pastures, to areas outside their home villages where they have other fields and houses, or to urban centers) with little sense of rupture to themselves or to the rest of the village. Without denying that there are structures and processes of "community" in Sherpa villages, in other words, the point is that such community must be achieved through *overcoming* the basic atomism and insularity of the component family units.

Gods, parents, and social sentiments

Parent/child symbolism weaves through the Nyungne ritual. The major locus of such symbolism is the figure of Cherenzi, the focal god of the rite. In the "Three Bodies" system[14] of Buddhism, Cherenzi is the creator of the present world. Because of this aspect of his role, Cherenzi is always depicted holding a lotus, and every Sherpa knows that the lotus symbolizes (divine) generative energy, if only because of their familiarity with their lotus-born hero, Guru Rimpoche. The creator function of Cherenzi is one aspect of the fact that, as distinct from many other gods of the Sherpa pantheon, he may be particularly symbolic of parental figures.

But Cherenzi's dominant attribute in Sherpa thought is his merciful compassion. The only other major deity identified with mercy and compassion in the Tibetan Buddhist pantheon is Drolma (Tib., sGröl-ma; Skt., Tara), a goddess, and she is generally said to be Cherenzi's consort. Thus although Cherenzi is male, mercy and compassion are "feminine" attributes, and Cherenzi qualifies well to function as a composite symbolic parent, indeed the perfect parent, male but merciful.[15]

The term for this mercy or compassion is *nyingje,* and it has a broad range of connotations. It includes love, devotion, concern, and caring, as well as mercy and compassion — sentiments that share the element of purity of motive, or altruism, particularly on the part of a stronger person for a weaker or helpless or dependent one. Nyingje has enormous religious significance. It is one of the key concepts distinguishing Mahayana from Theravada Buddhism, the former representing itself as more "compassionate" and less self-centered than the latter. And in both Sherpa thought and Mahayana orthodoxy, "compassion" is virtually always illustrated by mother–child metaphors. One Sherpa lama defined religious nyingje as "like the feeling of a mother who has no arms and sees her baby drowning." A Tibetan Buddhist text says, "You must develop compassion and loving-kindness which are far stronger and deeper than the love a mother has for her only child" (Guenther: 107; from the text, "The Specific Guidance to the Profound Middle View".) Many other textual examples could be cited.

As these metaphors for nyingje indicate, the primary love bond is conceived to be that between mother and child, and particularly, among the Sherpas, the bond between mother and son. This relationship is culturally emphasized as one of ever stronger mutual love and perfect harmony, and in fact mother–son relationships are often exceedingly close. My notes are scattered with observations of mothers lavishing affection on baby sons. On one occasion a man was discussing the futures of the five boys who were graduating from the village school. He remarked that the top boy didn't want to go away to high school, that he wanted to stay home where his mother lavished nyingje on him. There is even a lurking cultural suspicion, not far below the surface, that mothers like their sons to become monks because that way they do not have to break the tie and give the son over to another woman. A monk was asked if his mother was happy that he had become a monk "Yes," he replied, "very happy." Why? "Because if I had taken a wife, she and my mother would fight, because my mother would envy the young wife, criticize her work, and so forth." This, he pointed out, had happened with his older brothers' wives. The problem seems most acute with youngest sons, who must bring their wives home to live in the parents' house. Youngest sons are particularly babied and favored:

Of the three sons, S.'s horoscope showed he would succeed in Nepalese learning and affairs, and T. in religion. But if the parents send any of the sons to the monastery, according to the guess of the informant, it would be A.T., the youngest, because his mother doesn't want to give him away. [Note: I have noticed that she plays with him and fondles him incessantly, and he in turn makes himself irresistibly cute to her.]

This rather hyperdeveloped mother-love for sons in Sherpa culture is explainable largely by the fact that, in this patrilineal, virilocal system, a woman may have little initial status in the local social structure to which, as an incoming wife, she must adapt. She may tend to overvalue her sons partly because they are a source of status for her: In contrast to her husband, they provide her with "natural" ties to the local patriline and village. Further, because she owns no land and is likely to outlive her husband, sons are her potential economic security as well.[16]

But while it is possible to see analytically that mother–son love in Sherpa culture is not necessarily based on purest altruism, and further that it may be socially and emotionally manipulative (as the monk's comments suggest), nonetheless the image of this relationship, as well as very often the subjective experience of it, is one of great nyingje, of purity of motive, lack of self-interest, and mutual care and concern.

Nyingje, then, is *modeled* by the ideal mother–child relationship; at the same time one's ability to feel and express it *derives*, in the cultural view, from early experience with the mother. In some cases it may be seen as deriving from a bad early childhood experience:

I saw P.H. coming back from making lunch for the old nun who takes care of the temple, the nun being laid up with various complaints. I remarked to Norbu that P.H. was very kind. He responded that when P.H. was young she had had much suffering. Her mother died when she was small, and her father remarried, and the stepmother wasn't very nice. So now P.H. has *nyingje* for other people.

The more basic assumption, however, seems to be that one's capacity for feeling nyingje derives from having directly experienced it oneself as a child.

But the cultural (and especially the religious) point is that nyingje must go beyond one's early relationship with mother, to become a generalized social sentiment, an ability to transcend the normal egotism of social life and empathize with and have compassion for others. Certainly the term is frequently on people's lips in a variety of social contexts — listening to any sort of sad tale, observing a painful situation, hearing of another's grief — all these situations evoke sympathetic facial expressions and constant murmurs of "nyingje." Yet beyond such verbal expression (and even genuine feeling), *acts* of true empathy and compassion — as people lament, as the religion insists, and as much external evidence shows — are rare in Sherpa society. The religious attack on "egotism" remains relevant and meaningful.

Ascetic ideology and the crisis of the children's marriages

Nyungne is explicitly a microcosm of the highest ascetic ethic of the religion, normally observed only by monks and even higher adepts. The two renunciations of Nyungne, from food and conversation, embody the two basic dimensions of monasticism transposed into terms appropriate to the conditions of lay life. The abstention from conversation, symbolizing the renunciation of social intercourse, parallels the monk's more dramatic actions of breaking completely with family and society, and forswearing marriage and the formation of new family bonds. The abstention from food, symbolizing the renunciation of sensuous gratification, parallels the monk's more dramatic vow of celibacy and the renunciation of sexuality. In fact, the folk interpretation of the efficacy of Nyungne for gaining merit tends to focus heavily on the fasting, as signifying the transcendence of physical need and sensuous desire. But fasting, like silence, may also be seen as an antisocial gesture, not simply not eating, but not receiving food.[17]

The ideals of monasticism are the highest ideals of Sherpa religion. While their stress is on personal purity and spiritual development, they imply a critique of virtually every aspect of normal social life. And the family is perhaps their chief target: "The family, as a biological unit, is permitted but not truly sanctioned with the highest blessing and, in theory, should be discarded as soon as possible in the individual's progress toward liberation" (Ekvall: 68). The religion is opposed to the family partly because the family is so heavily founded on sex, and partly because it is so heavily involved with material concerns. But its major corruptive aspect, from the Buddhist point of view, is that it is the locus of the strongest, most binding and blinding, but ultimately (like all the others) disappointing and betraying of all human relationships.

Every relationship inherent in the family as an institution — sex, marriage, parenthood — will (according to the religion) ultimately turn out badly: Sex brings marriage, and marriage seems exciting, but this pleasure will not last:

> At first a wife is a goddess wreathed in smiles
> and her husband never tires of gazing at her face.
> She soon becomes a fiend with corpse-like eyes;
> if he casts a reproach at her she gives two in return;
> if he takes her by the hair she has him by the leg;
> if he strikes her with a stick she beats him with a ladle.
> In the end she becomes a toothless old hag
> and her fiendish look of anger preys upon the mind.
> I have renounced such a devilish scold
> and I do not want a maiden bride.
>
> Milarepa, Tibet, twelfth century (Clarke: 30)

Further, marriage brings children and children bring joy, as well as theoretical insurance in one's old age. But children require hard work to support them, and worse, they fail to reciprocate in one's declining years:

> At first a son is as pleasing as a scion of the gods,
> irresistible to the loving heart.
> He is soon relentlessly hounded for debt,
> though his parents give their all he is never content.
> He brings home the daughter of some strange man
> and turns outside his kindly father and mother.
> Though his father calls he gives no answer,
> though his mother cries out he speaks never a word.
> At last he becomes a hasty-tempered lodger
> and drives them away with false complaints.
> Now this foe sprung of their loins
> preys continually upon their minds.
> I have renounced such wordly swill, and I do not want a son.
>
> Milarepa (Clarke: 31)

Thus children, according to one of the saints of the religion, betray one in one's old age, and one is left alone, old and weak, with nothing but death before one and the reckoning of all the sins committed in the course of lay life.

The second poem in particular would be found deeply meaningful by a contemporary Sherpa parent. Not only does it capture the sense of betrayal and abandonment most Sherpa parents feel as they get old, but it specifically links the problem to the marriages of the children. In the context of Sherpa family structure, children's marriages indeed pose severe problems for parents, and we must now reexamine problems of the Sherpa family from yet another angle. We have already looked at it "externally," as a "closed" and strongly bounded unit. And we have looked at it from one internal angle, taking a sort of child's eye view of a strong emotional tie, nyingje. Now we must look at it again internally, but this time from the point of view of the parent whose children are approaching marriage.

Children's marriages pose threats at a variety of levels. There is for the mother rupture of the nyingje bond, already discussed. (We may also recall here the monk who said that his mother was happy to have him become a monk because, in effect, their bond would not be broken by the introduction of another woman.) But the threat is also, and very saliently, a matter of "hard" economic realities. There is, first, the simple point of breaking up the work team. Every able-bodied member of the household, male and female, participates in productive labor; with the exception of the fact that women do not plow, both males and females engage in all other aspects and phases of agriculture and dairying. Further, every member of the family does some share of the domestic work — women do more, but men help with cooking and child care as well. Older brothers as well as sisters take care of younger children, and fathers often carry around the next-to-youngest baby. Once all the property transactions and ritual stages of marriage have been completed, however, the children have no formal obligations to work on the parent's property, for by definition their responsibility is now to their own estate.[18]

Second, and more critically, the inheritance system system is, as I have noted, directly tied to marriage, and the marriage of a child thus means the breakup of the family's property. Upon marriage, a son must be given his share of the family's land, and a daughter a quantity of cash, jewels, and utensils. A son should ideally also be given a house. Practically speaking, splitting up the family's field holdings may be very problematic. And buying or building a house, as well as putting together an adequate dowry, may be quite beyond the means of the family. There is no question that a child's marriage may cause real economic hardship.

Given both emotional and economic factors, then, it is not surprising that we find strong evidence for parents resisting their children's marriages. While on the surface most Sherpa parents are eager to marry off their children — parents go on the market for mates for their marriageable children when the children are in their early twenties or even before — nonetheless we get quite a different picture when we look at other sorts of data. We note first some striking statistics on the late ages at which people, despite their parents' early show of effort, actually wind up getting married: 22 percent of lay men in the 30–34 year age group are unmarried, 29 percent of lay women in the 30–34 year age group are unmarried (Oppitz: 128). Oppitz classified as unmarried not only people who had not yet entered into the marriage process, but any individual who, though having begun the process, was still living without his or her spouse in his or her natal household. It is probable indeed that most of the people in the statistics had already gone through the early stages of the rites. But the minimal condition for joint residence is that the groom be given his inheritance of house and land;[19] in addition, even when this may have taken place, the bride's family must be willing to let her go. Thus 22 percent of lay men between the ages of 30 and 34 either have not yet been given economic independence by their fathers, or are allied to wives who have not been released by their parents.

A second piece of evidence for parental resistance to children's marriages is more suggestive than conclusive, but it contributes to the overall picture: Marriages are fragile, especially (apparently) in the early stages. One observer reports a 30 percent divorce rate for Sherpas (Oppitz: 124), and this parallels another ethnographer's 30 percent figure of broken "engagements" (von Fürer-Haimendorf, 1964: 44). While I do not have independent figures, it seems likely that most divorces take place during the "engagement" period, while the bride and groom are still living in their respective parents' homes, and during which time the natal families still maintain, or try to maintain, the primary loyalties of their sons and daughters.

If the parents are indeed trying to hold onto their children, they get a great deal of support from the traditional, greatly protacted structure of the marriage process. Marriage consists of as many as six distinct stages,[20] and not infrequently drags on for ten or twelve years. The various wedding events themselves are expensive, and parental foot dragging is often rationalized in terms of not being able to afford the wedding.[21] But the most commonly wielded parental weapon in this struggle is simply moving slowly on putting together and turning over the son's inheritance and/or the daughter's dowry. Theoretically this is not legitimate, and the person who overtly flaunts the rules is an object of social scorn. Hlakpu, for example, had plenty of wealth, because a number of his brothers and sons had become monks, thus not taking their full shares of property. Yet Hlakpu never formally separated his other sons when they got married, giving them their shares of the property, nor did he provide a dowry for his daughter. Hlakpu was widely disliked for his general miserliness, and his failure to cooperate in his children's marriages was something of a scandal, but only – I would suggest – because he carried it to the extreme, and not because the basic impulse was foreign to people's imaginations.[22]

Yet even if parents acquiesce with relatively good grace to the marriage of their older children, the system is virtually designed to hit them with "crisis" at the end of the line. For the inheritance rule is such that the youngest son will receive the parental house. He is theoretically obliged to feed and care for the parents out of this last share of their estate. In fact, however, this arrangement often works out badly for the old people – they are reduced to the status of dependents, and sometimes almost servants, in the son's household, and there tends to be friction between mother-in-law and daughter-in-law. The Sherpas are quite conscious of these problems, and seem to expect little from their children in their old age. They may instead retain a small piece of land and buy or build a small house, even an animal shed, for themselves, so as to remain independent for as long as possible. Alternatively, widows and widowers may become *genchu,* old religious mendicants who abandon at last their worldly attachments and commit themselves totally to the precepts of the religion.

Thus elderly Sherpa parents are ultimately more or less abandoned, or at least neglected and treated with some callousness. [Another ethnographer noted this too, more politely: "An occasional casualness towards aged parents, though by no means frequent, mars to some extent the otherwise pleasant picture of Sherpa family life" (von Fürer-Haimendorf, 1964: 87).] And this is perhaps one of the great tragic themes of Sherpa culture. Milarepa's poem expresses it, as does an image used by a lama explaining a point of religious orthodoxy to me. He was telling me that the godly state within the Wheel of Life, though apparently attractive, is not really so, for the gods must, like everyone else, die and be reborn. He said that when they die, their bodies begin to smell, and the smell becomes repulsive to their children, who then throw their parents' bodies out of paradise.

The prospect of being metaphorically thrown overboard by one's children in one's old age is both tragic as personal betrayal and frightening in terms of economic security. And while the whole process climaxes late in life, with the marriage of the last child, it begins to unfold much earlier, as each child's marriage cuts a slice out of the family and its estate. The parents, as we saw, try to forestall the disintegration of the unit as long as possible, and one might be tempted to view this in purely rational–economic terms. But I would argue strongly against such a view. Losing the children's labors, giving them their shares of the family wealth, and financing expensive weddings are indeed economically problematic, but they also *mean* something disturbing to the parents beyond sheer economic loss. For in this private-property society where one *is* largely what one *owns,* social identity and status are largely bound up with heading and managing a thriving estate. Particularly given the absence of formal statuses of honor or authority as alternate loci of social identity, family and property are not merely sources of survival, or even comfort and luxury, but the very basis of one's social self. It is clear then that the parents' identities as social beings would be closely tied to the identity and coherence of the family unit. The significance and worth of their life careers come to be identified with its career.[23] It seems important to stress these points, for the Sherpas know just as well as anyone that "you can't take it with you." The crisis of children's marriages, and of aging in Sherpa culture, is a crisis of personal identity as well as of personal survival.

The betrayal of aging parents is thus a virtually inevitable reflex of the structure and developmental cycle of the Sherpa family as a tightly bounded corporation. The relatively closed, corporate nature of Sherpa families in turn poses problems at a broader social level — difficulties in achieving interfamily cooperation, a fairly high degree of friction in interfamily relations, and a relative absence of community in Sherpa villages. And both the problem of aging and the atomism of the community are reflected in the cultural sense of the need for, but scarcity of, nyingje — love, compassion, empathy. All these issues were signaled by the symbolism of the Nyungne ritual, and we now return to the ritual to see how it deals with them through its symbolic structure and development.

The solutions of the ritual

Descriptively, Nyungne is a simple ritual. People gather in the temple, undertake a fast and other deprivations for a period of time during which they recite certain prayers and chants, and perform repeated prostrations. In the process they are meant to achieve identification with Pawa Cherenzi and hence gain much merit.

Despite the simplicity of the observance, however, it clearly involves extreme condensation of complex and profound feelings and meanings. All of this is reflected in the uncharacteristic seriousness with which the Sherpas treat Nyungne: Once committed to its observance, any given individual must and does remain in the temple for the full period and go through every aspect of it. In contrast to other occasions, there are few adults circulating in and out of the temple, no children dashing about and making noise, no delays between stages during which people joke and converse. Further, it is clear that the very nature of the observance is calculated to have strong effects upon the participants. Almost forty-eight hours of fasting, silence, and bowing could not, it would seem, fail to render the participants vulnerable to strong feelings. If one combines these effects with mental concentration upon Cherenzi — fostered by the no-conversation rule, the bowing, and the content of the prayers and chants, as well as the ten-foot-high idol of beautiful, benign, smiling Cherenzi before the worshipers in the temple — surely it is not difficult to believe that for many the observance of Nyungne is a profound if inarticulable experience.

In order to understand the nature of the Nyungne experience in relation to the problems of the Sherpa social world discussed above, the rite will be examined in three aspects. Beginning at the most orthodox level, the rite will be considered as a religious attempt to foster compassion and altruism in a society structured in favor of self-interested modes of social relations. Then, because Nyungne is largely observed by the elderly, it will be examined in relation to the particular life situation of these people, as a rite of passage to "postparenthood." And finally, the apparent polarity, but actual reciprocity, between ascetic ideology and the nuclear-family-based social structure will be discussed.

The fostering of altruism

The participants in Nyungne are supposed to achieve identification with the god Pawa Cherenzi, who is loving, compassionate, and altruistic. The contrasting complex of sentiments are those clustering about "egotism" — a sense of mine and thine,

of debt and quid-pro-quo obligation. The Sherpas see both of these sets of sentiments as orginating in the family experience, love or altruism associated with
mother, debt or obligation symbolically focused more on father.

Both a sense of love or altruism, and a sense of obligation (and obligating) are in
turn seen as central to the proper operation of full-scale social life. Every individual
must be able to experience and incur these sentiments in relations with many social
others. That is, according to the Sherpas, one must generalize or universalize sentiments that, while they originate in relations with one's parents, must become part
of one's emotional repertoire in dealing with the wider social world.

Now in the next chapter we shall see that the whole debt-and-obligation syndrome
seems very successfully to achieve this transformation to a universal social principle:
It is the cornerstone of village social process.[24] The generalization of love, on the
other hand, seems much more problematic for the Sherpas, and perhaps for all
human beings. The religion, however, through vehicles such as Nyungne, claims
the responsibility — and the credit — for furthering this process as much as possible.

It seems immediately significant that such a small number of people participated
in Nyungne. The Sherpas say that Nyungne is hard or rigorous, primarily (according
to them) because of the extended deprivations and exertions, but perhaps also (I
would suggest) because people might not be particularly open to having their sense
of altruism expanded. In the context of this suggestion, it is interesting that when I
asked my neighbour why she wasn't observing Nyungne, she replied, "I don't have
any money." The reply seemed somewhat nonsensical, partly because Nyungne, as
a microcosm of the ascetic ethic, subsumes the message that material concerns are un-
important, and also because it doesn't cost a penny to observe the holiday — one
consumes none of one's own food, and indeed when one eats one is fed by others.[25]
But her reply makes sense if one assumes that people might be resistant to having
their altruism and generosity inflated if they cannot really afford to give things
away. To put the point slightly differently, one may feel if one is poor that it is not
oneself that needs to feel altruistic. One may be resentful about one's own economic
position, and not particularly open to experiencing the sentiments that Nyungne is
intended to foster.

Yet Nyungne may nonetheless be interpreted as an attempt, however unsuccess-
ful, to inject at least some measure of the religious values into lay life: compassion,
nonegocentricity, non-self-interested modes of relating. Nyungne is meant to turn
lay people, who have already cast their lot with the secular world, into at least better
lay people than they are.[26]

In performing this transformation, the rite utilizes aspects of classic "rite of passage" structure and symbolism. In particular, there is important usage of the retrogression–progression movement common to such rites, in which the person is in
effect reduced to a presocial state in order to be reformed as a new sort of social
being. In the case of Nyungne, the point seems to be to resituate the worshipers in
the context of the early relationship with mother (or some idealized version thereof),
from which position they may recapture the purity of love and mutuality of caring

in that relationship. The first move of Nyungne is the withdrawal of the participants into the temple, where they are immediately given a meal by the sponsor-volunteers. Thus the first experience of the ritual is that of being fed by altruistic others who (like mother) demand and expect nothing from one in return.

During the main period of observance, the participants are under the rule of no-conversation. This too may have a retrogressive association, particularly in the repetition of mantra, socially meaningless (although religiously meaningful) syllables, akin to – although the Sherpas would surely resent the parallel – a child's pre-language syllable-noises (see Paul n.d.c).

Also during this period one repeatedly recites the "Refuge Formula":

> I go for refuge to the Buddha
> I go for refuge to the Dharma
> I go for refuge to the Sangha
> I go for refuge to the Triple Gem
> So that I and all sentient beings, my mothers,
> May be led to complete and Perfect Enlightenment.

(Willis: 9)

While there are many minor variations on the basic formula, this particular text makes explicit the point that the worshiper is situated as child vis-à-vis the universe of "all sentient beings," called "my mothers." Further, throughout the observance one performs repeated prostrations expressing, among other things, one's weakness before the religion and the gods, and one's deep dependence upon them. (I will return to prostrations below.) But because the focal god in this case is Cherenzi, a mother-symbol god, one is specifically expressing – and presumably reexperiencing – one's early dependence upon one's mother, in the context of a relationship of pure love.

Now the point about love, analytically, is that it is a relationship of mutuality, rather than reciprocity. The parties in a love relationship are interchangeable; either could be the other and their status/role in the relationship would be the same. Thus when the religious explication of Nyungne claims that the participants identify with Cherenzi, this is quite literal. Insofar as they recapture the primal experience of mutual loving, they become identical – "identified" – with the other with whom this experience is shared. They "become" Cherenzi.

But let us explore the logic of this transformation more closely. I am suggesting that the reattainment of the subjectivity of infancy and the achievement of universal altruism as universal mother are one and the same act, for mothers and children are united and identified with one another in a relationship of pure love. Two points may be adduced in support of this interpretation. One is that the Sherpas see infancy not as a period of egocentricity but as a period of purity, innocence, and precorruption (Paul, 1970: 154). The second point, more directly relevant to the Nyungne analysis, lies in the body of imagery surrounding nyingje: When we read Buddhist texts, we find nyingje, great religious compassion, illustrated not only by images of mother-love for a child, but also accompanied by injunctions to love the whole world "as if all beings were your mother."[27] The version of the "Refuge Formula" cited above also embodies this point. That great pure love is thus not only like a mother's love for a child, but also like a child's love for its mother, indicates the interchangeability of child and mother in the love relationship. And thus the apparently paradoxical moment at the heart of Nyungne, where one regains infancy to become identified with the universal Cherenzi-mother, is not actually a paradox, but a symbolically powerful transformation point.

If one achieves identification with Cherenzi through this process, then, one ideally becomes universally compassionate, loving, generous, merciful, altruistic. This is the essentially religious intent of Nyungne. Interestingly enough, however, the ritual seems to provide no follow-up for this transformation. It would make sense, for example, if the people who went through the Nyungne observance then traditionally volunteered to sponsor the following year's observance, thus demonstrating and expressing the altruism they have come to feel, but this is not the way it works. It would make sense, too, if those who had gone through the observance then distributed charity and/or made donations to religious causes, but again this is not the way it works.[28]

In fact, one informant reported that in his Khumbu village it was the practice for the villagers to come to the temple and distribute money *to* the worshipers. This detail seems highly significant if seen as part of the totality of "becoming monks," enacting as literally as possible the ascetic ideal. For in this ideal, the altruism or compassion of the ascetic has little to do with real material help for others. It is a matter of seeking one's own salvation and thereby providing an example for others of how they should go about seeking theirs. This, then, is the kind of "compassion" also achieved by Nyungne worshipers, as evidenced by the fact that others now give material things to them, as to monks, acknowledging the good they bring to the world by showing the way.

In the context of this point, a myth cited as the precedent for Nyungne may be introduced, the story of Gelungma Palma. It was first told me by the most learned of the local lamas, and was the most commonly cited precedent for Nyungne in the Solu area in which I worked:

Once there was a woman in India who had leprosy. Everyone made fun of her, and she was very unhappy. So she prayed to Pawa Cherenzi for help, and he actually appeared to her and gave her his blessing, and she was cured. In gratitude she took the vows of a *gelung* [fem., *gelungma*], the highest kind of monk. Now on Nyungne the people do as she did.[29]

The lama went on to explain that during the long prostrations the text reads as if the worshiper were the gelungma herself, talking to Pawa Cherenzi, saying "thank you" and other phrases of gratitude and obligation. But note that her mode of expression of gratitude to Cherenzi was neither to do anything for him in return (impossible at any rate), nor to go out and help others directly as Cherenzi had helped her, but rather to go off and take the vow of gelunghood.

The altruism or compassion of Nyungne, then, turns out to be a quite abstract and unsocial sort of sentiment: It is identified with *detachment* from normal social relations. This of course is the straight orthodox view, and we should not be surprised to find it embodied in Nyungne, the most orthodox of lay rituals. But it also relates directly to a second, less orthodox dimension of the meaning of Nyungne, to which we now turn.

Nyungne as passage to postparenthood

The religion in its highest ideals proposes one and only one solution to the problems of human experience: to break all social bonds, to refuse to form new ones, and to concentrate all one's energies on seeking enlightenment. It does not seem farfetched (nor is it particularly novel) to characterize the ideals of orthodox ascetic Buddhism, which are carried through quite intact into Sherpa Buddhism, as radically antisocial.

Specifically, however, we have seen that the religious attack is focused on one particular set of social relationships — those of marriage and family. The monastic ideal is actually aimed primarily at the young, to catch them before marriage and to offer them an alternative to family life. Yet it seems clear from our discussion of the Sherpa domestic cycle that the people best in a position to appreciate its message are in fact older people, who have begun to feel the disillusionment with and betrayal by family and children expressed in Milarepa's poem about the son who "turns outside his kindly father and mother."

It thus seems fair to consider Nyungne primarily in relation to the late-adult lay person, for whom its observance may be interpreted as providing a model of and for development beyond parenthood. In real life, as one gets old and one's children marry away; as one's property disperses bit by bit with each of their marriages; as one's physical powers, including one's sexuality, wane; and as the social structural realities of lay life are such that in fact one is not taken care of by one's children but is left to fend for oneself — as all of these things inexorably develop, the Nyungne observance, as a microcosm of the entire ascetic ethic and practice, provides a positive structure of accommodation to this process.

It is a model *of* this process, since in fact Nyungne, and asceticism generally, comes more and more to be a very close, almost isomorphic "reflection" of the real situation of older people: asexual, propertyless, not working, and perhaps not even talking very much to anyone.

But it is also a model *for* appropriating these realities and rendering them positive and meaningful. Only the religion has a solution: it has argued all along that precisely these traits — asexuality, etc. — are the conditions for realizing transcendence and salvation. Thus although the rite is open to all and could be interpreted in relation to any stage of the life cycle, I feel justified in interpreting it primarily in relation to this particular life stage, especially in view of the overwhelming predominance of older people among the participants. Specifically, I will argue that the rite moves the participants to an experience of "autonomy" — of personal separateness experienced not negatively as abandonment but positively as independence and dignified self-reliance. In this context, different dimensions of the classic "passage" structure become relevant. Where, in the context of the fostering of altruism, the retrogression–progression movement of this structure was critical, here the stages of segregation, liminality, and aggregation (see van Gennep) come to the fore.

The participants begin by withdrawing from their households and segregating themselves in the temple, where they will remain for the entire period. It seems directly significant for the present interpretation that the one category of people barred from entering the temple is children. Adults who are not participating may come into the temple at one point or another and perform one or two cycles of the expiation prayer and prostrations. But in contrast to all other ritual occasions, children may not come in. While the cultural explanation is that children will talk and thus break the no-conversation rule, the prohibition makes far more sense in the context of the postparenthood problem: Children are part of the problem with which the rite is dealing.

When the participants first gather in the temple, they are fed a meal by the sponsor-volunteers. It is immediately established that the participants, having taken refuge in the religion, will be cared for by others who have no personal ties to them and who, like the religion in general, operate on purely altruistic motives. The phase of segregation thus not merely detaches the participants from their normal social relations, but also embodies the implication of nondependence upon those ties.

In the liminal period, next, there is no linear sequence of events, but rather a cyclical repetition of certain prayers and acts, all encompassed by fasting and restraint of conversation. It is here that the detachment of the first phase is strongly consolidated and further transformed in the direction of genuine autonomy.[30]

All the observances of the liminal period — the fasting, the nonconversation, the repetition of mantra — may be interpreted in relation to this point. Insofar as one not only eats food but exchanges it, the fasting of Nyungne is a general gesture of nonexchange. (It is also an implicit assertion of autonomy vis-à-vis family in particular, because one's primary source of food, at any stage of life, is one's family.) And the abstention from conversation clearly signifies abstention from social intercourse — words, along with food, are the primary objects of exchange. Along these lines the mantra, the religious syllable-formulae that one repeats between prayers, are once again significant. Mantra are, as noted above, packed with religious significance, and indeed are much more meaningful than ordinary words. But from the sociological perspective it is noteworthy that mantra have no communicative value whatsoever — they are nonsense syllables. They establish a direct, vertical relationship between the individual and the highest cosmic processes. They are not simply noncommunication; they are directly counter to communication.

But the primary positive act of the liminal period of Nyungne is the performance of prostrations, *shawa*, and these lead us into more subtle dimensions of the process of detachment from the family. The normal object of prostrations is Konjok, a sort of ur-deity with strong and specific parental connotations.[31] Konjok in turn summarizes the gods and the religion as a whole, before whom or which one prostrates oneself.

Prostrations have a complex set of meanings. They include apologizing to the gods for sins and begging for remission of or forgiveness from sins; expressing gratitude for the bounty and aid of the gods; and "taking refuge" in the religion — placing oneself wholly and unconditionally within its strictures and under its guidance. The sum of significance seems paradoxical, containing both expressions of dependence ("refuge") and independence ("forgiveness," release). It might be noted, however, that these are precisely the components of the paradox of old age itself, in which a full-grown socially and culturally competent adult is nonetheless physically incompetent like a child. But the signs are inverted. Old people are seeking release from their children, who are lower than themselves. Yet in prostrations to the gods they seek release from beings who are higher than themselves.

Herein, then, lies the symbolic dynamic of the ritual. Postparents find their status inverting. They are, or begin to realize that they soon will be, in a position of debt and dependency vis-à-vis their children rather than the other way around. At the very least, even if they are not yet materially dependent upon their children, they may experience the symbolic/emotional dependence described above. The prostrations then reestablish the "proper" order of things, reorienting the participants' dependence, gratitude, etc., upward in relation to higher forces, rather than downward onto lower powers — one's children. And here precisely is where the religious message and meaning has great force: It breaks the natural cyclicity of the life course, from dependence to independence to dependence, and offers instead a linear progressive movement — a realm beyond the normal infantilism of old age, a higher order in relation to which one may place oneself, an upward movement beyond society.[32]

But while one thus places oneself in a position of what might be called "higher dependence," this turns out to be in essence "autonomy" — freedom from all needs, desires, obligations, responsibilities, and relationships. For the effect of the whole process, if it has worked properly, is that one achieves identification with the god Cherenzi. And the significant fact about Sherpa gods is that they "need nothing," they are wholly fulfilled and satisfied, they are the only truly autonomous beings in the universe.

But Cherenzi is not just any god; he is a parent-symbol god, the creator of the universe who has compassion and love for all benighted beings, compassion and love like — as Sherpas and texts endlessly tell us — a mother has for her children. Thus while one may have begun to lose one's own fleshly children, in becoming Cherenzi one gains instead the whole universe as children needy of one's gifts, help, love, and compassion. One becomes, when one achieves identification with Cherenzi, the universal parent.

The liminal period concludes with the participants exhausted, hungry, and presumably spiritually transformed. As the final act of the ritual, there is what appears to be a classic rite of reaggregation, a collective feast, *tso*. The tso, which is the concluding phase of all Tibetan Buddhist rituals, is explained as a party for the gods and the congregation. It consists of offering the gods a variety of foods that are then distributed to all the worshipers and collectively consumed. Virtually the entire village came to the tso at the conclusion of the Nyungne I observed, and in that sense it was a genuinely communal event. Yet it is noteworthy that no special attention was paid to the individuals who had observed Nyungne. They were not feted or honored in any way, nor were there any gestures that might be interpreted specifically as reaggregating them into the group. This final act of Nyungne, then, does not fully undercut the significance of the liminal phase. It does not involve symbols and gestures of reintegrating the participants back into normal social roles and structures. In this sense it may be said that the experience of autonomy of the participants is to some extent left intact. And if Nyungne has worked at the deepest religious level, this autonomy may be considered "real" — a genuine detachment from the particularistic sense of social abandonment, and a restructuring of one's subjectivity in the direction of a benign universalistic attitude.

Ascetic ideology and family structure

Monastic asceticism is founded on the vow of celibacy. As one monk said, if you break the other vows, it's like cutting the limbs of a tree, but if you break the vow of celibacy, it's like chopping down the trunk. And in Nyungne, the participants are said to become monks for the period of the observance. They do not have any sex during the entire period, of course, but the stressed abstention of the holiday is fasting rather than celibacy. This makes sense on a purely practical level — three or four days of abstention from sex would hardly be much of a sacrifice,[33] while the religion can hardly demand that monks fast for an entire lifetime. And the symbolic interchangeability of food and sex also makes sense, because the overt point is renunciation of the sensuous world in general; both fasting and celibacy may symbolize this point.

Yet I have already suggested that the stress on celibacy in asceticism is less an attack on sex in general than on the institution of marriage in particular, and the culture obliquely seems to recognize this. The Sherpas themselves see asceticism and marriage as directly opposed and mutually exclusive choices confronting an individual at a given moment in life. One decides that one will become a monk *instead of* getting married, or one finds oneself moving toward marriage and realizes that one is losing one's chance to become a monk. Either forecloses the possibility of the other, and one is forced to make a choice (Paul, 1970: 440).[34]

The point that it is marriage rather than sex to which the ascetic ideal is opposed may also be supported in a somewhat different way: by noting the striking polar contrast between the ritual of Nyungne and the rites of marriage. (Interestingly enough, weddings ignore sex just as much as Nyungne does, for while sex is assumed in marriage — and once married, *only* in marriage[35] — the central point of marriage is the formation of socially and economically independent property units.) The two rituals are inversions of one another on every dimension.

In terms of style or tone, Nyungne is ascetic, austere, and inward turning. There are no sensuous gratifications, and there is no social communication between the participants. Weddings, on the other hand, focus largely on eating and drinking, singing and dancing. They are happy, noisy, sensuously gratifying events, and intensely social. Further, quite simply, Nyungne is religious and weddings are avowedly secular. There is minimal religious ritual at a wedding, and the lamas' main function is to carry banners to ward off the evil demons who are attracted by all the food, drink, and wealth displayed at the event. When, before having attended a wedding, I asked a woman whether there would be any religious ritual, she replied that religion was for funerals, that at weddings there is eating and drinking and fun.

In terms of structure, Nyungne stresses vertical ties of dependence on a parent-figure deity, and operates against any sort of horizontal bonding. Weddings, on the other hand, deemphasize parent–child ties and stress horizontal bonds in various modes. Space forbids including a full analysis of weddings here, but suffice it to say that at every ritual stage of the protracted marriage process, the key transactions are either between the two sets of parents, or between the parents and their respective mutual-aid networks, or, at the end, between the new couple and their newly acquired mutual-aid network. Vertical transactions are minimized or undercut in various ways, including the point that the actual transfer of property from father to son is unmarked by ritual or public notice. Parents and children scarcely relate to one another at all throughout any of the official events of the wedding.

What is noteworthy in the sociology of weddings is in fact the prominence of mutual-aid (*tsenga tsali*) relationships throughout the proceedings. At the broadest level the religion is, I have suggested, against not just marriage but all sorts of social bonding. Mutual-aid relationships, based in turn largely upon kinship ties, are the most enduring sets of bonds in Sherpa society. A tsenga tsali crystallizes around each family at marriage, and it will be, at the practical level, the most important larger network within which the family will operate for the duration of its existence. Weddings, then, stress the "openness" of the family, its participation in wider social relations, while Nyungne and asceticism, as I will show in a moment, reinforce its tendencies toward "closure" and "autonomy."

Finally, the contrast between weddings and Nyungne may be drawn in terms of the comparative popularity of the two events. Nyungne drew only eight people the year I was in the field, and although it was said that there had been more participants in other years, and in other villages, it is clear that it is not a highly popular ritual. Weddings on the other hand draw vast, noisy throngs, and the Sherpas consider them their favorite social events.

The opposition between asceticism and society is thus dramatized sharply by the contrast between Nyungne and weddings. And yet of course most people get married. And yet too the ideal of celibate monasticism gets reproduced and passed on from generation to generation. Here indeed is a major puzzle: Why should people keep subscribing to a system of ideals that devalues marriage and the family, when the overwhelming majority of people in fact get married with much rejoicing, and in fact invest a great deal of affect and energy in the family?

In answering this question, I will argue that, despite the appearance of opposition between ascetic ideals and family structure, there is in fact a sort of closed dialectic, operating over time, between the two, each actually engendering, or at least reinforcing, the other. Both sides of this process are rather subtle, but it is perhaps easier to see some ways in which ideology and symbolism affect — reinforce, and even reshape — social structure, and I will begin with that side first.

It seems inescapable to note, first, that the overall shape of Nyungne is a more or less direct reflection and validation of the "closed family." The rite stresses ties, only minimally symbolically transmuted, of parent–child relations, and urges not merely connection between the parent-divinity and the children-worshipers, but total identification between the two. Further, the ritual manages to imply that one can have family and parenthood without the intervening horizontal transaction of marriage, that the family can emerge ex nihilo and then reproduce itself without either loss or addition of members through marriage. For note that Cherenzi is androgynous, a merciful loving father, a male mother. The family in Nyungne symbolism is truly a closed, magically self-reproducing unit.

But the intent of the family symbolism in the religious context is very specific: It is being used to evoke the sense and experience of nyingje, of altruism, love, and compassion. Insofar as religion cannot reject sociality altogether (however much it may tend in that direction), it wishes to stress the altruistic over the self-interested modes of sociality. Because the family, but particularly the maternal relationship, is the primary context in which nyingje is experienced in lay life, the religion winds up symbolically validating family relationships for this reason, however much it may ideologically fulminate against them.

But it actually goes further than this. In reality the family contains both the debt-and-obligation mode, identified largely with the father–child relationship, and the love-and-compassion mode, identified with the mother–child relationship. In Nyungne, however, the debt-and-obligation mode that generates most of familial conflict largely disappears, and the family is identified almost exclusively with altruism, its most desirable characteristic. Nyungne in other words does not validate the undifferentiated family, but rather stresses one element and thus in fact idealizes it. In this context then, the parental symbols point beyond themselves to the larger structure: Mother is a symbol not only of the altruistic mode of social relations, but also of the family as an institution, while father in turn is a symbol not only of the self-interested modes of social relations, but of the social world beyond the family where such modes of social relations are considered to prevail.

The effect then is once again to reinforce the closure of the family, in this case both by idealizing its internal relationships and by polarizing it against society at large. Sharpening the opposition between family and society, in turn, works to downgrade and render less meaningful those few secular modes of social coopera- tion, mutual aid, and collective pleasure that exist. This is clearly in religion's "interest" – it implies that once one loses one's family, or in some other way finds it less than fully supportive, one has nowhere else to go, no other "refuge" than the religion. And in many ways the religion is not misleading people even on this point, for although there are mutual-aid groups, or at least networks, these have no social- welfare functions: If an individual loses all productive members of his or her nuclear family, for example, the mutual-aid group will not care for him or her. Both orphaned children, and old people whose children have completely died off or dis- persed, are not objects of collective secular support.[36] Monasteries on the other hand can, and especially for old people often do, perform social security functions, for old people may attach themselves to monasteries in a special status and receive both material and spiritual assistance.

By portraying the image of the closed family in its symbolic forms, by idealizing the emotional quality of family relationships, and by symbolically polarizing the family against society at large, Nyungne belies its theoretical intent: Though it em- bodies an ideology that attacks the family, the ritual actually makes a contribution, through symbolic processes, to its reproduction. Yet it is perhaps even more of a puzzle that the ascetic ideology itself gets reproduced from generation to genera- tion, when so few people become monks, when monks (as we shall see in Chapter 6) get so little support from the laity, and when so few people make even the minimal gesture of observing Nyungne. I would argue, however, that just as asceticism in- directly reproduces the primary institution – the family – it attacks, so the primary sources for the reproduction of the ideology lie in that same institution.[37]

I begin once again from the point that Nyungne is observed largely by older people. The Sherpas do not find this abnormal, and in fact in other contexts say quite explicitly that it is only as one grows older that one comes fully to appreciate the importance of doing meritorious work and living up to the religious ideals. Children are said not to "understand" payin and dikpa, virtue and sin, and only to develop this understanding gradually. Even – or especially – young people in the prime of life, while understanding the moral precepts, nonetheless are assumed not to appreciate their full import. Young men and women are said to be caught in the throes of sexuality, especially distracting during adolescence and young adulthood. But later, as one's body begins to degenerate, and as one sees one's contemporaries dying, one becomes increasingly aware that one will die too, and that one must per- force be concerned with one's fate after death. Thus Sherpas consider it "natural" that it is primarily late-adult and old people who participate in Nyungne, because old people facing death, they say, realize the importance of making merit.

The culture then recognizes that the generations will have divergent investments in the religious ideals, but the cultural explanations for this rest on biological fac- tors – the natural ignorance of children, the sexual urges of adolescence, the bodily decay of old age foreshadowing physical death. All of this has some truth to it, but it is not analytically the whole story. For young people have an interest in marriage that is more than a sexual urge — an interest in being just like everyone else in Sherpa society, socially and economically independent, in their own households, on their own property, out from under the parental economic and emotional hold.[38] Parents on the other hand, as discussed above, have interests *against* their children's marriages. Not only will they lose members of the work team, but the marriage of a son will actually break up the family property. Further, the dispersal of the children and the breakup of the property will have emotional as well as economic implications: The parents have invested much of their adult identities in the family as an intimately bonded unit. This heavy investment is no doubt sustained by the actual cooperation of all members of the family in economic production itself. But it is also fostered by various aspects of cultural ideology that emphasize the mystical corporateness of the family and the special committed, enduring, and solidary quality of its relationships as opposed to those in society at large.

It is at the point of the children's marriages, then, that the parents may actually tighten their grip on their children, attempting to delay their marriages in various ways. Increased parental possessiveness and delayed wedding stages, however, will intensify conflict between parents and children; a son often becomes, in Milarepa's phrase, a "hasty-tempered lodger," which in turn sharpens the parents' sense of betrayal. All of which seems to fulfill religion's prophecies about the inevitable pain of social, and particularly family, life. And suddenly the religion begins to make sense in a profound, and very personal, way.

There are of course a number of ways to discover and enact a deepening religious commitment, of which observance of Nyungne is only one, although it is the most dramatic and meritorious of them. And Nyungne may, if it works at the profound religious level at which it aims, actually liberate people from the disturbing emotional investment in their children, once and for all. If it does not work at this level, however, it may still be effective in helping them at least to deinvest in the child whose marriage is most imminent. Thus they feel aided by participation in the ritual, and grow further committed to its ideals.

Here then we have the key to the process of reproduction of the ascetic ideology. It happens in a sort of discontinuous cycle, depending for its operation on the developmental cycle of the domestic group, and the process of generational passage. ("Wait till you grow up. Then you'll understand.") The religious ideology remains for a long time quite abstract to most people; it is encapsulated in Nyungne, in monasteries, and in the notions of sin and merit which, while more pervasive in everyday life, might still not be taken terribly seriously. But as one ages, and conflict develops, silent or overt, over one's children's approaching marriages, one "moves into" the ideology, one's life intersects with it. The ideology, and rituals such as Nyungne, seem to offer the parents a subjectively satisfying "refuge" from the conflict, helping them at least to achieve some distance from it, if not full detachment.

It would thus perhaps not be too strong a statement to say that virtually the entire system of religious ideals is, among many other things, a model — an ideology, if you will — of and for the situation of aging parents. Its message would be most meaningful to them, and it would be appropriated by them as a way of coping with, but also perhaps as a weapon in, the conflict produced by their children's movement toward marriage. Such conflict seems virtually inevitable in this system, a system where property is divided at marriage, property that is private and that becomes to people a matrix of personal identity in their lives. And thus although for young people there is conflict and opposition between the interest in marriage and the ideal of monasticism, for parents with children approaching and moving into marriage, there is actually convergence between personal interest and high religious ideals. Parents' interests against the marriages of their children in fact coincide nicely with religious salvational precepts. And we can understand now both why, in *social* terms, Sherpas tend to "get religion" as they get older, and how it is that ascetic ideology continues to be meaningful for, and reproduced by, Sherpas who do not and will not ever enact that ideology.

We must now, however, temporarily depart from the sphere of religion. One of the themes of this chapter has been the introversion of the Sherpa family, and the relative atomization of society that this family structure both produces and is produced by. We must now explore this social atomization from a different perspective, and at the same time counterbalance to some extent the image of utter lack of cohesion in Sherpa society that has perhaps been conveyed. We shall thus turn to the Sherpas at their most social, in village hospitality practices.

4. Hospitality: problems of exchange, status, and authority

From one, not inaccurate, point of view, the key fact of Sherpa social structure is its relative "atomization" into nuclear family units and estates. At the same time, however, a Sherpa village is a community, with lively social interaction, a reasonable degree of order and solidarity, and often a certain collective identity. Such communal solidarity and identity is reproduced in many contexts: in the periodic macro-events of village temple rituals, and in the countless microinteractions of day-to-day social life.

But there is also an intermediate level of social event in which the community reproduces itself, with its distinctive structures, processes, and style, as a community: in formal parties privately sponsored by individual households, with most of the rest of the village as guests. A household will give a formal hospitality event in conjunction with a wedding, a funeral, or a privately sponsored New Year, mid-year, or other seasonal ritual. While only the wealthier households commission seasonal rituals and entertain large numbers of people on those occasions, even the poorer families will sponsor major parties in conjunction with weddings and funerals, if they are not to drop out of community membership altogether. Giving and receiving hospitality are among the major acts of sociality in Sherpa culture.

The party

Guests are invited to a party only a few hours before the event is to begin, the host/hostess sending their children around to the village households to tell people, "Come, they said!" When the guests arrive later in the day, they are seated and served tea or beer. The men sit in status rank order around the periphery of the room. Because the status of individuals may fluctuate, however, the seating process is not as casual as it may appear, although it is all done in the usual Sherpa style of hearty jocularity. The women sit in the center of the room, with little apparent ordering.[1]

The food is not served for several hours, but beer flows continuously during the period before the meal, and conversation is loosened and heated by the alcohol as time goes on. Often someone will initiate a sort of scathing "joking" with another that may become quite vicious. It may or may not culminate in an outright quarrel,

Men eating in status order at a picnic

but it nonetheless generates, as time goes on, a fair amount of tension and antagonism. Eventually, however, the food is served, and this interrupts, and usually puts
an end to, the repartee. (The food is served in a distinctive manner to be discussed
below.) The meal itself is enjoyed and appreciated, and after the meal there is often
singing and dancing, engaged in with pleasure and enthusiasm. Finally people begin
to drift out, with no particular formality. Such, in brief, is a Sherpa party, with its
highs and its lows.

   Hospitality is the most generalized form of "being social" in Sherpa society.
Enacted time and again, from small-scale visiting and entertaining to vast and lively
events such as the one just sketched, hospitality is the central "ritual" of secular
social relations. It is perhaps best seen as being on the border between ritual [the
latter a special (sacred) context removed and bounded off from everyday life] and
everyday life itself, the ongoing flow of work and casual interactions that simply
happen as people go about their business. The ritualism of hospitality is etiquette,
a trivial term in our own culture, but a tremendously fruitful domain of analysis
for the anthropologist. In etiquette, certain social interactions have been shaped,

formalized, and raised, one might say, to the level of statements about the meaning
of sociality in the culture.

While a party such as the one described is noninstrumental — is not conducted
with any goal or purpose other than to be a pleasurable social event — hospitality
also functions as the model for conducting most of the critical instrumental transactions in the society: manipulating neighbors, propitiating gods, pacifying demons,
making merit, discharging (and regenerating) mutual-aid obligations.[2] When one
manipulates one's neighbors for cooperation of various sorts, one casts oneself as
host in an institutionalized transaction called *yangdzi*. When the community petitions the gods for protection, it casts itself as a collective host to the gods. When a
household, or the community, wishes to rid itself of accumulated demons, it hosts
the demons to a party. When a family makes merit for a newly deceased member,
it does so by giving a special sort of party called a *gyowa*. And one of the important
sorts of help a mutual-aid group provides for its members is giving parties to supplement the hospitality of a member vis-à-vis the rest of the community. Most of these
applications of the hospitality structure will be discussed in the course of this and
the following chapters.

I will not have occasion to discuss shamanism at any length in this book, but
would simply note here that, again, hospitality provides the framework for the
critical rituals of this institution, in this case transactions between the shaman and
the gods whom he contacts to help him cure the patient:

Hlawa Norbu said a *hlabeu* (a curing seance) is like a party. He first throws rice (as
during the invitation to the gods in offering rituals), sets everything out for the
gods, and invites them all down.

Purbu said that when the gods visit him, he receives them exactly like human guests,
with tea and other hospitality. Then he and the gods discuss the fate of the sick
person.

Karma Renzing said that when the gods come, it's like having your friends come to
visit you. You sit and chat, have a nice time, discuss the patient's problem.[3]

The host — the shaman — in these contexts gains the awesome powers over illness
and health of the gods themselves. We thus glimpse here, and we shall see more
fully as we proceed, some of the astonishing effectiveness hospitality is assumed to
have in bringing about the successful consummation of a transaction.

The Sherpas are so aware of hospitality's cultural meaningfulness and social pervasiveness that they parody it, joke about it, and, when they are not immediately
caught up in its tensions, laugh about it. I witnessed a little scene at a family meal,
for example, in which the daughter passed some potatoes to her mother, saying
casually, "Eat, eat," in ordinary, nonhonorific language. The mother refused the
potatoes, at which point the daughter jumped up and put on an exaggerated parody
of hospitality serving, crying "Eat! Eat!" in honorific language, and pressing, indeed
shoving, the plate into her mother's hands. The rest of the family burst into laughter. More significantly, at the largest and most elaborate of the Sherpas' festivals,

Mani-Rimdu, there is a traditional comedy dance during which one of the characters, using a stooge from the audience, puts on a detailed parody of hospitality etiquette, to the great glee of the spectators.

As the jokes and parodies perhaps indicate, the Sherpas have mixed feelings about their hospitality practices. Indeed, I would characterize the cultural attitude toward hospitality as one of radical ambivalence. Thus on the one hand there are cultural associations between hospitality and paradise, the image of ultimate, incomparable pleasure. One informant defined *dewa,* happiness, as like "when everybody is happy eating and drinking at a family celebration." The term dewa is often used specifically with reference to the bliss of heaven, in contrast to the mortal human realm of *dungal,* suffering and anxiety. One monk, explaining dream associations, volunteered the point that, "If in your dreams you are drinking tea in a pleasant and happy way with friends, it means you will go to heaven."

Yet if hospitality has paradisical associations, it also has associations with lethal danger: Hostesses, it is thought, may poison one in the course of hospitality. They do this not out of any social animus, but simply because, in cultural belief, poisoning others is a magical way of getting rich. Theoretically only certain evil persons would actually do this, but of course one never knows, as the Sherpas always insist, people's inner motives, and in theory one could get poisoned in the course of accepting any hospitality at all. People, do not, of course, approach every party with fear and trembling. But the existence of and fascination with poisoning beliefs (which are quite elaborate; see Ortner, 1970: 171–5), indicate a sort of diffuse anxiety about hospitality, the other side of the diffuse pleasure indicated by the paradise associations.

The ambivalence concerning hospitality is reflected in the complex meanings and powers attributed to food in cultural thought. Food is so richly endowed with significance that I have written nearly 200 pages on the subject elsewhere (Ortner, 1970); some of that material is summarized below. Here I simply wish to stress that the range of meanings of food manifests a radical ambiguity that parallels the radical ambivalence of Sherpa attitudes toward hospitality. On the one hand, food has major positive powers, in being vital to health, well-being, life itself, and in being considered immensely sensuously pleasurable. On the other hand, food has dangerous negative powers: It is actually/potentially polluting, and thus debilitating to vital energies; and it is actually/potentially morally corrupting, thus engendering sin with consequences of misery and even torture in the next life.

Enough has perhaps been said to indicate the central place of hospitality in Sherpa social life and thought. It is not only the primary "ritual" of generalized social relations; it also provides the model for conducting a wide range of special transactions. Further, it is a focus of parody and laughter, of fantasy, and of fear. Yet finally it must be stressed that hospitality is usually greatly enjoyed, and engaged in with gusto. We must now explore the structure and dynamics of this powerful and meaningful event.

The problems of hospitality

The problem of giving and receiving

Social exchange is one of the distinctively human processes. Both Marx and Durkheim considered that exchange only became socially significant with the advent of specialization in the production of the material needs of the community. It was Lévi-Strauss's powerful insight, however, that people articulate symbolic differences serving both to generate and rationalize exchange relationships even where there is no material necessity for them (1963b). Thus in some ways it may be said that giving and receiving are existentially interesting questions for all human beings, things about which to speculate and ruminate, to mythologize and ritualize, in all societies. Yet the ways in which exchange will be problematic in cultural thought will obviously vary with the particular modes of social exchange practiced in the society.

The Sherpas, as we have seen, have a subsistence economy within a system of private property. Thus there is little practical pressure for exchange of material goods, and at the same time a strong and culturally encouraged sense of possession of one's property. In such a system, we would expect giving and receiving to be particularly uncertain and troublesome, and indeed, for the Sherpas, they are. There is great cultural elaboration of the notions of generosity, greed, and stinginess. And while these are all on the side of giving, we find too that there are problems with receiving, for receiving puts one in a position of debt and obligation, and this is considered uncomfortable.

Generosity, first, is highly valued, both in ordinary social intercourse and as a source of religious merit. Because, however, it is rarely practiced consistently by anyone, the few generous people develop widespread reputations. People still talked of Dawa's wife, who had died several years previously, as having been very generous, in contrast to Dawa himself, whom we shall meet in a moment as a local example of stinginess. Another legendarily generous person was Mingmu's mother, who died during my stay in Dzemu. It was said that when she was younger and running her own household (now she was living with and wholly dependent on her son) she had been very kind — whenever people dropped in for a visit, she went beyond the usual hospitality of tea or beer and, despite not being very wealthy, served people fine whole meals. Yet another case was a woman whose house was a traditional sleeping place on the main trail. She would never take any money for firewood used by travelers, but would give it with the comment that giving was merit-work — a rare phenomenon these days, added the man telling the story.

Despite the high value placed on generosity, the normal state of affairs is believed to involve, unfortunately, a great deal of stinginess and greed. People are loath to give away what they have, and furthermore they always want more. Both stinginess and greed are great sins; both will doom one to a variety of unpleasant rebirths.

Stinginess, first, might lead to being reborn as a *yitak*, a being whose fate it is always to be very hungry, and never to be able to satisfy itself. Equally undesirable, stinginess might lead to becoming a *nerpa*, a "ghost" that does not have a realm in the six spheres of existence, as yitak do, but that must wander without material incarnation in the sphere of humans, very hungry and uncomfortable, and causing illness and sometimes death. Villagers recount the case of a powerful nerpa named Tangar, who lived in a house above the neighboring village of Phungmo. Tangar had once been a living man who had been a miser; he had had two wives and no children, and had amassed much wealth. He never gave anything away, died intestate, and thus had become a nerpa.

Just as with generosity, cases of extreme stinginess and miserliness were discussed at length in the community. There was the case of Dawa, mentioned above, who was known to be stingy but who, it was thought, surpassed acceptable bounds when his penniless, ancient stepmother died and he let it be known that he did not plan to make a funeral feast for her. There was gossip about this for days, and he was finally shamed into making the feast by some other villagers who said that if he didn't, they would, for not to hold such a feast would bring demerit on the entire community. And there was Hlakpu, discussed in the last chapter, who had formerly been moderately well off, but who was now thought to be extremely wealthy, all of his male relatives and several sons having renounced worldly wealth and gone into monasteries, leaving him most of their property. This notwithstanding, it was widely known that Hlakpu "never gave anybody anything." He never formally separated his sons from him and gave them their shares of his wealth, and never gave his daughter a dowry. Furthermore, he attended every temple event for the distribution of food, but never acted as a sponsor for any such event, and never had any guests in for private hospitality either.

Not only are there individuals who do not like to give. It is also difficult to get people to lend and even to sell things. We are familiar with the idea that it is difficult to get people to lend, particularly to lend money, and that therefore the prospective borrower must be persistent. But we are accustomed to thinking that a seller is generally a consenting, if not an active, party to the sale. Yet among the Sherpas it is not uncommon that people will browbeat others into selling them things that they want, even if the seller himself needs or wants to keep the item and had no intention of selling it.

Greed, finally, like stinginess, is sinful and, if indulged in, will also cause one to be reborn as a nerpa, or in the sphere of the yitak, the insatiable beings. In contrast to the situation with respect to generosity and stinginess, however, one does not hear tales of exceptionally greedy people. Rather, greed is considered to be somehow more basic and universal, part of essential human nature. To put it another way, unlike generosity and stinginess, which particular people might go out of their way to practice, greed seems to be conceived of as a latent trait in everyone, and can be stirred up at any moment. The simple sight of money is said to arouse greed, and people will theoretically be more eager to sell things if they see cash.

The Sherpas will often remark matter-of-factly that people are greedy, always wanting fine clothes and good food. There are a few basic (and not always consistently held) ideas about the incidence of greed, such as the notion that women, monks, and nuns are greedier than other people. Yet, as noted above, there are few instances of singling out individual cases of greedy people for discussion, and the idea of ordinary human greed is rarely elaborated upon. What we find instead is a great proliferation of greedy supernatural creatures, each of whose variations on the basic theme are spelled out in great detail, and are well understood by Sherpas of all ages. There are at least seven types of greedy non-human beings in the Sherpa cosmos (Ortner, n.d.). While we shall come back to the question of greed in society in the next chapter, it is clear simply from these points that a materialist drive to have more things, to keep them for oneself and at the same time to get them from others, is a pervasive concern in Sherpa social thought. And this notion of the power and universality of greed, and of its barely controlled nature, is not surprisingly taken into account, used, and played upon as a means of manipulating other people.

But if there are difficulties with giving, or getting people to give, there are also difficulties with receiving. Mostly these are elaborated around the processes of borrowing and lending. Debts weigh heavily on the mind of the borrower, and borrowing and the state of being in debt have strong negative connotations in the culture. People develop reputations for being bad debts, and are disliked for this trait. Conversely, the good life is defined in part as being free of debt to anyone. Lending is considered somewhat sinful, in causing hardship for others, and thus on Losar, the Sherpa new year, a day on which one's sins and virtuous deeds are multiplied a thousand times, no debts are collected.

Perhaps the best indicator of the Sherpas' discomfort with borrowing and being in a state of debt is the following local legend, mentioned above:

Tangar was a quasi-historical local personage whose spirit now inhabits a ruined stone house high on the ridge above Phungmo. This house, though appearing empty to some people, is seen by others to be completely stocked with every possible utensil and appurtenance. (When it appears empty, it is said that the spirit is hiding the things.) You could borrow anything from this house, as long as you brought it back on time. But if you did not bring it back on time — if you were so much as five minutes late — the spirit would strike you dead. Before, it is said, people from Phungmo used to borrow a lot of things for funeral feasts and weddings, when one naturally needs a lot of pots and plates. But then many people were remiss in bringing back the things, and were struck down within five minutes. So they stopped borrowing things from the spirit's house.

While the discomfort with the state of indebtedness is articulated primarily around the specific cultural category of borrowing, any sort of prestation, even freely and voluntarily given, is felt to obligate the recipient to the giver. And while there is little explicit cultural lore on the problems of this sort of receiving, there is much evidence that it is also felt to be problematic. We shall see, for example, that the gods must be forced to accept their offerings. But we shall also see that in ordinary hospitality etiquette people must be "forced" (and occasionally there is genuine coercion) to eat and drink.

Viewed externally, however, the problem of giving and receiving may be translated back into the picture of a community of relatively self-contained units, each protective of its property and its social boundaries, cautious about giving, and cautious about the obligations it may incur by receiving. The picture, in other words, is another view of the situation described in the preceding chapter. There we saw the closed or introverted family structure largely in terms of its resistance to breakup through the marriage of children; here we see its resistance to the exchange of material goods, and to the social bonds such exchange might produce. While stinginess and greed are culturally seen as individual personality quirks, or even as "human nature," they are clearly in large part reflexes of the economically based shape of the community as, at least at one level, an aggregate of would-be autonomous units.

The power of food

At the core of any hospitality event, there is a material transaction: A host gives food to his guests. Feeding is culturally considered to be an act of great power, and although in a large wedding or funeral party, for example, the host has no immediately manipulative intent, most of the other usages of the hospitality framework are explicitly manipulative. The coercive power of feeding is best summed up in a statement addressed to a god during the Dumji festival: "I am offering you the things which you eat; now you must do whatever I demand" (quoted in von Fürer-Haimendorf, 1964: 193).

The manipulative power of food and feeding is embodied in the Sherpa institution of yangdzi. In a yangdzi transaction, an individual brings a token gift of beer and/or food to another in a culturally formalized manner, and then asks the other for a favor — anything from lending a small sum of money to giving some sort of extended lessons, from promising to dance at one's wedding to dropping a legal suit, from selling something at a cheap rate to giving a daughter in marriage.

Yangdzi has the same sort of centrality — intense meaningfulness and broad pervasiveness — as hospitality itself. It was practically the first term I learned when I arrived in the village, and very few days went by that I did not hear of it, see it enacted, or find myself involved in it. The archetypal yangdzi prestation is a bottle of beer, and the recipe for beer was a gift of no less a figure than the Guru Rimpoche, the founder of Tibetan Buddhism, the culture-hero of the Sherpas' Nyingmawa sect, and the personage considered literally to have brought civilization to the Tibetans and their descendants. The Guru Rimpoche taught the Sherpas' ancestors how to make beer so that they could offer it to the gods to gain protection, and the yangdzi prestation is felt to be the supreme mode of effectively generating civilized social exchange. Its presumed effectiveness is illustrated in the Sherpa proverb:

> First, request: state briefly;
> Second, soften up: talk sweetly;
> Third, clinch: give yangdzi.

The basic yangdzi transaction is of a classic Maussian nature. The donor shows up, bearing his wooden bottle of beer, at the house of the person from whom he wishes a favor. Everyone acts as if it were just a friendly visit, and the visitor is seated and given basic hospitality. After a polite interval, however, the visitor gets up, makes the householder sit down, and pours him a serving of the beer. The householder must drink some, and the visitor keeps refilling his glass as many times as he can. Finally, ideally, after the beer has begun to take effect, he enters the request for the favor, which was the intent of the visit all along, and which all concerned knew was coming sooner or later. If the recipient refuses the request (which is considered psychologically very difficult to do), he may try to give back the remains of the gift, at which point the donor will insist that the gift had nothing to do with his request, that it was "just a present." Here are a few examples of yangdzi from my notes:

Dorje brought yangdzi to Mingma Zangbu and some of the other good dancers of the village, and begged them to come to his wedding to liven it up with their dancing. (They agreed.)

Purbu Dorje is known to have stolen certain items, among them Phu Tenzing's silver-lined teacup. Phu Tenzing was going to go to the government office about the cup, but Purbu Dorje's older brother went to him, gave his cup back, gave him a bottle of beer, and begged him not to report the theft as it would shame the family. (Phu Tenzing agreed not to go.)

About five or six years after Purbu Zangbu's grandfather's third wife left him to live with Lama Ngawang's grandfather, the latter died, and the wife started bringing beer to Purbu Zangbu's grandfather in hopes of being taken back by him. He kept accepting the beer and drinking it all up, and the ex-wife would go home thinking that any day he'd send for her, but he never did. (Big laugh among all the listeners to this story.)

I was formally invited up to Tsala monastery, as they were hoping to sell me some rugs. They gave me an enormous meal, including rakshi, brought in especially for me since they're not supposed to have alcoholic drinks in the monastery. (I bought seven rugs.)

The yangdzi transaction is simple, but it contains a revealing little twist. It was noted that, at the moment of initiating the transaction, the visitor stands up, makes the householder sit down, and serves the householder the beer to drink on the spot. It is clear, then, that the visitor has become a host, and the householder a guest, and that the power of yangdzi actually resides in the asymmetry of the host–guest relationship. The sources of power of the host role is in fact one of the problems of this chapter, but as far as the Sherpas are concerned the answer is simple: It derives from serving food, which itself has innate natural powers. The power of hosting is seen largely as the power of food, and we must thus explore the cultural notions surrounding this stuff. As the food and beer lore of Sherpa culture is extensive and elaborate (see Ortner, 1970), only its barest outline can be given here.

The significance of food in Sherpa thought rests first and foremost on the natural powers it is assumed to have to affect one's being in direct causal ways. Food actually operates upon people, entering and transforming them for better or for worse. That food has real material effects upon the human organism is something few cultures have ignored. But the Sherpas consider it to have a wider range of effects, not only on one's physical well-being, but also on one's psychic energies and one's moral and spiritual welfare. The presumed natural powers of food actually to transform people in various ways is the core of its significance for Sherpa social action.

The transforming effects of food are both positive and negative. On the positive side, food sustains the health of the physiological organism, and provides pleasurable stimulation of the senses. On the negative side, food pollutes the energies of one's total system, and contributes to one's moral corruption. Health and pleasure on the one hand, pollution and corruption on the other — these are the meanings of food in Sherpa thought, and the modes of operation of its powers.

The relationship between food and physiological well-being, first, is well elaborated in Sherpa culture. Ordinary food, that is, the average Sherpa's daily fare, will sustain one's basic good health; it will not make one sick, but neither will it have any extraordinary positive effects upon one's physical condition. "Bad foods," which seem to be defined largely by the status of those who are providing them, may actually make one ill in some minor way. "Good foods" on the other hand (generally expensive foods, but also beer which is relatively cheap and available), will actively promote better health in the individual, and will rapidly restore strength to people in weakened states — pregnant and postnatal women, sick people, ascetics weak from fasting, and so forth.

The relationship between food and physiological well-being is compared to the relationship between compost and good crops — the more fertilizer one puts on, the larger the plants. Similarly, rich men who eat good and plentiful food are said to grow better than poor ones. Further, eating promotes strength as well as growth, causing people to be able to work well. People involved in hard work — heavy physical labor, fine craft work, the performance of religious ritual — must be kept supplied with regular meals as well as snacks, and especially with an ongoing stream of tea or beer, to sustain their endeavors. And finally, good and plentiful food will cause one to grow fat, and fatness (at least within limits) is considered not only a sign of good health, but attractive as well. Health, strength, beauty — all of these are aspects of one's physiological well-being that may be promoted by the powers of food.

The promotion of health and material well-being is one part of the positive power of food for people. The other part, the stimulation of sensuous pleasure, is less well elaborated in Sherpa discourse, although ultimately it is more important as a factor in the use of food for social manipulation. Eating in general is felt by the Sherpas to be one of the major pleasures of life, and eating good-quality, tasty, and aesthetically prepared food in particular is considered the epitome of enjoyment. Many accounts of existence in the heavenly paradises stress limitless exquisite food as a major part of the *kirmu*, bliss, of being in heaven, and high-ranking monks were said by one informant to have a kirmu existence because "they just eat and read, and don't do any work." Further, it is clear in other descriptions of heavens that fine food also represents and conjures up images of the entire range of sensuous pleasures — fine fabrics and soft rugs, sweet smells and sounds, beautiful visions.[4]

In addition to the pleasure of food, there is the pleasure of intoxicating drink. For the Sherpas intoxication often provides a temporary sense of release from inhibitions and escape from humdrum existence, making one feel light-headed and gay. While no Sherpa articulated this point in precisely these terms, it was clearly indicated in many contexts. Beer is used to liven up parties, and guests are plied with beer explicitly to make them lose their inhibitions and participate in singing and dancing. Weddings, for example, are meant to be the most joyous and uninhibited events in community life; everyone is supposed to get drunk, and the success of a wedding party is considered to be in direct proportion to the amount of beer served and consumed. Many stages of Sherpa weddings are named as one or another type of beer transaction. In short, intoxication is a pleasurable state, and beer is valued for its pleasure-giving properties.

The great pleasures of food and drink, then, derive directly from the effects of food on the senses and drink on the spirit. But it is important to note that both eating and drinking are fundamentally social acts. Eating a meal alone is considered at least pathetic, if it means that one simply has no one to eat with, or at worst a matter for derision, if it means that one is being greedy and trying to have a lot of food for oneself when no one is around. Drinking alone is considered rather shocking, indicating an antisocial attitude or a lamentable uncontrollable habit, either of which is upsetting to others. Thus the full pleasure of eating and drinking derives not only from the direct effects of the food and drink, but also from the social conviviality which those effects in turn produce. These points are extremely important. On the one hand sociality heightens, indeed is part of, the pleasures of food and drink; on the other hand the effects of food and drink are such as to generate social conviviality among the people eating and drinking together.

But there are negative aspects to the powers of food: It may pollute one's energies, or corrupt one's moral will.

Regarding moral corruption, the broad overall point that interaction with food, all food, is sinful is made in the general notion, known to every Sherpa, that in working the land one perforce kills thousands of tiny creatures. Killing is the "heaviest" Buddhist sin, and the injunction against killing is taken very seriously by the Sherpas. They never slaughter animals, and avoid as much as possible killing insects, worms, and pests. The only things they systematically kill (in self-defense) are lice, which are considered a legacy of the demons. Nonetheless, one must have food to survive and one must work one's fields to obtain it, but in so doing one treads upon, or cuts up in hoeing and plowing, the myriad tiny creatures that teem in the soil. This point is the basis for the injunction against monks doing manual labor; working the land is unavoidably sinful and impedes one's quest for salvation. The point is simply that even with the best of intentions, and with all the worst aspects of one's nature under control, one cannot avoid being corrupted when one deals with food.

The moral corruption one feels about plowing the land may be rather abstract. But the role of food in causing one to sin can be experienced much more directly as food in fact or in fantasy stimulates one's greed. Greedy thoughts and acts are also great sins in Sherpa culture, so much so that one informant said that theft ranks as an evil (in a generalized way, including sin, shame, and some pollution) higher than brother–sister incest (although in practice people would be far more horrified by the latter). And he said this is true no matter how little one steals nor how hungry one is.[5] One's moral life is in large part defined in terms of not letting the ever-present greedy elements in one's nature take the upper hand (Ortner, n.d.). One of the primary villains in the struggle of decent people against greed is food; reciprocally, a primary negative meaning of food is as tempter, as arouser of greed and corrupter of souls.

The power of food to arouse our sensuous greed is evil in itself. But it is also a model for other sorts of sinful temptations. One monk drew the explicit analogy between the temptation of food and the temptation of sex:

The monk said that, in his opinion, not having had intercourse before taking the celibacy vow is best because, just as when we see someone eating a lemon our mouth puckers, because we have tasted lemons, just so, if we've had intercourse, we can picture doing it again. But if we've never tasted lemons, then our mouth doesn't pucker when we see others eating them.

But another monk said:

Perhaps it is better if men have had sexual intercourse before taking a vow of celibacy. Just as someone who has eaten or drunk too much will retch at the sight of food or beer, so people who have had much sex will find it easier to renounce it.

Neither monk was aware of the other's statement. But despite their conflicting views, both used food analogies in order to formulate a point concerning sensual temptation.

More generally, the verb "to eat" in the past-complete conjugation (eat-finished, "ate up") is the standard term for any sort of excessive or illegal consumption of wealth:

Pemba Zangbu has been asked to run for Panchayat (district council) next time. He said he didn't want to, that Panchayat officers all get rich *eating up* other people's money in bribes, thus committing much sin . . .

The monks did a memorial *tso* ritual for T. for three years after he died, but then (it is said) the sponsor of the ceremony *ate up* all the money for this in his government work, so they had to stop.

While Nyima Dorje was away, his brother's wife *ate up* almost all his fields. Nyima Dorje had said that she (his sister-in-law) could reap his last year's potato crop if she gave back an equivalent amount of seeds for a tenant to plant in Nyima Dorje's absence. But she only gave back six fields worth of seeds.[6]

The evilness or morally corrupting power of food is thus encoded in a variety of beliefs, assumptions, and usages. Simply producing food by labor in the fields automatically puts one in the position of committing the heaviest sin in the culture. Simply contemplating food arouses one's greed for the sensuous pleasure of eating. The greed for food in turn is a model for other sinful lusts and urges — the desire for sexual pleasure, and the coveting of others' wealth and property.

Of all the various foods, two are specifically more sinful than others — meat and beer. Both must be renounced if one embarks upon the most direct road to salvation, monkhood or any more austere form of asceticism. Meat is sinful because of the slaughter of the animals. Beer (I will use this term to cover distilled spirits as well) is much more complicated. The actual creation of beer does not involve slaughter, although because it is made from grains, the point of killing the tiny creatures of the fields is still relevant. Much more important, however, is the direct experience of intoxication and the consequent weakening of the spirit in all its aspects — it is a culturally explicit point that under drink one loses one's sense of shame, one's physical coordination, and especially one's ability to make both utilitarian and moral discriminations. Here is the paradigmatic myth:

Once there was a very high and holy lama who was approached by a *dirnmu,* a demoness. The dirnmu appeared in the guise of a beautiful woman, carrying a bottle of beer and leading a goat. She forced the lama to choose — kill the goat, drink the beer, or have intercourse with her. The lama chose the beer as the least of the evils, but then he got drunk and in his drunken state he killed the goat and had intercourse with the woman.

It is clear that beer is used to manipulate others on the basis of its "naturally" corrupting powers. Beer is the basic yangdzi — manipulative giving (see above) — prestation, and in theory the effectiveness of yangdzi in gaining the cooperation of another depends upon the effects of intoxication: the artificial heightening of feelings of camaraderie, the blurring of judgment, the undermining of willpower. In fact, whether or not a particular yangdzi attempt is successful generally depends more on social factors than on the quantity and potency of the beer. Yet the Sherpas act as if it is the beer that does the trick, and thus, logically enough, because intoxication is ephemeral, beer is less important when one has no immediate request: There is less use of beer, and more of food, when one uses yangdzi to establish longer-range good will.

Finally, food may pollute one's being, weakening one's vital energies, as well as corrupting one's moral spirit. While theoretically only certain foods are "dirty" or polluting, in fact when one tries to get informants to provide specific examples of dirty foods, their answers are vague, inconsistent, or simply not forthcoming. This suggests, among other things, that just as all food is ultimately corrupting, so all food is also ultimately polluting. In the myth of the fall to the human state, for example, people are said to have originally been like the gods, incorporeal and needing no food to survive. But then they killed animals and ate "dirty food," and in consequence acquired bodies with all the ills attendant thereon. The contrast "no food/dirty food" suggests that dirty food is simply food.[7]

The effects of pollution on one's being include various forms of debilitation, of loss of vital powers and energies. If one has any special powers, pollution may temporarily or permanently undermine them: Men may lose their sexual potency, shamans may lose their powers to contact the gods, children who appear to be vehicles for important reincarnating souls may lose the capacity to function as vessels for those souls. For ordinary people, however, the primary effects of pollution are to weaken one's faculties of active and appropriate responsiveness — one becomes either lethargic, dull, and stupid, or agitated and emotionally churned up, in either case unable to make critical evaluations and discriminations.[8]

From these points it is clear that pollution and moral corruption are closely related, and indeed they interact in a variety of ways in Sherpa cultural thought. This is in no way surprising from any general overview of human religious evolution; as Ricoeur has said, "the stain [defilement] is the first schema of evil" (46). Thus, for the Sherpas, pollution often operates as a precondition of sin. In the myth of the demoness and the lama, for example, the disorientation (an essentially polluted condition) produced by the beer causes him to commit the "real" sins of slaughter and the breach of his vow of celibacy.[9]

The negative powers of food thus include the interrelated operations of pollution and corruption. At the same time, we saw above that food has positive powers of promoting health and being sensuously pleasurable and gratifying. Thus food as a total symbol embodies polar meanings. It is both good and bad, both enjoyable and dangerous, both pleasurable and problematic. I would argue that this ambiguity is a reflex of the problems discussed in the preceding section, the cultural difficulties experienced with giving and receiving. For food is the primary exchange item, that which is, more than anything else in the society, given and received. There are reasons for keeping it and reasons for giving it away, reasons for wanting it from others and reasons for not wanting to want it. The semantic ambiguity of food grows largely out of this social ambivalence.

Problems of status, power, and authority

Dissecting hospitality in terms of the problem of exchange and the powers of food tends to focus attention on the host–guest relationship. Yet from another point of view, the critical dynamics of hospitality take place largely among the guests themselves. The host has merely created a structure in which certain types of interaction among guests will tend to happen. And such interactions have largely to do with status.

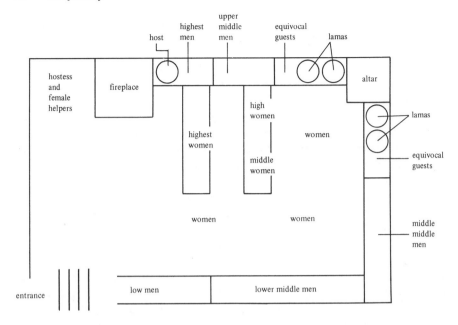

Figure 1. A seating arrangement

Status interaction begins with the seating process. Everyone is supposed to sit in his correct status position, and everyone knows generally where that will be. The host himself is by definition the highest-status person at the party, and has the highest seat, almost always next to the fireplace. The highest-status men are seated nearest him, and so on around the room to those of lowest status, who are usually near the door. Lamas are clustered about the household altar (if the structure of the room will allow this), and men of ambiguous status around them. The women are clustered in the center of the floor, and do not get involved in the machinations of the men's seating. A model of a fully developed seating pattern is shown in Figure 1.

Yet the seats are neither assigned by the host nor fixed by tradition, and in fact gaining one's rightful status location involves a certain amount of renegotiation on each occasion. It is good manners to try to sit *lower* than one's proper place, whereupon one's neighbors, with pushing and pulling and many hearty ejaculations of "Here, older brother!" and "Ho, older brother!" will try to pull one into one's rightful seat. This may go back and forth for some time, but eventually, despite all the pulling and shouting, one usually winds up in the same relative position one had before. Occasionally, however, shifts of relative seating position do occur. In such cases, the man who tried to sit lower than his position at a previous party is allowed to "win," while the man he displaced up the line allows himself to "lose." When this happens, there has been one microshift in the status hierarchy of a Sherpa village.

Hospitality in short is, among other things, a political arena, and the status hierarchy and other aspects of political structure and process in Sherpa society must now be explored.

The first point to be noted is that there are no *formal* political institutions, offices, roles, or mechanisms in a Sherpa village. There is no official headman, no official governing or decision-making unit, no formal judicial body or process.[10] Further, there is no class structure, such that landowners might have indirect (economic) power over tenants or wageworkers.[11] In short, no one has the right or the power to command, legislate, or arbitrate vis-à-vis other members of the community.

Yet Sherpa villages can hardly be called egalitarian. There are broad differences of wealth within most communities, and these differences have social, as well as economic implications. Loosely, the Sherpas speak of "big people," "small people," and "middle people."

High status, "bigness," has two culturally defined bases — wealth, and generosity, the latter symbolized and/or epitomized by large religious gifts. In addition, there is always a genealogical factor, such that the descendants of one who achieved high status through meeting those two criteria will retain, all things being equal, the high status of the ancestor. His descendants will be ranked according to their genealogical distance from him: The line coming out of his oldest son should be higher than the lines coming from his younger sons, all of which should be higher than the lines coming from his brothers, which in turn should be higher than the lines coming from his father's brothers, and so on. One can see that things will become quite complicated, even among those whose genealogical connections to this ancestor are clearly established. If the key ancestor had older brothers, for example, their descendants may try to make claims of being higher than his direct descendants, because lines coming from a group of siblings should be ranked according to birth order. Thus in Dzemu, all the "big people" are descended from an *older brother* of the key ancestor who established the high status of the Lama clan in the nineteenth century. They try to claim, on that basis, higher status than the men of nearby Ghirpu, who are *direct* descendants of this ancestor, although it is perfectly clear that the men of Ghirpu, if they were to attend a party with the men of Dzemu, would sit higher than Dzemu men.[12]

The case of Ghirpu is instructive for the next point, namely that given this sort of system, a newly rich and newly charitable man will not automatically spring to the top of the status hierarchy, because he does not have the genealogical heritage that the other "big men" already have by birth, even if he is wealthier and more charitable than all the rest. His rise in status will take time, and perhaps will not be socially granted until his children's generation, if then. Indeed, perhaps it will never be granted within the already established hierarchy of a given village, and this among other factors may account for village fission. Thus the village of Ghirpu is relatively new, and it seems that the key nineteenth-century ancestor moved out and built his mansion in Ghirpu because he was a younger brother, and was not accorded the status he came to feel he deserved on the basis of his manifest wealth and piety (the latter expressed by endowing an entire monastery). Currently, the woman

whose name was given as "the richest man in town" had bought some fields a day's
walk to the south, and had built herself a house there. One suspects that this
family might move out of Dzemu altogether eventually, because by genealogy
they do not rank among the highest people in town, yet by wealth (if not generosity)
they clearly belong up there.

As for nonbig people in the community, everyone else in Dzemu is descended
from more temporally and/or collaterally remote ancestors of that key sibling
group, and is "middle" or "small" depending primarily upon wealth and active
community-mindedness. "Smallness" becomes absolute, or close to absolute, when
a family is no longer able to support itself by traditional economic activities (agriculture, dairying, trade) and begins to do wage labor for other families. Wage labor
is by and large the key criterion of "smallness." In fact, Sherpas dislike working for
wages for other Sherpas, and rarely do it.[13]

There are of course always exceptions to these rough, general rules. If a man is
of previously highish status, is well liked, and has become poor through no fault of
his own (perhaps his father squandered the family fortune), he may perform wage
labor and still be accorded a reasonable seat in the status hierarchy, and otherwise
be treated with respect. People say they have nyingje, compassion, for him, although
it might more cynically be viewed as the "big people" sticking together and not
wanting one of their own to slide down. The same would not happen for some previously "middle" person who had mismanaged and squandered his resources, and
who anyway was not well liked. He would slide down and no one would take much
notice. Like the rising rich with status aspirations to "bigness," the sliding poor
sinking to "smallness" would likely move out of town, probably to Darjeeling to
find work and a bit of social obscurity.

It must be stressed again, however, that high status does not systematically generate real political power. While the wealth of the big people clearly gives them advantages — material comfort, a certain amount of deference from others, greater economic freedom and security — it does not give them authority to make decisions
for the community, to legislate the behavior of others, or to adjudicate disputes. In
fact, when the community does on rare occasions manage to organize some ad hoc
attempt to settle a troublesome dispute (and there is a little ritual for performing
this function), the peacemaker is rarely selected from among the biggest people, but
is generally a well-respected middle-status person.[14]

Yet just as the absence of political and economic power structures does not mean
that a Sherpa community is egalitarian, so the absence of systematic dispute-settling
mechanisms does not mean that a Sherpa community is at all times peaceful and
harmonious. While many disputes occur over real material resources, others are often
expressions of status rivalry that seize upon some material factor as an excuse for an
argument. The Sherpas recognize, and lament, the fact that envy over wealth differences is rife in the community, and status competition and rivalry chronic. Occasionally, specific rivalries erupt into physical fights, or in destructive acts of vengeance: One man was said to have retaliated in a feud with his brother by going
into the brother's field one night and breaking the stalks of ripening grain in a large

area of the field. The Sherpas find such violence highly distressing. Fights, other destructive acts, and even angry arguments leave onlookers as well as participants shaken and disgusted, in a subjective state that they label pollution.

The problem of pervasive status antagonism is compounded by the social atomization of the community discussed above. The relative absence of sustained (as opposed to episodic) social bonding and reciprocity between families, and between individuals, manifests itself in the status arena in the fact that people rarely form political coalitions or factions. One's status struggle with one's neighbor is one's own problem, and one can expect no direct help from anyone else, unless by chance the neighbor is also more generally troublesome to the community, in which case people may back one on an ad hoc basis. How this process may work will be seen later in the chapter.

The big/middle/small system is primarily a set of economic categories. The terms are loose, vague, and shifting. At parties, however, each person must sit in a precise and unique position vis-à-vis everyone else. Hospitality, in other words, performs certain social and cultural operations upon the economic structure of the community, and one of the problems of this chapter will be to understand the nature of these operations. We now return to the hospitality event to analyze its relationship to this and the other problems discussed above.

The solutions of hospitality

The "empty mouth" principle and the etiquette of giving and receiving

Parties are supposed to be pleasurable events for all concerned. Yet the tradition of giving and receiving hospitality in Sherpa culture is backed by negative sanctions, suggesting that people must be threatened a bit into playing the roles of host and guest. It is actually felt to be dangerous to fail to enact either side of the transaction properly, and there are culturally articulated fears of both the "angry" (offended) guest and the "angry" (offended) host.

From the point of view of the host, guests are thought to become angry if they are not adequately fed or if they are otherwise improperly treated. This notion is formulated in the punning proverb, *kha tongba loksin, kha tong gasung*, which means, very loosely, that if one's guest goes away with "an empty mouth" (*kha tongba*), one is in trouble. Technically the proverb refers to return invitations – if one's guest goes away with an empty mouth, one will receive no further invitations from him. But the expression is used in numerous contexts, generally with an improvised ending, or with the ending trailing off: "Empty mouth . . . [meaningful pause] ," implying vaguer and more sinister possibilities.[15]

If one is a guest, on the other hand, the notion is that one must accept and eat all that is offered or the host or hostess will become angry. As one hard-pressed guest said, "All Sherpas are like this — very *hard* — they brook no excuses. . . . Even when you're full, people make you eat and get angry if you don't."

The fear of offending and angering the host (and especially, it seems, the hostess) is seen in a variety of beliefs. An offended hostess, it is believed, may make one ill through the activity of her *pem*, which may be translated as a force of "witchcraft" that exists latently in all women. More generally, a hostess who urges one to eat and drink too much may be seen as attempting to corrupt one's morals. She may be said to "have a little bit of dirnmu in her," dirnmu being the (female form of) demons whose special activities include, as we have seen, the seduction and moral corruption of lamas and monks. It was also noted above that all hostesses are in theory potential poisoners. While this belief might be thought to work against acceptance of hospitality, in fact it works for it, because to refuse food or drink would be to imply that one suspected a hostess of being a poisoner, thus gravely insulting her. It is said that an outspoken and/or drunken hostess may get angry and actually say to a guest trying to refuse food, "What's the matter, is my food poisoned?" And such a scene is of course to be avoided.

Yet it was clear from my own observations that a host or hostess whose hospitality has not been properly accepted suffers anxiety rather than anger, for he or she assumes that the guest's refusal is a sign that the guest is for some reason angry with the household. The anxiety is actually encouraged, as will be seen below, by the etiquette forms themselves, prescribing that a guest make several refusals before accepting food and drink. The host is thus forced to urge his hospitality on the guest, never being sure whether a refusal was a genuine indication of nonhunger, a simple expression of etiquette, or a veiled indication of personal animosity. He plays it safe by assuming the latter, and presses the food relentlessly, which in itself sometimes irritates the guest.

It was noted above that the Sherpas can joke, in certain contexts, about the tension and intensity of their hospitality practices. Yet all humor and perspective about this situation are lost when one is in the role of host oneself. A host sees nothing funny about his urging people to eat, and finds it difficult to receive a guest's refusal casually. Thus my assistant knew very well that I could not eat or drink as much as most Sherpas, and he frequently came to my rescue in the face of overabundant hospitality in other people's homes. Yet when, toward the end of my stay, I visited his parents' home, he immediately became the host, seconding his parents' pressures on me for three days of solid eating. When I finally became ill with gas, indigestion, and diarrhea, he felt his hospitality to be insulted, and was quite out of sorts about it for several days.[16]

All of which is to say that the giving and receiving of food in hospitality is a serious business, backed by threats of anger and even retribution for failure to play the game properly. The party must now be analyzed to show the way it develops, and finally resolves, this issue. Virtually all the etiquette of hospitality requires that the host play a pressuring and almost authoritarian role, while the etiquette of the proper guest entails resistance and struggle against the pressures of the host. A party may thus be seen as a tug-of-war between host and guests over giving and receiving, but the host always wins, and pleasure ensues.

Hostly pressures may begin with the invitation. The tradition of sending a small child to invite guests is partly a matter of convenience, but it may also be a pressure tactic, in that the child is generally not supplied with information as to the time or occasion for the party. Further, the child is often either too young and/or irresponsible to convey excuses back to the household if the guest will be unable to come.[17] Thus if the invitation is inconvenient it is difficult to communicate this to the host, and unless one is willing to insult him one is manipulated at the very outset into allowing oneself to be entertained, with whatever obligations may wind up being entailed. This point is particularly applicable to a small-scale party, where the host probably has some ulterior motive behind his invitation.

If the host is particularly anxious to insure that his invitation not be ignored (and invitations are ignored from time to time), he may decide that sending a child is too risky, and may take the tack of attempting to waylay the target guest as the person is passing the host's house. Waylaying is frequently done with travelers one knows who are stopping in one's village, but it is also done with fellow villagers, especially those of high status. "Come in!" cries the would-be host, in honorific language, from his doorstep or his window. The passerby indicates that he can't because he is on his way to wherever he is going, and must get there. But the householder presses his invitation as strongly as possible — simply repeating, with some urgency, "Come in! Come in!" — and the passerby often feels compelled to relent, and to come in and be served whatever the host sees fit to serve him. This may be anything from tea and a snack to a full-scale meal. Once the guest is in the house, further, he must carry through with the whole process, and if the hostess has begun to prepare something elaborate and time consuming the guest has no choice but to wait for however long it takes.

For large-scale parties, the invitation to the event may be relatively painless. People have been anticipating the event, and are more likely to feel offended at not being invited than put upon when the invitation comes. But similar pressure patterns prevail in the etiquette of the serving and acceptance of the food and drink. The first round of serving is generally quite matter-of-fact. The serving of seconds and thirds, however, brings out the distinctive etiquette dialogue of giving and receiving food.

A situation in which a host is trying to serve extra food to someone who does not want it makes for something of a scene. The person serving the food presses the plate upon the reluctant recipient, crying, "Eat, eat, eat," over and over again. The guest attempts to push the plate back into the hands of the server, babbling his excuses. The server pushes back, continuing to cry, "Eat, eat!" Finally the host and other members of his family chime in — "Eat! Eat!" The guest must ultimately relent to bring the scene to an end. His only resort at this point, if he really cannot eat, is to leave the food over, which is not well received although no comment will be made, or to wrap up the carryable food and take it home to his family.[18]

In the case of beer, the exchanges are occasionally even more violent. At some point in the party one may reach a saturation point and simply not want any more beer. Further, there are members of the community who have sworn off drink, and there are the village lamas who, while not having taken the monk's vow against drinking, nonetheless as an informal practice should really not indulge. But unless one has established one's credentials as a teetotaler over a long period of time, none of these excuses will have any force with a host and hostess, who feel it their absolute duty to ply people with beer at all costs.

Their method is sheer attrition; they simply will not take no for an answer. The person serving the beer — usually the wife, daughter, or servant of the host — attempts to fill one's glass, saying, "Drink, drink, drink," over and over again. One covers one's glass with one's hand, but the server tries to pry one's hand off, or to pull the glass out of one's hand, continuing to cry, "Drink, drink!" The guest may resort to hiding his glass under the bench, with the server dragging at his arm. Finally again the host and other members of the host family chime in — "Drink! Drink!" And again one finally relents.

What does all this add up to? The point is very simple. Guestly etiquette clearly reflects, and even parodies, the resistance to receiving (in turn a resistance to being placed under obligation) that prevails in everyday life. The pressures of hostly etiquette on the other hand communicate the urgency of overcoming those resistances. And the weight of cultural pressure is on the side of the host, who must at all costs not allow a guest to leave with "an empty mouth," and who of course always "wins" the symbolic etiquette struggle. "Losing," however, turns out to be pleasurable, for once the struggle is over, and people are filled with good food and beer, they wind up singing and dancing, and enjoying themselves immensely.

These pleasures, with which every really good party concludes, are attributed to the effects of food and drink, and the general stimulation of social interaction. I would argue, however, that this exhilaration is (also) the joy of transcending, if only in this safely noninstrumental or nonpractical context, the structurally induced difficulties of giving and receiving. The sense in which exchange is problematic in Sherpa society was discussed above. Given the property and production structure, and given the cultural notions of human nature as stingy and greedy, exchange cannot be taken for granted, but rather must actively be generated on each occasion.[19] Parties are precisely *not* genuine situations of exchange; there is a one-way transaction, from host to guest, although future reciprocity is implied. My point, however, is that party etiquette reproduces certain subjective *conditions* for exchange, the sense of its necessity, its difficulties, and finally its rewards. The reluctance about giving and the resistance toward receiving are, in the special context of party etiquette, broken and transcended. The result is an experience of collective social pleasure that is quite genuine, and that is clearly the basis of the Sherpas' insistence that parties are *hlermu* — fun, pleasurable, exciting — rather than stressful and pressurized as I have portrayed them. Sherpa parties *are* fun, and people do, most often, have a fine time. And precisely because such pleasure comes in part from having allowed oneself to lose a struggle against accepting the food and drink of another, one is perhaps a bit more receptive to such gifts in contexts in which they may have more specific entailments. From this point of view, party etiquette may be seen as a sort of rehearsal and shaping of consciousness for experiences of genuine (would-be) exchange, a symbolic mechanism in the service of facilitating difficult exchange relationships in the practical world.

Seating and joking: the party as politics

We must now shift our perspective and view the party from another angle, the angle of guest–guest rather than host–guest relations. Here, status and other aspects of politics come into focus.

As soon as each person is seated, he or she is served beer, and the beer continues to be served until the meal is ready, often a matter of two, three, even four or five hours. During this waiting period there is general conversation, warmed as time goes on by the effects of the beer. Often, eventually, someone begins "joking."

Now although the Sherpas have the concept of the innocent or friendly joke, as well as the concept of the amusing or funny story, the fact is that most Sherpa joking (*shaga gyaup, marchak kirup*) takes the form of needling or ragging another person. It consists of people zeroing in on one another's suspected or well-known weaknesses, and probing them with assorted verbal tactics. Such joking normally takes place only at parties, where people are gathered for a long period of time, and are under the influence of drink. It is expected that people will joke at parties, and joking is said to be part of the fun of the whole event.

The initiator begins by making loud statements to the room at large that are thinly disguised insults about another guest at the party. He concludes his statements with a hearty laugh and some phrases to the effect that it is all a joke, and isn't it funny? The object of the jokes may or may not start calling out equally pointed responses, depending on his glibness and self-assurance in such situations, but it rarely fails that, if the initiator of the joking is persistent and insulting enough, the object of the jokes will respond in kind, and often will ultimately lose his temper and attempt to take direct revenge. The other guests will usually be able to stop the fight before it comes to blows, but there will be bad blood between the principals for a long time to come (if indeed there wasn't already), and there will probably be a similar scene between them at the next party.

Virtually every large-scale Sherpa party has scenes of this sort. Many of them culminate in genuine quarrels in which the pretense of joking is dropped, although the participants rarely come to blows. The quarrels may cause the breakup of the party, although if they occur early one or both of the principals will be taken home by some kinsmen or friends and the party will continue without them.

Now, what is clearly going on in these engagements is that the participants are working out grudges while safely surrounded by virtually the whole village, who will see to it that things do not get out of hand. Further, as people chime in on one side or the other of the argument, both parties can get a sense of whether and to what degree public opinion is on their side, or at least who their friends are or will be on this particular issue. Alternatively, the person initiating the joking may be aware of gossip and public opinion concerning the issue being raised and the person being attacked, and the joker thus spontaneously functions as a vehicle for the expression of community disapproval. The institution of joking at Sherpa parties, in other words, is a rather classic social control mechanism. While it may be extremely funny, and while it is often enjoyed both for its humorousness as well as for the accuracy of some of its blows, it clearly performs a serious function and is probably appreciated for that as well. Grudges and disputes are aired in a safe context, public opinion is generated and tapped.

But there is more to the politics of a party than a simple social control function in relation to the behavior of individuals. Specifically, I would argue that the core of hospitality politics lies in the reproduction of that peculiar stringing out of individuals in a minutely graded status hierarchy. The "objective" economic bases of hierarchy in the community have already been described; wealth differences roughly grade people into "big," "small," and everyone else. The status hierarchy clearly builds upon these objective gradations, but at the same time, the production of an utterly unambiguous string of positions, each unique, entails and represents a set of further social operations upon these objective economic facts.

Status is a theme throughout the entire hospitality event. The process begins, as we saw above, with the seating. The little seating drama, where everyone modestly tries to sit lower than his rightful place, but then allows himself to get pulled into his proper seat, somewhat parallels the dramas of serving food — pressure, resistance, and finally acquiescence. Normally, people simply wind up where they were at the last party. Occasionally, however, when all the dust settles, two individuals have changed places, and an adjustment in the hierarchy has been made. Seating etiquette, then, is one of the means by which status, changed or unchanged, is actually socially and publicly bestowed and rebestowed.

The next phase of the party, after the seating has been ordered, is the long period of conversation and joking. The joking may be seen, beyond the way I have already interpreted it, as part of, and a further development upon, the reproduction and adjustment of the status hierarchy that began with the seating. It often entails putting someone who has status pretensions, or who has been from a community point of view illegitimately throwing his weight around, back in his proper place. Alternatively, the joker may be a community bully who initiates joking against some minor personage at every party as a way of inflating his own status pretensions. But in general, joking takes place between people near in rank to one another, in the upper or middle ranks, as a sort of verbal version of the same microstatus rivalry seen in the seating process. [20] And how well one acquits oneself in this process — ideally with wit (however heavy-handed) and self-control — may actually, if insensibly, affect one's status position.

The joking is broken up by the serving of the meal, which, because it follows the seating order, thus continues to express status order. But finally, after the meal, the whole thing is dramatically broken down: In the singing and dancing, people line up in random order, finally destroying the punctilious arrangements that have prevailed throughout the whole event. Dancing is always egalitarian, and is always, too, the most hlermu — fun — part of the affair.

Hospitality, then, is an almost unremitting play upon the theme of status. The community as a string of individually graded positions is assembled and displayed almost exclusively at parties,[21] and herein lies the real political function of hospitality. One is, in large part, where one sits. And one sits, by and large, where one's fellows let one sit — where the host indicates, where one's neighbors pull one, and where the joking might not let one remain the next time around. The status processing at parties — the seating and the joking — are best understood as the constant public, and in a sense democratic, translation of material "facts" (wealth, pedigree) into social and moral significance. Status is the social significance such facts will be allowed to have.

Disputes and status rivalries arise from the particular details of personality and fluctuations of fortune that weave in and out of everyday affairs. Any given individual may appear to be gaining status ground in informal interaction around the community. But it is not until a party that such ground gaining is or is not accorded legitimacy. Money is made or lost, acts of charity are performed or finessed, but the translation of these facts into the significance they will have for social relations within the community takes place largely at hospitality events. Status is the community's bestowal of moral significance, positive or negative, on the material facts of each and every individual's life.

From one point of view it may appear that the status hierarchy itself is, or embodies, the political order of the community. Certainly it is a cultural image of perfect social order, embodying the pious hope that everyone may be so justly arranged that there will be no cause for resentment, dispute, or crime. Such notions, further, would draw strength from religious ideology, for in the religious view everyone is and has exactly what he morally deserves, on the basis of behavior in past lives. In such a view, order — arrangement — generates order — regulation of behavior.

Yet in fact it could be argued that arranging people in such a way produces just the opposite effect: It may be seen as *over-ordering* people, stressing (or creating) minute differences among them, and setting up a situation in which competition is all but inevitable, even when there is nothing much to fight about. The status-string system thus reflects and reproduces the atomization and petty conflict that operate in ordinary social life. Yet it translates all these petty conflicts, whatever their actual issues, into a single idiom of social value that can only be arbitrated by the collectivity. People will rarely arbitrate between two neighbors feuding over a material issue. At the next party, however, the status processing allows the general community to indicate who is felt to be the better man in terms of overall social and communal value.

Thus the political ordering of the community is not *in* the status hierarchy, but in the quite democratic processes that bestow, legitimate, or withhold status in public hospitality contexts. Primarily this takes place in the joking. After someone initiates a sally against another individual, anyone may chime in: Old men who are by now "high" simply because they are old, respected older women, sharp-tongued matrons, judicious widows, all participate along with the active core of men directly involved. People add their jokes to one or the other side of the repartee, or at least contribute their laughter in appreciation of the aptness of one or another remark. People intervene, defend, or join an attack. And by and large this sort of participatory democracy works fairly well for the communal welfare, throwing weight on the side of the more decent and responsible of two economically indistinguishable individuals, cutting down potential bullies and autocrats, and keeping the big people in general relatively responsive to public sentiment — or even making some of them uncomfortable enough to consider moving out of town.

The status hierarchy, in other words, is not a political *structure,* but the reproduction of the status hierarchy that takes place almost exclusively at parties is a political *process*, and a reasonably effective one at that. And the process is communal, actually democratic, producing that peculiar political shape characteristic of Sherpa communities — democratic hierarchy, or hierarchical democracy. It is clear that the process is more important than the final results. The perfectly graded string of individuals does not carry over into, or have any functions in, any other domains of social life. "Big people" do not have any special perquisites, and there are no patterns of deference to be paid to the man who sat above one, or patterns of domination vis-à-vis the man who sat below one. The status string is clearly based on actual gradations of wealth, but it then becomes a symbolic medium for the enactment of collective political process, and this is its primary function and significance. And once it has served this function, at parties, people are able to relax and form the unranked line of dancers, singing, stamping, and kicking in obvious pleasure. It is then, most often, that one's neighbor will turn to one and say, "Isn't this hlermu?"

"Civilized" coercion and the reproduction of hosts

Civilization began with a hospitality event. In the paradigmatic myth of the founding of Tibetan civilization, the people learn how to make offerings to the gods, and the offering rituals take the form of parties. The myth was first spontaneously told me one afternoon by a lama, as he was explaining the various altar items he was constructing for a household ritual, and it was also recounted publicly by lamas in the course of a number of temple rituals. It concerns the building of Samyang (Tib., Samye) monastery, the first Buddhist monastery in Tibet.

The people, so the tale goes, worked hard every day building the monastery, but every night evil demons came and destroyed their work. The people were making no progress at all, so they called the Guru Rimpoche and asked him what to do. The

Guru Rimpoche said it was no wonder they were having trouble, they weren't making the gods happy, only spending a lot of money. So he taught them how to do an offering ritual, and then the gods helped the people build the monastery. Not only did they keep away the demons, but they also helped carry the heavy things, and worked while the people slept, so that the monastery was completed in a very short time.

Offering rituals are explicitly cast as parties or hospitality events for the gods (see Chapter 6). They are also explicitly manipulative, designed to get the gods to help, although one particularly articulate lama informant was careful in his phrasing to play down the manipulation. According to him, people are simply evincing goodness and generosity in doing the rituals, and the gods are pleased when they see this and so agree to help people. Yet the lay people do not (as the lama himself said) understand things in this spirit. They see the effectiveness of the rituals as analogous to the effectiveness of yangdzi transactions wherein one manipulates others through the powers of food and the evocation of a sense of obligation. The yangdzi analogy is reinforced by the stress upon beer as one of the central offering items, just as it is the most basic yangdzi prestation. Another of the Guru Rimpoche's gifts to the people was the recipe for beer to be used in the offering rituals; during the distribution of beer in every ritual a little chant or blessing is sung commemorating the Guru Rimpoche's gift of beer.

Now, although there are no formal structures or roles of power and authority in a Sherpa community, the yangdzi process is a culturally legitimate mechanism of (attempted) coercion. It is considered psychologically and even mechanically persuasive, and is the proper way of trying to get things from others that they might be reluctant to give. Further, if the yangdzi recipient agrees to the request of the giver, there is a strong moral obligation to follow through and deliver the goods — money, labor, cooperation, or whatever has been agreed to. Because there are, however, no systematic sanctions against failing to live up to the bargain, the whole thing depends entirely on belief, on the moral authority of the idea. Yangdzi can only work as long as everyone believes it is both powerful and legitimate.

Yangdzi, as noted above, is a special form of hospitality; the yangdzi giver is a host. And the Sherpas assume that the powers of hosting derive in large part from the food and drink the host serves. Food is "fetishized" — endowed with what are seen as natural and intrinsic powers — and he who serves it, in the cultural view, merely rationally appropriates its powers for his own ends. From a post-Durkheimian perspective, however, the point must be inverted: The power of a host makes for the power of the food. Yet the virtue of the culture's perspective is its anchorage in "natural" processes, and once we have cut this anchorage we must now ask whence, if not from the food, does the host's power derive?

The myth of the origin of offering rituals gives us the clue. In the myth, as in all offering rituals, the host is actually the collectivity, the assembled community. For the remainder of this chapter I will argue, then, that the coercive authority of the host role is reproduced at noninstrumental, large-scale hospitality events of the sort analyzed thus far, and that the reinvestment of hosts with legitimate power, necessary for effective yangdzi manipulation in other contexts, involves a sort of absorption by the host of the collective social energies that are exercised at his party.

The power and centrality of hospitality in the culture thus derives not only from the direct and almost visible effects of a party — creating experiences of pleasurable exchange, allowing for the democratic exercise of social control, and temporarily resynthesizing an image of order in the status hierarchy. Its more far-reaching significance lies in the fact that, at parties, the socially vital role of host itself is reproduced, reinvested with legitimate coercive authority. We must now once again reexamine the party to see how this process occurs.

The host is seemingly endowed with high status from the outset. He is the *zhindak*, a term that means not only householder and host, but also master, lord, the man in charge and responsible. And his seat is at the head of the seating order, the highest seat in the room. Yet we can see another dimension of meaning in his seat location: Unless the host is also the highest man in the village (a purely hypothetical case, because the "highest man" is rarely firmly established), his seat actually places him out-of-status, and renders him temporarily neutral in relation to the status machinations of the rest of the guests. Further, in hosting a large-scale wedding or funeral party, or a celebration of a seasonal ritual, he has no material interests, no hidden manipulative motives. Such parties represent hospitality in its purest form, a simple social entertainment, in keeping with tradition and in expression of community participation. Thus again the host has a certain disinterested neutrality for the duration of the event. And finally it might be noted that, in actual behavior, a host generally stays in the background during the early stages of a party. He does not necessarily greet most of the guests and show them to their seats; in fact, given the delicate maneuvers of seating among the guests themselves, it seems important that he stay out of the whole business and simply allow it all to happen. He often busies himself with a show of supervising the food preparations, or in any case keeps a low profile.

These aspects of hosting — status neutrality, material disinterestedness, and initial demeanor of relative self-effacement — all render the host a sort of cipher, a structurally neutral element in the social process of the event, a sort of vessel or receptacle that will gradually be filled.

We have seen that the politically dynamic portion of the party takes place largely before the meal. There is first of all the series of individual negotiations, in the idiom of good manners, in the seating process. In the course of these negotiations, the status of each member of the community is rebestowed or a new status is publicly bestowed, as symbolized by the seat that a person winds up occupying. Then there is the long period of conversation and "joking." Despite the fact that the joking is both genuinely amusing and socially functional (and even assuming that its social functions are somewhat evident to and appreciated by the community), nonetheless the net effect of joking upon the development of the party is generally negative. Tempers and tensions rise, and the whole business may become quite distasteful, for the Sherpas are really not very comfortable with overt expressions of aggression. And while the unpleasantness might be felt by all present, there is one person for whom, if it really gets out of hand, it would be a disaster — the host.

Now, although I would not want to claim that the timing of the serving of the food is deliberately geared to the tension level of the party, nonetheless it often seemed that somehow, rather magically, just when things were approaching flash point, the food would start being served.[22] The serving of the food, for a variety of reasons, almost always works to defuse the situation. For one thing, everyone is by now very hungry, and the food is genuinely distracting. For another, the responder is no doubt looking for an excuse to cut off the interchange. Further, the servers are now moving about in front of the guests, getting in the way of the conversation. In addition, one must receive one's food politely, and at least stop calling out long enough to make some gesture acknowledging that one has been served. Next, when everyone has been served the lama or host must say a brief blessing, dedicating the food to the gods, and people should be silent during this. And finally, although there is no rule against speaking while eating, in general it is considered impolite to carry on sustained conversation during a meal. The food, in short, effectively cuts off the joking and undercuts to some extent the tensions that had been building. The individuals directly involved are no doubt still smoldering, and the joking (and ultimately a fight) might erupt again after the meal. But usually the meal effectively does the trick, and the worst is over.

The host then is, in a sense, the deus ex machina of the party, the magic agent with his magic panacea, the food. And the serving of the food is his grand entrance, the moment at which the whole focus of the party shifts. During the long period of joking, the dynamics of the party operate among the guests, and the host remains in the wings. But when, after three or four hours of beer and repartee, the service of the food begins, and breaks the heightened tensions (or, in the case of dead parties, breaks the deepening boredom and restlessness), the whole attention structure shifts to this central figure and the pleasant, sensuous gratification he is providing. It is here, then, that social energy almost visibly flows into host and food, both of which seem charged with power. And of course it is only after this point that the host turns his pressures on the guests to "Eat, eat," asserting the power that he has now absorbed.

The period before the serving of the meal is, as I said, the "political" period of the party. It embraces a variety of processes of communal self-regulation. It is the energy of these processes, I am arguing, that the host comes symbolically to embody, and the point may be supported in other ways.

When a shaman goes into a trance and hosts the (lower) gods to a party, he actually embodies the gods: They enter him and speak through him, and express their will. If the gods, from the classic Durkheimian perspective that pervades this entire chapter, are expressions of the moral force of the community, then the shaman, who is explicitly said to be "hosting" the spirits, dramatizes in extreme form the literal embodiment of social sentiment that hosts normally come to embody more metaphorically at parties.

More directly to the point, when the people collectively give offerings to their gods they do so, as noted above, in the framework of a party of which they are the collective hosts. Here, then, host and community are one and the same, and the host role is isomorphic with the expression of collective will. Further, the individuals who materially sponsor any given offering ritual, by providing the food, labor, and money for the event, are called "servants"[23] of the congregation. The true host of the ritual is the collectivity. Those who merely provide the materials for the event get no particular power or status (although they do get merit) from doing so. The point seems to confim the analysis that the host's power not only does not derive from the natural powers of the food he provides, but that it specifically derives from the social energies of the collectivity.

This analysis is also supported by a different set of data. We have seen that much of the political process of a party operates around the issue of status. Of course there are many things that generate social antagonisms, from simple personality conflicts to complex disputes over real material resources. Yet because there are no social mechanisms to resolve most of these problems, all of them tend to be translated up into the more generalized idiom of who is the "bigger" — the better, the more congenial, the more livable-with — person, that is, who shall be granted generalized social support and respect through an acknowledgment of higher status. This is in fact the "political" process that takes place at parties, this translation of particularistic antagonsims into a general idiom of status, and the collective arbitration of what has now been redefined as status rivalry.

Now, if the communal self-regulation energies are primarily in terms of status antagonism and status arbitration, and if these are the energies that the host comes to embody, then it is interesting to note that in certain kinds of party-like social events in which status expression is for particular reasons muted, the role of host may be seen, correlatively, to recede and lose marking. Thus funeral feasts, as will be discussed more fully below, have rules against discrimination between the guests by status, and in these contexts the host loses most of his hostly prerogatives. And in dancing get-togethers where there is no status ordering among the participants, there is also no host — the dancers buy the beer collectively. In these cases the downplaying of status (for reasons specific to the nature of the events) coincides with a weakening or disappearance of the role of host, thus articulating with the overall argument being presented here: That the host's powers in normal party contexts derive from his structural relationship to the status dynamics of his party.

I have argued that the management of status antagonisms is accomplished in a relatively "democratic" way at parties, through various interventions of the other guests in any given status "debate." The host has provided the conditions for this process to happen. His space and time embrace the event, his food and beer fuel it. He provides both the media and the catalysts for whatever social arrangements or rearrangements get worked out. Further, he himself is symbolically "neutral," in terms of both status and material interest, for the duration of the party, thus being a sort of social vacuum into which the collective energies may flow. When after several hours of intense social politicking among the guests, the host serves the food, the whole focus of the party shifts. Joking repartee, having perhaps gone as far as it could safely go, and having covered a good bit of disputed ground, now ceases, as people engage in vertical interaction with the server, rather than in horizontal interaction among themselves. The host seems to absorb these intense social energies, to be infused with "natural" power.

Thus hosts make parties, but analytically parties make hosts. The point is not, however, that any particular host gains any particular powers as a result of his relationship to the dynamics of his party; it is rather that host and food as symbols come to be invested anew on these occasions with the coercive power and authority required for the successful enactment of any situation of social manipulation. Yangdzi — manipulation of others by food in a hospitality format — is the basic mechanism for generating exchange in Sherpa society, whether from selfish neighbors, passive gods, or predatory demons. Yangdzi is assumed to work because of the "natural" powers of food, and the intrinsic authority of a host. The analysis of hospitality, however, has allowed us to see the social sources of such coercive power and authority, in the dynamic processes of the ordinary Sherpa party.

The Sherpas' myth of the origin of themselves as a civilized community embodies the basic hospitality relationship, with the community as a whole playing the host. We saw earlier the pervasiveness of hospitality as both social practice and cultural metaphor. And we have seen now some of the vital functions it performs in this uncentralized and atomized society. Hospitality dramatizes order (in the status hierarchy), produces order (in the political functions of party interaction), and reproduces a mechanism — yangdzi — for generating order beyond the party itself.

Yet the forces of anarchy and disruption periodically return, in the form of demons, to wreak chaos and pollution in society just as they did when the Sherpas' ancestors were trying to build Samyang monastery. The exorcism of demons is the distinctive focus of the Sherpas' Nyingmawa sect of Tibetan Buddhism, and it is to these rituals we now turn.

5. Exorcisms: problems of wealth, pollution, and reincarnation

The discussion of hospitality in its status, as opposed to exchange, aspects raised the point of wealth differences in Sherpa society. In the context of the hospitality analysis, these differences of wealth were seen merely as the objective basis, the point of departure, for status ordering, which in turn was seen as providing the idiom of political self-regulation in the community. Yet differences of wealth which, along with pedigree and piety, place people in the categories of "big," "middle," and "small," also have other ramifications, which must be taken up here.

It is important to begin by noting that although these categories or strata are not true classes (defined in terms of any sort of surplus-extraction relationships), there are nonetheless real structural differences — and not just differences of comfort and life-style — generated by relative wealth and relative poverty. The immediate advantage of wealth is greater economic flexibility. The wealthy can take advantage of market opportunities when the poor cannot. The wealthy can also absorb a few bad economic breaks without being seriously undermined, whereas for the poor a few bad breaks may send them over the brink. It is clear that at some point a Sherpa family may pass a point of "take-off," where its wealth sustains itself and even increases, and where anxiety about staying afloat and simply maintaining what it has becomes insignificant. Such a family is clearly among the "big people." And thus wealth, even without a systematic surplus-extraction mechanism of reproducing itself, tends to make more wealth, while poverty tends to keep declining. The Sherpa proverb, "The rich get more money, the drunks get more beer," perhaps expresses this point.

With these prefatory remarks, then, we turn to an analysis of exorcism rites, in which issues of wealth differences, along with other problems, are symbolically raised and manipulated. Exorcisms, in contrast to Nyungne, are highly popular rites, indeed are the most popular of the orthodox calendrical events. In addition to being held annually, however, exorcisms are also connected with funerals, and here, as we shall see, certain significant heterodoxies enter in. It is on these funeral-connected, heterodox/orthodox exorcisms that we shall focus.

A wealthy woman and her daughter

The rituals

The variety of malicious, aggressive, violent, and otherwise downright unpleasant beings in the Sherpa world is somewhat overwhelming. Even the highest gods can take nasty forms, while the legions of evil beings do not correspondingly have good sides. The weight of the system, in terms of sheer numbers and types, is on the side of evil. Correlatively, the preponderance of Sherpa rituals is concerned with combating the various evil beings, and the modes of dealing with them are almost as diverse and numerous as the types of evil beings themselves.

It will be useful to distinguish between rituals of offering to gods, to be discussed in the next chapter, and rituals of exorcism of demons, although this does not correspond to a native distinction. In rituals petitioning the gods for assistance, the chief type of help requested is the gods' alliance with humanity against the demons, and in fact rituals of offering and rituals of exorcism would both be classed by the Sherpas as *kurim*:

In one kind of kurim, you call all the gods, give them offerings and ask them to join your side in getting rid of the offending spirits. Then when the spirits see how powerful your side is, they realize they are outdone, they are frightened and go away. In another kind, you ask the offending spirits what they will need to satisfy them [and then you give it to them].

The informant who made this statement includes rites of offering, in which the gods are asked for help, and exorcisms in which the demons are confronted directly, within the single kurim category.[1] Nonetheless, he does make a distinction – in the first type the emphasis is on mobilizing the gods, and the reaction of the demons is merely implied; in the second type, the demons are confronted directly. I will take this as a measure of justification for the division I am utilizing analytically here. There is, further more than one mode of direct confrontation with demons. The informant indicates "giving them what they want," which is indeed the explicitly preferred mode, but exorcisms also include threats, forcible ejection, and attempts at outright destruction as well. To reiterate the distinction I will be using, the emphasis in offering rituals is upon mobilizing the gods and not on confronting the evil beings themselves; in exorcisms there is always direct enactment of confrontation with the forces of evil. The mobilization of the gods remains important, indeed critical, but the dramatic thrust shifts to the confrontation itself.[2]

The do dzongup

Some funerals conclude with a single rite called a *do dzongup.* For this, laymen construct, from mud and dough, an effigy of a tiger in a standing or striding posture on a slab of wood. Often the tiger's tail is erect, and its testicles prominent. Three small anthropomorphic figures of dough are placed around the tiger, one in front leading, one astride riding, and one behind driving the tiger out of town (See Figure 2). The figures represent humans, said to be asserting man's authority over the demons. Paper banners are stuck into the tiger's back, or into the human figures, inscribed with the names of the illnesses and demons being got rid of. Thread crosses are also sometimes stuck into the figures along with, or in place of, the banners.[3] Each person present takes a small lump of dough, passes it over his or her body, then squeezes it in the fist, and places it on the tiger's tray. These lumps, called *pak*, are said to remove all the "bad smells" from the body, and are thrown out with the tiger.

The tiger is placed in the center of the floor of the large main room of the funeral house, where everyone is gathered. It is set up facing the door, with a flour "road" leading from it to the door. The demons are conjured to enter it. Several young men, usually adolescents, dress up in caricatures of "poor clothes" to act as the *peshangba*, who are said to be "like soldiers" but have many comic and other-

Figure 2. The tiger figure (sende) destroyed in the first exorcism (do dzongup) (drawing by Lydia Chen)

Figure 3. The effigy (lut) of the sponsor in the second exorcism (gyepshi) (drawing by Lydia Chen)

wise ambiguous aspects. They escort the tiger out of town and enact its destruction.
The lamas are chanting the appropriate text. The peshangba line up in crouching
positions in front of the tiger, carrying swords or knives, or brandishing sticks. They
keep poking one another lewdly with the weapons, and otherwise acting silly, but
they grow more and more serious as the rite develops.

The chanting is accompanied by a steady rhythm on the large drum. Periodically
the drumming accelerates, joined by the loud clashing of large cymbals, approaching but not reaching a climax. This occurs six or seven times, and each time the
peshangba rise and dance toward the door, seemingly trying to get out but unable
to. Their dance consists of frenzied foot stamping, in a sort of forward–backward,
stop–start motion (with much behind wiggling, to the amusement of the children
present) which then, as the rhythm of the music decelerates before climax, modulates into a more stately hopping dance. On the last few sorties, the peshangba and
others present give loud piercing whistles and shouts of ha-ha-ha! ho-ho-ho!

Finally, the music moves to climax. One of the peshangba takes the cymbals and,
to great hooting, the dance is repeated. Another man (theoretically and sometimes
in fact a poor, low-status man) picks up the tiger, and the procession— peshangba
with weapons, peshangba clashing cymbals, man with tiger, several men carrying
torches, and assorted young people hooting and whistling — dances out of the
house. They dance down through town with much clashing of cymbals to the shrine
at the entrance of the village, where the tiger is tossed down and hacked to pieces by
the peshangba. As soon as this is done, the peshangba peel off their costumes, and
the entire procession sings and dances its way back to the house whence it came.[4]

The gyepshi

In addition to the do dzongup, a wealthy or pious family may also commission a
gyepshi rite.[5] The gyepshi is virtually the polar opposite sort of exorcism, in that it
operates by lavishing the demons with valuable, beautiful, and tasty offerings, and
treating them in a manner bound to soothe and pacify them, rather than threatening
and overpowering them with rage and brute force.

A complete gyepshi altar is a very complex affair, and takes many hours to set
up. The focal item is a large anthropomorphic dough effigy of the sponsor, serving
as a substitute offering to the demons in place of the sponsor's flesh and blood.
The effigy is called a *lut* (Tib., *glud*), generally translated as "scapegoat." It should
be a perfect model of a human being (or sometimes two, a man and a woman),
and as attractive as possible. It should have precious stones for its facial features,
and should be dressed in fine clothes and thread crosses, the latter said to represent
"rainbows," thus making the effigy even more attractive than its human counter-
part (See Figure 3). The most elaborate lut I saw was decorated with thread crosses,
jewels, and ceremonial scarves; it stood on a platform heaped with real clothing,
valuable jewels, shells, money, grain, and a small ritual food cake. Attached to a
stick stuck into the lut is a piece of paper containing horoscopic data to identify

the sponsor properly. On one side the lama writes in the sponsor's name, year of birth, and other particulars, and on the other side is a printed request to the demons to leave the real sponsor alone.

The altar is laid out on the floor, on a gigantic diagram of the open palm of the Buddha. The ceremony is said to operate against a demon grouping known as "the four Dü," and there are dough effigies of these four figures as well as the effigy of the sponsor. In small-scale versions of the ritual, the demon effigies are pressed from a mold, and are simple anthropomorphic figures; at the great Dumji festival, they were elaborately sculpted figures, apparently androgynous, with a variety of terrifying features, but outfitted with items meant to represent offerings of fine clothes.

The lut, the effigy of the sponsor, is placed on a tripod in the center of the palm diagram, an idol of the Buddha is placed on the wrist (as if it were the body behind the hand), and the effigies of the four dü are placed on the four fingers of the hand, or sometimes at the four corners of the altar. All the effigies have thread crosses stuck into them. Surrounding the central effigy of the sponsor are four concentric rings of offerings — 100 miniature clay shrines, 100 ritual food cakes, 100 butter lamps, and 100 miniature lut (dough effigies of the congregation). Each type of offering is said to be specific to the taste of one of the four dü.[6] Figure 4 is a sketch of a model gyepshi altar.

Once the altar is set up, the lamas read the text, establishing alliances with the gods, presenting the offerings to the demons, and commanding the latter to be satisfied and depart. The onlookers, the lay people on whose behalf the ceremony is performed, shower the altar with kernels of grain and with flower petals at appropriate moments in the chanting. When this text is completed, the effigies and offerings are collected and lined up on a flour "road" leading to the door.

At the conclusion of the rite, the items are taken out in procession: The big sponsor-effigy is carried at the head of the procession, followed by people carrying baskets laden with the other types of offerings, each with its appropriate demon effigy atop. The carriers are, or should be, low-status people, ideally non-Sherpas. The big lut is carried to some prescribed spot and set down, and the other four demons-cum-offerings are each carried to one of the four directions. At Dumji the four demon effigies were kicked around and roughed up (though not chopped to bits as the tiger had been) but the sponsor-effigy was carefully placed up on the ledge of the village shrine, and the lamas in their god costumes danced around it, expressing, according to one of the lamas, "the happiness of the people at having got rid of the demons."

The entire gyepshi ceremony emphasizes the placation and soothing of the demons, rather than threats and violence. They are given elaborate and beautiful offerings to satisfy all their needs and make them happy, so they will not bother people. The effect of the altar, with its perfectly symmetrical arrangement of offerings and its glowing circle of butter lamps; the slow and steady rather than accelerating–decelerating rhythm of the chanting; and the participation of the onlookers

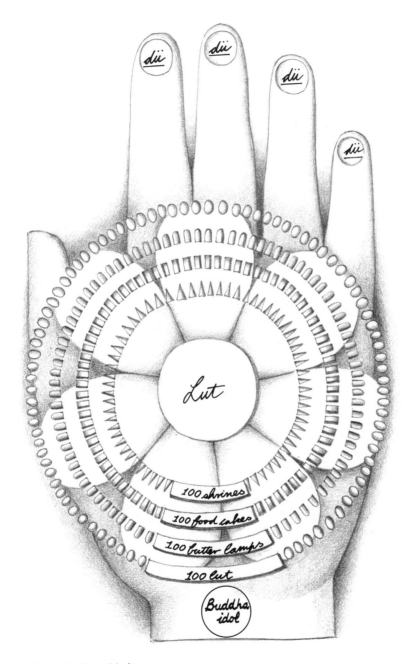

Figure 4. Gyepshi altar

in showering flower petals and grain upon the altar, combined to generate a feeling of warmth and good will. Yet in the end, as in all dealings with demons, the dü are hustled out of the party, together with their offerings, and commanded to be satisfied and depart. They are told that if they do not accept the offerings and allow themselves to be pacified by them, and if they then try to return and cause trouble, the lamas will chop them up in little pieces.

When one asks Sherpas about the meaning of exorcisms, there is general agreement even among lay people that the correct way to get rid of demons is to feed them, to satisfy their greedy desires, so that they will go away and leave people alone. It is understood, but not fully accepted, that demons cannot be killed; they can only be controlled by feeding and bribes:

Q. Why do they chop up the tiger?

A. (Lama) They're ignorant. In the book it doesn't say to do that, but they don't understand. They think the tiger is a demon, and they can kill it and it will never come back. . . . You don't kill demons, just pity (nyingje) them and give them what they want, satisfying all their needs.

The gyepshi exorcism, then, in which the demons are fed, is the more orthodox of the two exorcisms,[7] while the tiger exorcism is quite heterodox, and indeed monks (as opposed to village lamas) will not perform this ritual. Although the Sherpas sometimes perform the tiger rite alone, more often it is conjoined with and encompassed by the gyepshi, and for this as well as other reasons that will become clear as we proceed, I shall treat the two together.

A number of questions arise from a consideration of this complex material. First, who (or what) are the demons? Second, among the Sherpas exorcisms are specifically considered rites of purification; the Sherpa purity/pollution system must thus be examined, specifically as it relates to death, funerals, and demons. And finally, as exorcisms are part of the funeral process and hence connected with death, the third problem will be to examine "the problem of death" in Sherpa culture. Demons, pollution, and death are the three keys I will use to gain access to the meaning of exorcisms. We shall see that each of these is, simultaneously, an issue of cultural, social, and psychological import. We shall also see the ingenuity of the ritual in interarticulating ultimate existential concerns, immediate personal and affective concerns, and ongoing social structural problems and conflicts.

The problems of the rituals

Demons, greed, and social predation

Demons are insatiably greedy, vicious, predatory creatures who roam the world causing trouble — illness, death, corruption, and destruction. They were in the world before humans came into being, and exist independently of any human endeavors.

Buddhism, when it came to Tibet, undertook to bring the demons under control, and to provide people with means of defending against them.

While the Sherpas have names for many different kinds of demons, the distinguishing features of the various types are not all that clear. In the case of funerals, the chief villains are creatures called *de*. It is de who are attracted to the corpse, who are attracted by all the religious ritual, and who are attracted by all the feasting that goes on in the course of the funeral. The tiger exorcism (do dzongup) is directed against de, although the gyepshi is directed against a different type of demon called dü.[8] For present purposes, however, demons may be treated generically without losing too much cultural subtlety. I shall interpret them first as ethnopsychological symbols, and secondly as social symbols.

In the first instance, then, demons are images, projections of human psychological forces, particularly the greedy, voracious, predatory tendencies of the self. The concept of projection is in fact culturally articulated, at least at the higher levels of Buddhist theory. The Buddhist point is that while these beings appear objective and external to the ignorant individual, they are really aspects of the self. High-level Buddhist meditation and teaching is aimed at achieving an understanding of this point, and at "defeating" demons by learning to control, "quiet," and ultimately eliminate these interior impulses. Controlling the demons is thus, for high adepts, not a matter of external ritual actions, but of concentration and self-control.

The point has filtered down into popular consciousness, albeit not fully understood. Men who have had some contact with religious teaching had been told this point in some form or other, and one occasionally hears seemingly skeptical remarks among lay people about the existence of demons and other evil beings. One man said that when you are nervous, walking home in the dark for example, every rock and tree looks like a demon, but this is a projection of one's own nervousness. His comment may be compared with this Tibetan textual verse:

> When one is shaken with wishes, fears and sorrows,
> worried by thieves and dreams,
> then one will see them as if placed before one
> even though they are not there.
>
> (Beyer: 76)

And there is a lay proverb that goes, "Say there is and there is, say there isn't and there isn't," the implication again being that the nonobjective beings and forces in the world are creations of human thought/speech and do not exist in themselves.

Thus, it does not do violence to the culture to view the demons as psychological projections, or more precisely as culturally provided symbolic modes of conceptualizing certain psychological processes (thereby, in effect, creating, or at least shaping, those processes). But it must be kept in mind that for most lay people the demons are really "out there," and are felt to prey upon people from without. Thus, the most common lay mode of drawing relationships between human psychological processes and evil beings is by analogy: People, they say, are *like* demons in various ways — hungry, greedy, violent, anarchic, attempting to corrupt others and to subvert others' fragile good intentions when they stand in the way of getting what one wants.[9]

Along with violence, greed is the demons' most salient characteristic. They are insatiable for food, preferably flesh and blood, but ultimately for any sort of food and any other form of material wealth, luxury, and satisfaction.[10] But if demons are genetically greedy, so are people: Greed is considered a basic impulse of human nature, present in all people, and threatening to get out of hand at all times.

The pervasiveness of greed is articulated, as we saw in the preceding chapter, again and again. People are conceived not only to need food for survival, but to desire food for sensuous pleasure and satisfaction over and above their basic needs. From the religious point of view, greedy thoughts and deeds are highly sinful (as are violent ones) and a major portion of the religious effort for the individual is devoted to conquering and subduing the ever-present greedy elements of one's nature. The proper way of going about this is asceticism, training oneself to want less. Even in lay etiquette, as opposed to religious practice, every child is taught, and every adult feels, some responsibility for controlling their greedy impulses, if not by actually extinguishing them, then at least by masking them with good manners and having a sense of social shame about letting them show. In all of this, the emphasis is upon self-control, and the responsibility lies with the individual. Greed is conceived to be a psychological problem, and sophisticated religious specialists will say that the greedy demons represent this problem to the unsophisticated lay mind.

But the problem is, of course, social as well. For greed is not simply a matter of wanting objects that exist outside a social matrix. With few exceptions the objects of desire are sought by others from oneself, or by oneself from others.[11] Further, greed is considered to be more prevalent among certain categories of people, and other social categories, though not culturally specified, fit well the description of being heavily motivated by greed and desire. This brings us to the question of demons not as psychological "projections," but as social "reflections."

To treat demons as reflections of elements of the social structure, one must again raise the question of whether there is any cultural ground for doing so. Unlike witches and ghosts that arise directly from the human community, and unlike the various nasty beings and states within the Wheel of Life that again derive from human beings (through bad reincarnations), the demons existed prior to and independent of humanity, a completely separate order of beings. Further, though they bother humans, they do not bother any particular group (except perhaps the religious specialists, because they want to undermine the religion that wages war on them). But, as exorcism texts show, demons are often considered along with problematic humans; the two categories are frequently jumbled together, and destructive magic is directed rather indiscriminately against both:

> Let us all, yogins and our retinue,
> avert the vindictive enemies of the past,

the barbarous enemies of the present,
the foreign enemies mobilized against us, . . .
avert the 80,000 hindering demons.
I pray you avert them all, every one: . . .
the demons who follow behind,
the demons who bring shame to a mother and her son,
vindictive enemies and hurtful hindering demons . . .

(Beyer: 354)

It seems clear that the demons are a sort of catch-all *social* projective system for any category or group that is threatening or problematic. But one may also ask more specifically whether there are elements of Sherpa society, permanent features of its social structure of which, in an ongoing way, the demons might be symbols. That is, from the point of view of the ordinary lay villager, what are (to sharpen the question very strongly) the structural hungry, greedy, predatory elements of the society, that threaten to "eat" one's vitality and resources, and against whom one needs protection?[12]

For present purposes, I will restrict the discussion of this question to one dimension of Sherpa social structure, the socioeconomic hierarchy. As explained above, there are no formal stratification distinctions within Sherpa society. There are no castes, and the clans are considered to be of relatively equal status. But there are individual differences of wealth and status — there are, as we have seen, "big people," "middle people," and "small people." The big people are a handful of wealthy high-status families, the small people are a handful of very poor, property-less families (they are "Sherpas," but generally of ethnically mixed origins) who do wage labor for the other families of the village. And the middle people are everyone else in between, "not-rich-not-poor" as they often describe themselves.

In what sense may any of these sectors of Sherpa society be interpreted as referents of the demons? At the most obvious level, the "small people" are good candidates because they, like the demons, are always hungry, they never have quite enough to eat, and can probably never, given the total situation, be fully satisfied. And it is clear that others fear and distrust the poor to some extent — they assume that the poor will steal, that they are sneaky and "dirty," that they will take advantage of one if they can, and so on. These views are supported by reincarnation theory, which says that these people were immoral in a previous existence; thus one is somewhat justified in mistrusting them now. In fact, I never saw anybody give charity to the poor families of the village, or voluntarily do them a good turn. Even hiring them for wage labor was done grudgingly, because it was feared that they would be more trouble than help — they might steal, they would bring along their small children who would disrupt work and would have to be fed along with the parents, and so on.

The middle people (who comprise the majority of the population, and who are taken here as the reference point, the "ego" from whose point of view the ritual is interpreted) are, and consider themselves, different from the "small people" in that they own property and are self-supporting. Of course within this group there are still broad differences of wealth — some are barely scraping by, while others are quite comfortable. Yet ultimately, in relation to the "big people," *everyone* considers himself "small," poor relative to the rich, and always potentially poorer. The specter of increasing poverty, of downward mobility, is fed (as we shall see) by reincarnation theory and the sense of one's own less than morally perfect life, as well as by the actual observation of families that have mishandled and lost their fortunes within living memory, themselves perhaps examples of karmic retribution in operation. Of course, theoretically there is at least some basis for optimism about upward mobility. There are also families that have made their fortunes within living memory of the members of the community. But given the structural advantages of greater wealth, discussed briefly above, and given certain aspects of reincarnation theory (to be discussed below), upward mobility is both relatively less probable and less conceivable.

But then, what of the rich? While certain theoretical presuppositions might lead one to suspect that the rich are comparable to the demons, greedy and sucking resources from the general mass of the society, certain peculiarities of the position of the "big people" make it seem more likely that the gods are their correct symbolic analogue. Specifically, the gods (as will be discussed more fully in the next chapter) have the attributes of self-absorption and relative lack of concern with wordly problems; they threaten to detach themselves from the top of the system and "float away." The same, mutatis mutandis, may be said of the rich, and we must now briefly examine their position to show that this is the case.

It was noted in Chapter 2 that the rich men of Dzemu gained their economic advantage by virtue of a particular set of historical circumstances. What happened is not exactly clear, but it seems that one T., late in the nineteenth century, did some favors for the prime minister of Nepal, and in return was given large holdings of land. His direct descendants now form the community of Ghirpu, near Dzemu, and they continue to have strong ties to the central government of Nepal (one of them has been a cabinet minister). Many of the men of this lineage spend relatively little time in the Sherpa region, and their relationship to the rest of the Sherpas seems somewhat distant and superior, if not outright condescending. The big men of Dzemu are descendants of the older brother of this important ancestor, and somehow, as part of this same process, also acquired extra landholdings, setting them, too, above the ordinary folks of the village. They continue to live in Dzemu and participate in village affairs, but they seem to consider themselves somewhat above it all. Both the Ghirpu and Dzemu village lineages still regard themselves as Sherpas, but they are Brahminizing in several ways. The Dzemu big people, for example, tend not to drink alcohol, which they explain largely in Buddhist terms, but which may be interpreted as a gesture of Brahminization.[13]

The source of wealth inequalities in the Khumbu region is somewhat different, but I would argue that the net effect is roughly the same. The wealthy Khumbu men made their money largely from trading. Indeed, initially the early Khumbu Sherpa villages were largely settled by traders, middlemen in an extended system

between Tibet and India. Some were more successful than others, and while
they eventually invested in land and livestock, they continued to focus more upon
their lucrative trade. The less successful settled into the less profitable but economically adequate modes of subsistence farming and dairying, while the traders, at
least until the closing of Tibet by the Chinese, continued to do well. The trade base
of the wealthy Khumbu men and the land base of the wealthy Solu men is thus very
different, and Solu and Khumbu show very different economic configurations. But
the point that, I would suggest, unifies them, and that gives unity to "the problem of
the rich" in Sherpa culture, is that their economic base is not located within the
local society, indeed, within the Sherpa ethnic boundaries. The traders' base derives
from Tibet and India; the rich Solu men's additional lands are all located outside
the original boundaries of Sherpadom, are generally worked by non-Sherpa tenant
farmers, and produce crops (especially rice and tea) not native to, but important in,
the local diet.

The upper stratum of Sherpa society, in short, is analytically quite comparable
to the gods – beings whose connection with the society is tenuous, remote, and
potentially utterly detached – and not easily comparable to the demons. Because
they are not rich by virtue of extraction of resources from other strata of Sherpa
society, it is difficult to see them as greedy predators upon the group. Because their
economic base is largely elsewhere, they have few real ties or bonds of a hard
material sort with the local society, nor, given the peculiar political structure do
they systematically take roles of power in relation to the rest of the community.
They are, in short, relatively unintegrated into the local society. Like the monks, as
will be discussed in the next chapter, they seem to form an exclusive group with
little concern for what happens to everyone else. And like the disinterested and self-
absorbed gods (and the monks), they form an upper stratum of beings who "need
nothing," and who threaten to "float away" from the top of the system.

I have suggested, then, that there is a fairly neat correlation between the supernatural and the social hierarchy. This shall stand for the moment, although ultimately the analysis of the ritual will reveal that things do not remain so neat. Gods
and demons lose some of their apparently clear-cut distinctiveness from and opposition to one another, and the rich (disliked and envied for their inaccessibility and
their comforts) and the poor (disliked as images of where, on some future turn of
the karmic wheel, one might wind up) merge as objects of rage, to be exorcised.

Pollution, disintegration of self, and subversion of the social order

Culturally, exorcisms are considered to be rites of purification, "to clean all the
dirty things out of the village," "to clean all the bad smells out of the village." The
system of purity/pollution beliefs in Sherpa culture is primarily a theory of the
integration of the self, the person. Death is one of the situations of great pollution

for the living, and we may interpret that this is primarily because the deceased as a person, a self, has disintegrated, modeling and prefiguring the disintegration of the selves of the living. At the same time, however, it is possible to show that not only the person of the deceased, but also the social order itself has been symbolically disintegrated over the course of the funeral, and this is of equal significance in understanding why death (but actually the social process connected with death) is considered polluting, and why there must be exorcisms at the end of a funeral.

Sherpa purity/pollution beliefs posit that the primary effects of pollution are on the individual, although ultimately if pollution is rife and widespread, the community as a whole may suffer. And the effects are particularly what we would call mental or emotional, rather than physical. If one has been polluted, according to the Sherpas, one tends to become dull, lethargic, and stupid; alternatively, one may become touchy, agitated, and prone to violence. To be pure, on the other hand, is to be free of both of these tendencies, to be absolutely calm, peaceful, and yet alert and sensitive. In cultural metaphors the image of complete dullness, lethargy, and stupidy is the domestic beast of labor (cows, yaks, and cow-yak crossbreeds), while the images of complete violence, agitation, and aggressiveness are the demons. Hence, I call the two types of polluted states (or the two forces which, if they become dominant in the person, result in the symptoms of the polluted states) the "physical" and the "demonic," respectively. The force that transcends these two states, and that is dominant in a state of purity, I call the "spiritual."[14]

Everyone should strive to be pure, that is, to diminish the physical and demonic tendencies of the self, and to enlarge and render dominant the spiritual tendencies. A state of purity conduces both to better pragmatic functioning in the world, and to the pursuit of salvation. But in lay life, it is difficult to avoid experiences that exaggerate either the physical or the demonic tendencies. Hence, the aim is not so much to eliminate or demolish those aspects of the self, but to keep them in an integrated balance and to keep the spiritual forces from being overwhelmed by the physical and the demonic. The purity/pollution structure thus refers primarily to the proper *hierarchy* of psychic integration, the ascendance of "spiritual" functions or forces (control, moral purpose, spiritual striving, etc.) over both the "physical" forces (tendencies toward dullness, inertia, passivity, stupidity, etc.) and the "demonic" forces (tendencies toward violence, anger, greed, etc.). The system of the self may be represented as a triangle, as in Figure 5.[15]

In the context of death, pollution is said to come from two sources: the corpse

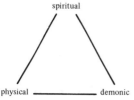

Figure 5. The system of the self

and the demons. This is consistent with the analysis of pollution as having two poles, the "physical" and the "demonic." We can see that the corpse would be considered highly polluting because it is at the ultimate extreme of the physical dimension, not merely dull and sluggish, but utterly inert. Further, the corpse attracts the cannibalistic demons, because flesh and blood are their favorite fare, and the demons themselves are filthy and polluting. It must be noted, however, that the demons are not said to be released from the self of the deceased, but rather attracted *to* him. How shall this point be interpreted?

I said above that the demons are culturally considered projections of aspects of the self, at least in the sophisticated religious view, and it was noted that even lay people are aware of this view in some vague way. There is certainly the notion that one aspect of the self consists of violent, aggressive, greedy, predatory — "demonic" — tendencies. And I have even heard Sherpas use the expression, "So-and-so has a little bit of dü in her." Thus demons are, or reflect or project, an aspect of the internal self. Yet as we shall see in the discussion of the funeral, although the body and the spirit of the deceased are directly dealt with as parts of him, the demons are viewed as coming upon the scene from without, descending upon the corpse and the funeral. Where, then, are the demons — in or out?

I would suggest that this ambiguity accurately reflects the situation that demons (and pollution) are in fact both psychological and social symbols. Before moving to the social question, however, it will be important to explore in greater detail purity/pollution as an ethnopsychology, a cultural theory of the self.

With the departure of the soul or spirit at death, the body becomes polluting because (it can be interpreted) the deceased has moved to the extreme end of the "physical" dimension, organic but utterly inert, undirected by purposive intentions, and defenseless against attacks by the demons. I would suggest that this defenselessness is the primary fear expressed by the notion of pollution of death, and indeed the notion of pollution generally. Although in theory, when one is polluted, the danger is that either one's physical or demonic tendencies will become exaggerated, and although in fact various myths, texts, and rituals indicate that both these tendencies are considered parts of the self, nonetheless for any given ego it seems that the pollution danger in *oneself* is the tendency toward the physical, toward weakness, inertia, and defenselessness; the demonic tendency is what one worries about in *others*. If one is polluted, one's fear is that one will be weakened; if others are polluted one's fear is that they will become "demonic" against one. The view of pollution as comprised of both tendencies is thus in fact an external, analytic (although still cultural) view. It is the total system seen from a position outside of both ego and alter, and comprising the views of both.

These considerations clarify at least two points. In the first place they explain why, although the exaggeration of both the physical and the demonic tendencies in the self are equally considered possible effects of a polluting experience, nonetheless the physical tendency receives far more elaboration from informants when they discuss the dangers of pollution. The prime examples given of persons who have suffered polution are cretins and people with physical deformities, and the Sherpas seem to find both types of people disturbing. They treat them rather callously, and we can see that both types would easily model the problem of defenselessness. Violent persons (who are in any case rarer) are not particularly pointed to as examples of the effects of pollution, although *acts* of violence pollute both the participants and the onlookers. Again, then, although ego should theoretically worry about becoming either weak *or* violent through pollution, in fact he is worried primarily about himself becoming weak and others becoming violent.

All of this also helps to explain why the demons, at death (and on all other occasions), are seen as coming from without. The relevant disturbing aspect of the deceased is the departure of his spiritual dimension and his move toward the physical dimension, leaving him defenseless against the demons – this process is what ego himself fears most. The funeral treats the deceased as composed of only two aspects, his body and his spirit, and indeed any given ego perceives only these two aspects to be the relevant parts of his person. Aggression, violence, and other demonic tendencies are primarily threatening in others, and then only if the self is in fact in a weak or defenseless (highly "physical") state.[16]

The pollution of death, then, may be interpreted on the psychological level as the fear of personal disintegration, and the deceased models this problem. But because the deceased can no longer be integrated, then the most desirable alternative is total disintegration, indeed destruction of the entity that held together the various elements in the first place, such that there is no longer any entity that can be seen as "that which has disintegrated." It is significant in this respect that the deceased after the funeral should no longer be referred to by name but rather by the term, "empty." The explanation for this is that hearing his name would "startle" him, but it also reaffirms his complete nullification.

This disintegration of the deceased, while begun as a natural process (death among the Sherpas is largely, and in orthodox Buddhist theory entirely, seen as "natural"), is taken over and guided by the community of the living, with all the resources at its disposal (money, group effort, religious ritual). Thus, the community takes it upon itself to promote and further the process of disintegration of a self. But from this point it is intuitively clear that, insofar as the funeral ritual works its effect not (only) upon the deceased but on the living, then the ritual would simultaneously be exaggerating in the living the fear initially created by the death: It would carry forward, symbolically and psychologically, their own sense of disintegration. In this context, then, it is perfectly clear why the demons are felt to attack or crowd in upon the living *in their performance of the funeral,* and specifically at two points: once at the conclusion of the processing of the corpse, and once at the conclusion of the processing of the soul. If pollution is a problem of disintegration of the self, and if these are the moments (cremation of the body, dispatching of the soul) of fullest disintegration, then these are the moments of greatest pollution, and in fact of the influx of the demons. And it is the job of the exorcisms, at these moments, as rites of purification, to put the selves of the living back together again and hence, by definition, to repel the demons' attacks.

Thus far I have treated the problem of the pollution of death (including the influx of the demons) as a psychological problem, a treatment that the Sherpas would find resonant with their own explicit notions. But I have suggested that the referents of pollution are as much social as they are psychological. To see this, the moments of the arrival of the demons (and the performance of exorcisms) must be examined not as moments in the sequence of treatment of the self, but as moments in the social process of the funeral. I will show that these are moments not only of greatest psychic disintegration, but also moments at which the social order has suffered the heaviest symbolic attack, and indeed may be said to have "disintegrated" much as the self has. In particular we shall see that, on the one hand, the deceased is symbolically treated to a great deal of (illegitimate) status elevation, while on the other hand status distinctions among the living are systematically denied and negated.

In the first part of the funeral — the first two or three days after death — attention is focused largely upon the corpse. It is bathed, purified (nonexorcismically), trussed in a white sack, and housed in a little structure at the front of the altar. The little structure, the *pungbo*, is said to be like a god's house. There the deceased sits upon a lotus mandala, as gods sit on lotus thrones and as gods' palaces and heavens are designed on mandala plans. He is continuously offered food, and this is explicitly said to be in part "like making offerings to the gods." Members of the family prostrate themselves before the altar, ambiguously directing their prostrations to both the gods of the ritual and to the deceased. In light of the discussion of prostrations in Nyungne, the divinizing significance of these gestures is evident.

After several days of all this, the deceased is taken to be cremated. He is carried in a litter chair like a high personage, wearing a ritual crown like the lamas wear in certain ceremonies when they "become" gods, and accompanied by the temple orchestra. His lotus mandala is beneath him in the chair, and then is laid at the base of his pyre. The pyre, like the altar structure, is said to be "like a god's house." At the pyre, the family performs continuous prostrations before the corpse while the final preparations are made for his cremation.

Finally the pyre is lit, and at this point the status of the corpse goes into sharp decline. As one lama succinctly put it, "Before the burning he's a god, then when they burn him he becomes an offering." Further, the demons are invited, just before the fire is lit, to come and feast upon the corpse, and for them he is simply a hunk of meat.

The sequence of the treatment of the corpse is thus one of massive status elevation. The early purification reduces its grossest physical emanations; it is fed and pampered and bowed before, and it is decked in symbols of royalty and divinity. At the point of cremation the deceased is virtually a god, and it is highly significant that it is at this point that the demons descend (in fact are invited to descend) upon him.

Attention now turns to the soul.[17] While this portion of the funeral is, in religious terms, more important than the treatment of the body, it is perforce less visually dramatic and colorful, for the soul cannot be seen, handled, decorated, and sent up in a huge conflagration. The main proceedings during this phase consist of recitations of texts for guiding the soul to a good rebirth. The basic text is the *totul*, "The setting-face-to-face to the reality in the intermediate state: The great deliverance by hearing while on the after-death plane, from 'the profound doctrine of the emancipation of the consciousness by meditation upon the peaceful and wrathful deities.' " (Evans-Wentz: 83). The Sherpas are familiar in a general way with the contents of this text. They know that it contains (among other things) descriptions of frightening encounters with gods in their ferocious forms, encounters that the deceased must successfully pass through if he is to achieve a good rebirth. They generally summarize its contents as "showing the road" to the deceased.

The text moves from early attempts to project the soul directly to salvation. Then, assuming that for ordinary mortals these attempts will have failed, it guides the soul through progressively more frightening encounters. Finally, it realistically assumes that the deceased is about to enter, as the best that can have been accomplished, another human incarnation. Even at this stage, the deceased has one final opportunity to achieve a pure Buddha state, if he realizes disgust and horror at the prospect of being reborn and meditates upon the divine. Failing this, however, the guide gives its final pragmatic instructions:

If birth is to be obtained over a heap of impurities [i.e., the sperm and the ovum in the impregnated womb], a sensation that is sweet-smelling will attract one towards that impure mass, and birth will be obtained thereby.

Whatsoever they [the womb or visions] may appear to be, do not regard them as they are [or seem]: and by not being attracted or repelled, a good womb should be chosen. In this, too, since it is important to direct the wish, direct it thus:

"Ah! I ought to take birth as a Universal Emperor; or as a Brāhmin, like a great sal-tree; or as the son of an adept in *siddhic* powers; or in a spotless hierarchical line; or in the caste of a man who is filled with [religious] faith; and, being born so, be endowed with great merit so as to be able to serve all sentient beings." (Evans-Wentz: 190–1; brackets in original)

Thus the reading of the totul may not have achieved instant salvation for the deceased (as it realistically acknowledges), but even at the end it puts him back within the human realm (which is probably more than he deserves), and further as nothing less than "a Universal Emperor; or as a Brahmin, . . . or as the son of an adept in *siddhic* powers; or in a spotless hierarchical line . . ." and so forth. There can be little question that this key funeral text carries forward the symbolism of the treatment of the corpse, and that together the treatment of the body and the soul involve attempts to elevate the deceased's status beyond what he morally deserves.

Further, at the close of the first phase of the funeral in which the corpse was elevated to royal/divine status, and at the close of the second phase in which the soul winds up as a would-be Universal Emperor, there are feasts in which the family of the deceased performs meritorious acts in the deceased's name, to help him gain a better rebirth than he deserves. Just before the cremation, they give a feast at which they distribute coins of equal value to all present, young and old, high and low; they may distribute coins again in the same manner at the cremation. And at the end of the reading of the totul, when the soul is finally dispatched, the family holds the enormous gyowa feast, for which there are rules stipulating that there be no discrimination in invitations, seating, or feeding of guests. The host should see to it that as many people as possible come to this feast, that all are fed, and all fed exactly the same amount of food. Local Nepalese untouchables show up at gyowa and are fed (outside the house); trekkers or tourists who happen to be passing through the village are pressed into coming (to their delight); even the host's enemies are sent for. The guiding principles of the gyowa are universalism and egalitarianism. The more people fed, and fed in this egalitarian nondiscriminatory manner, the more merit for the deceased.

Thus the dealings with both the corpse and the soul involve extended symbolic status elevation, and at the culmination of each of the two sequences of status elevation there are feasts which, in a variety of ways, deny social status and hierarchy. At the feast before the cremation, while there seem to be no explicit rules concerning nondiscrimination, the distribution of money to all comers foreshadows the rules of the gyowa. And at the gyowa, there are the explicit rules against discrimination by status among the guests.

Now it is following each of these feasts that the exorcisms are performed in funerals, and this brings us back to the point of this lengthy excursion. The exorcisms qua purifications, in other words, follow upon sequences in which not only psychic but also social hierarchy has been undermined. The deceased has been projected to overly high status, while status differences among the living have been, in the two feasts, pointedly ignored and crosscut. And it is precisely this sequence, enacted twice, that is followed by attention to demons and concern for purification, in the first case dealt with through the cremation ritual, in the second case dealt with by the large-scale exorcisms at the conclusion of the funeral.[18]

In sum: Exorcisms are considered rites of purification. Purity is culturally conceived primarily in terms of the proper hierarchical relations among the parts of the self. In the case of a death, the hierarchical relations among the parts of the self of the deceased have as a natural process begun to disintegrate, and the funeral process involves further disaggregation of the deceased. All of this is a threat — a "pollution" — to the living, in preenacting their own disintegrations and ultimate deaths. Exorcisms, as purifications, will in turn be seen in part as rituals of reintegration of the selves of the living, reestablishing the proper hierarchical order among the elements of the self. Examination of the funeral process, however, reveals that the pollution of death is a matter not only of disintegration of the hierarchy of the elements of the self, but also of subversion, in various ways, of the social hierarchical order. In the course of a funeral, as part of the process of "helping" the deceased to achieve a good rebirth, aspects of the social hierarchy are attacked. Careful analytic attention to the timing of the exorcismic elements of the funeral reveal that they come directly after sequences and events in which this occurs. Pollution, in the form of the attack of the demons, is as much a social as a psychological threat.

Reincarnation theory and the social order

Both demons and pollution have here been interpreted as in large part concerned with the social hierarchy. But why should problems of social hierarchy cluster about the problem of death? In fact, for the Sherpas (and other thoroughgoing Buddhist believers) death and the distribution of privilege in the social order are *directly* linked to one another through reincarnation theory, the theory of the universal law of karma.[19]

According to orthodox reincarnation theory, one could be reborn into any of the six states on the Wheel of Life, from the (finite) heavenly paradises to the demonic hells. (For the Sherpas, "salvation" is simply an infinite heavenly paradise beyond the Wheel of Life, as opposed to the finite one within the round.) In fact, however, it is more or less assumed by most people that one will be reborn in the human realm, and simply in a better or worse physical and/or mental and/or social state than one presently has. Thus, people who are very virtuous in this life will be reborn beautiful, intelligent, spiritually well-motivated and, most importantly, rich and of high social station, while people who are very sinful will be reborn crippled, stupid, with low spiritual motivation and, most importantly, poor and of low social station. The system is perfectly self-fulfilling, for one need simply look about and see people both better off and worse off than oneself, just as the system "predicted," and for which it offers a thoroughly logical explanation. Reincarnation theory thus accounts, quite simply, for why some people are better off than others. In time-honored and time-worn anthropological parlance, it is a charter for and a justification of the status quo of the distribution of privilege and wealth.

Further, the theory suggests and justifies certain attitudes toward this situation: not envying the rich, and not pitying the poor. If people are poor, it must have been their own fault (in a previous existence), and they are getting their just deserts. One need not feel concerned for their plight, nor take any action to ameliorate their situation; indeed, there is justification for not associating with them in any way at all. If people are rich, on the other hand, they are reaping rewards for past good actions, and they cannot be begrudged their wealth and privilege. Indeed envy is sinful, although it is general wisdom that people frequently indulge in this sin. One informant said, however, that it only occurs between people of similar status, and that "a low man never envies a high person," presumably because a rich man must really deserve what he has. And perhaps if one keeps one's envy and other sinful impulses under control, one will have a chance of getting such benefits oneself next time around.

Reincarnation theory thus effectively disengages actual present behavior and moral tendencies from actual present social status, denying in effect that there *is* such a thing as injustice. If the immoral are rich, this is not an injustice; their wealth pertains to their past morality, and their present immorality will reap its punishment in the future. And if the good are poor, this is not unjust; it means they were bad in the past, and will be rewarded in the future.

Now, from the orthodox point of view, the chief implication of the death of another, particularly of one who is emotionally or geographically close, is that it raises the question of one's own moral fate. As one lama put it, "Every instance of death near us increases our *dungal*"; dungal simply means suffering, but the lama specified it in this context as meaning the preying fear of receiving retribution in the manner in which one had done ill before. The Sherpas are fond of giving vivid examples of quid pro quo karmic retribution; here are some examples from my notes:

If you plow now, in the next life you will be beaten by oxen [in hell], or else you will be an ox. Similarly, if you kill a goat, in the next life you will either be a goat, or will be beaten by goat demons.

Killing results in miscarriage of the subsequent rebirth, or, if born, early death (no later than age 15–16) in the next life.

For every louse you kill, you will be bothered by 1,000 lice in your next life.

If you smoke, you will be reborn in hell with an inextinguishably burning tree in your stomach.

If you shirk carrying loads, then you'll be reborn as an animal and have to carry.[20]

Ideally, then, the death of another stimulates all to review their sins and reform their behavior, before it is too late. And in theory the process of karmic reward and punishment works wholly automatically, not subject to human or divine interference. Yet virtually the entire funeral process systematically undercuts the orthodox point that one's fate depends purely and simply on one's own moral behavior. If the lamas can read books that send one, if one listens carefully and follows instructions closely, straight to eternal paradise, and if one's family can create vast quantities of merit for one after one dies, then something must be amiss with reincarnation theory itself. I would suggest that, for most people, rather than stimulating self-scrutiny and self-reform to bring themselves in line with reincarnation theory, what the funeral process does is call into question certain aspects of reincarnation theory itself, specifically the ways in which it is perverted by social advantage and disadvantage.

In addition to the notion that karmic law is wholly just and automatic vis-à-vis particular deeds, there is also the implication that it is self-regulating vis-à-vis the population as a whole. That is, no situation in an individual's present life necessarily gives him any special advantage or disadvantage for the next time around.[21] Theoretically, in other words, both rich and poor have equal opportunity to be moral, make merit, better their situation, and achieve salvation. The system presents itself as radically egalitarian and democratic, an equal-opportunity system of salvation. Thus the wealthy are not necessarily in a better religious position than the poor, for there is the notion that wealth corrupts: The more worldly goods one has, the more one tends to be attached to them, to engage in sinful manipulation to obtain more, and so on. And by the same token, there is the notion that poverty makes it easier to be virtuous: One has less to be attached to, and it is easier to concentrate on moving toward enlightenment. That is why it is better to be poor and propertyless, the condition of monkhood.

Yet one need not look very closely at all to see that the system cannot work out in a self-regulating, equal-opportunity sort of way. The poor have in fact little chance of ameliorating their state in the next life, for they are caught up in sheer survival and must perforce spend most of their lives mired in the most negatively valued material concerns. Further, they are barred effectively by their poverty from two great sources of merit: donations to religious institutions (monasteries, events, personages), and entering the monastic life. On the first point it is clear that, however nasty and evil a rich fellow may be, he can still give large donations to monasteries to offset his sinful words and deeds, and thus have a better chance for salvation than a poor man. And on the second point, monasticism too is clearly a rich man's game. Sherpa monasteries are not self-supporting, nor endowed, nor tax-supported (as they were in Tibet); one must have kinsmen who can spare one's labor and contribute to one's support as a monk. (Paul, 1970: 423–9). It is thus not difficult to see that the poor are handicapped in the working out of the reincarnation system, and doomed to further poor rebirths. The rich keep rising and the poor keep sinking.

Now in theory this analysis is incorrect. The Sherpas are forever saying that the most important thing for one's fate is one's state of mind, one's moral intentions, that a poor man who gives a few rupees with a good heart (actually "mind," *sem*) and a generous spirit will gain more merit than the rich man who gives thousands of rupees and yet whose mind is full of evil and impious thoughts. As one monk said,

When we die, what good are riches? Rich men have big gyowa feasts at their funerals, but do they really profit by them? We don't know, we never see what happens after a man dies.

Yet, there is evidence that Sherpas do not, at some level, believe their own skepticism. There is certainly a conscious awareness that the best way to achieve salvation is through monkhood, yet that poverty bars one from monkhood. Many men complain that they wanted to become monks, but their families could not spare their labor. More directly, there is the straightforward view that once one begins sinking down the karmic ladder, it is very difficult to reverse the trend. As one lama put it, "It can get worse and worse, and you finally wind up in a hell eighteen levels down, from which it is very difficult to escape."

The "sinking" tendency of the system, which means that people who are down are on the way toward even lower conditions, is abetted by one further aspect of karmic theory: the point that it is possible to commit sins without knowing it, while virtuous deeds are on the whole not recorded unless there was conscious intent behind them. Indeed, one is committing sins all the time without knowing it. That is why one must do as many meritorious deeds as possible, merely to keep even. In theory this point works equally for (or against) rich and poor, and the factor of indeterminacy, of not knowing how many sins one has committed, is on the side of downward mobility for everyone equally. The tendency of the whole system, for all, is toward "sinking," and only those who escape from secular life into monasticism, in which all one's efforts are consciously and single-mindedly directed toward virtue and salvation, really have a chance to counteract this tendency. Yet this brings us back to the point that the rich have greater opportunity to become monks than the poor, and second best, have greater means for making donations to monasteries and other religious institutions. Once again then, although the indeterminacy factor and the sinking tendency of the system theoretically work equally against all, the rich are in a better position to escape the operation of this tendency.[22]

In sum, reincarnation theory ties the problem of death directly to the problem of social inequity, because present differences of wealth and privilege are products of the past working of the reincarnation system, and one's own fears about death include concern about where one will wind up on the social ladder the next time around. Thus the interpretation of demons who are exorcised after funerals as being involved with the problem of rich and poor, and of pollution as also being involved with the problem of social hierarchy, both accord with cultural logic and have cultural justification. The fact that both demons and pollution are culturally seen primarily in psychological terms does no violence to these interpretations. It will be precisely my concern to show how the cultural view that these are psychological problems is correct but partial, and that the psychological and the social are integrally interrelated. Each is the condition for the operation of the other.

The solutions of the rituals

Imagine that we have just concluded a funeral. Last night was the grand gyowa feast, in which the family of the deceased fed hundreds of people indiscriminately, without regard to status distinctions.[23] And tonight the host commissions the performance of exorcism rites, to banish all the demons that have gathered over the course of the funeral, and to purify his house and indeed the entire village from the pollution that has accumulated. The exorcisms are the focus of much excitement. Everyone looks forward to them as the climax and conclusion of the long, drawn out, and thus far unresolved funeral process. They are truly popular rituals, in the sense of being enjoyed by many, and also in the sense of involving more active participation of the congregation than most other Sherpa rituals.

We have already seen the issues involved in exorcisms, through discussion of the significance of demons, pollution, and death, and through analysis of aspects of the funeral process revealing the structural and narrative moments at which exorcisms are performed.[24] Before turning to analysis of the exorcisms, however, one note must be entered. I pointed out above that the do dzongup, the first exorcism, seems to be a relatively heterodox ritual. It receives little treatment in the literature of orthodox Tibetan Buddhism, and monks will neither execute nor attend performances of this ritual. On the other hand, the second exorcism, the gyepshi, is an orthodox Tibetan Buddhist ritual. The Sherpas will often perform the do dzongup by itself, although ideally both should be done. The significance of these points will be apparent in the analysis of the two rituals, and I will sum up and discuss the relationship between the two in more general terms in the concluding section.

We now turn to these final exorcisms to see what, precisely, they do, and how, precisely, they do it.

Exorcisms as purifications: reconstituting the psychic hierarchy

Pollution is culturally conceived primarily in terms of its effects upon the self. The self appears as a system in which there are "physical" and "demonic" tendencies (or passive/defenseless and violent/predatory tendencies), both of which are kept in check by the dominance and control of "spiritual" forces. Pollution is conceived as a situation in which either of the lower tendencies has for some reason gained ascendance. In the context of death, I interpreted the fear of pollution specifically as the fear that one will, like the deceased, move toward the "physical" pole, leaving one prey to the "demonic" forces of others, as the deceased is prey to the attacks of the demons. How can the exorcisms be seen as countering these threats, or in cultural terms, how do exorcisms "purify"?

Beginning with the first exorcism, the do dzongup, the first act is the construction of the *sende*, a mud and dough sculpture of a tiger surrounded by anthropomorphic figures (see Figure 2). The demons will be conjured into the tiger. Although I have no exegesis from the Sherpas on the choice of a tiger as the vehicle for the demons, and although in fact there are no tigers in Sherpadom, wild (as opposed to domestic) animals have a variety of affiliations with demons in cultural thought. Gods in their fierce manifestations, geared up for fighting demons, generally have tiger skins wrapped around their groins. And in another context I located wild animals as intermediate between domestic animals and demons on the spectrum of pollution symbols, because they integrate both aspects of pollution – the physical imaged by dull, stupid domestic animals, and the demonic, imaged by demons (Ortner, 1973a).

The little anthropomorphic figures surrounding the tiger, leading, riding, and driving it out, are always said to be "men" asserting authority over the tiger, that is, asserting human will. The total complex may thus be seen as the first attempt to reintegrate the structure of the self, placing will in a position of dominance over a physical/demonic synthesis (the wild beast). But it is a very "weak" version: The human figures are disproportionately small in relation to the size of the tiger, suggesting the precariousness of the control established thus far. And indeed the weakness of this construction is evident in the fact that the demons actually come and enter it, precisely the situation that is feared in a weakened ("polluted") state.

Before the action starts, as the tiger is being set up, the people attending draw lumps of dough down over their bodies, "to draw out all the bad smells," squeezing these lumps in the hand so as to leave the imprints of the finger and palm joints, and depositing them on the tiger's tray. The finger-joint imprints are explained as in effect personalizing each lump, but the resultant little squiggly elongated pieces of brown dough look like nothing if not pieces of excrement. The gesture would thus seem to be both an acknowledgment of a relationship between the people and the tiger, and at the same time a rejection of it (excreting it, or excreting on it) as a weak and unacceptable version of the self, prey to the invasion of the demons and fit only to be given over to them and destroyed.

The ritual begins with the chanting of the text for conjuring the demons into the tiger. The music strikes up. Enter the young men got up as peshangba, ritual clowns, pushing and shoving one another, the first wielding a knife or cleaver, the others brandishing sticks. They are comic figures, and everyone is delighted with their entrance. They bat at one another with their sticks, make lewd gestures, wiggle their behinds, and otherwise act silly. While the Sherpas say they are "guards" or "soldiers," this does not provide much elucidation. We must examine them a bit more closely.

The peshangba quite clearly derive from ritual figures in Tibet who were themselves scapegoats. That is, the scapegoat role now played by the dough effigy, the lut, in the second exorcism was played in one major Tibetan state ritual by real human beings, dressed exactly as the Sherpa peshangba now dress.[25] The Tibetan human scapegoats were

dressed in rough fur-coats and wearing conical hats, one-half of their faces being painted black . . . (Nebesky-Wojkowitz: 508)

At one Sherpa exorcism,

Both peshangba have straw basket hats. Pemba Gyelwu has a woolly rug-robe. Their faces are painted white.

At another,

They are outlandishly got up with straw wigs, and overturned baskets for hats. Their behinds are stuffed with pillows. Their faces are painted white with black spots and they have huge black fur mustaches stuck on.

And at the Khumjung village Dumji exorcism, the man who escorted the demon offering out of town was

dressed in a sheepskin coat, worn with the fur outside, and a conical cap made ostensibly from the skin of a *yeti.* (von Fürer-Haimendorf, 1964: 202)

At least one Sherpa lama was aware of the connection between the peshangba, concerned mainly with the destruction of the tiger in the first exorcism, and the dough effigy (lut) that functions as the scapegoat in the gyepshi, the second exorcism. In an exorcism, he said,

You really need to give everything to a real man and then send him very far away, out of Nepal, never to return. But since you can't do this, you do it with the dough figure, the lut. If there is a rich sponsor he gives real clothes [i.e., dresses the lut in real clothes], and the peshangba get to take them home and keep them.

The lama is aware, in other words, that the lut ideally should be a human being, as were the Tibetan scapegoats upon whom the Sherpa peshangba are modeled. And he connects the disposal of the lut with giving things to the peshangba, though in fact the peshangba do not play a role in the disposal of the lut. The relationship between the Tibetan human scapegoats, the Sherpa peshangba, and the Sherpa dough scapegoat effigies, lut, may be summarized as shown in Figure 6.

Continuing the analysis of the first exorcism, the do dzongup, the peshangba may be seen as another, more powerful version of the schematized human being (a set of spiritual, physical, and demonic forces) than the tiger construction. Their animal-fur costume stresses their physical, animal dimension (as does their lewdness and sexuality), while their weapons (and their subsequent treatment of the demons) express their violent demonic dimension. They are also human, however — that is,

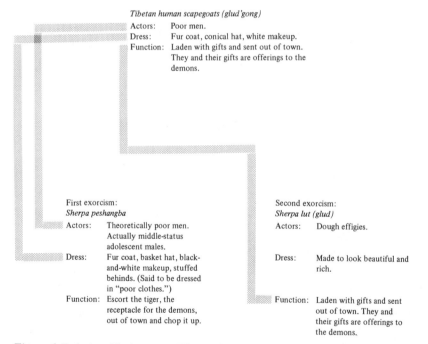

Tibetan human scapegoats (glud'gong)
Actors: Poor men.
Dress: Fur coat, conical hat, white makeup.
Function: Laden with gifts and sent out of town.
            They and their gifts are offerings to the
            demons.

First exorcism:
Sherpa peshangba
Actors: Theoretically poor men.
            Actually middle-status
            adolescent males.
Dress: Fur coat, basket hat, black-
            and-white makeup, stuffed
            behinds. (Said to be dressed
            in "poor clothes.")
Function: Escort the tiger, the
            receptacle for the demons,
            out of town and chop it up.

Second exorcism:
Sherpa lut (glud)
Actors: Dough effigies.

Dress: Made to look beautiful and
            rich.

Function: Laden with gifts and sent
            out of town. They and
            their gifts are offerings to
            the demons.

Figure 6. Relationship between Tibetan human scapegoats, Sherpa peshangba, and Sherpa lut

they are played by real live human beings — and thus have at least the rudiments of will or control. But only the rudiments. If we recall their dance, in which they seem to attempt to escape, but are controlled by the music that decelerates before climax and thus slows their gathering momentum, we realize that most of the control, the "spiritual" element, lies outside them, in the text and the music of the ritual.

The peshangba then are a slightly — but only slightly — stronger version of the integrated person than the thing they destroy. They are more integrated than the sende (tiger) construction, which represents the person as a small weak-willed being riding a wild beast, but they are still very clearly low-level, patched-together sorts of beings, as stressed by their black-and-white makeup. Nonetheless, they do triumph over the people/tiger construction, and the spectators are clearly on their side. Indeed, my impression is that the Sherpas identify more closely with the peshangba than with any other figures in their ritual repertoire: The peshangba provide some comic relief on the whole death situation, a relief from both the moral condemnation of the religious perspective, and the stress of the direct reaction to death. In any case, the ritual concludes with the peshangba rushing the tiger out of the house and chopping it to bits, with everyone cheering them on.

Now, although the Sherpas often perform the first, do dzongup, exorcism alone after a funeral, we can immediately see that its solution to the purity problem might be considered unsatisfactory, because the peshangba have triumphed by brute force and not by an act of the higher spiritual faculties. Indeed, the impression is that they have broken away from the spiritual control of the music and text of the ritual, especially because, on the final sortie, one of the peshangba takes the cymbals away from the lama, and in a sense forces the music to its climax himself, crashing away on the cymbals. But if this is the case, if in fact the demonic tendency has triumphed, then the ritual could hardly be said to have solved the pollution problem, even though the people may feel they have adequately handled the demons by running them out and chopping them up. But the lama quoted above expressed the "higher" view: "They're ignorant." They may feel that they are strong, and capable of defeating demons, but it is the brute strength of the demonic forces of the self, and not the strength of spiritual calm and control.

From the sophisticated religious point of view, then, which the Sherpas accept (although not necessarily wholeheartedly, because sometimes they end with the do dzongup), a further ritual, the gyepshi, is required. The gyepshi may be seen to replay the purity/pollution integration structure yet one more time. Here the two unsatisfactory integration attempts of the first exorcism — the people/tiger construction and the peshangba — are cancelled. The entire system is disaggregated again to its extremes, and then reintegrated sequentially, establishing the proper hierarchy of relations among the elements. Each element receives separate representation in pure form: The demons are represented with their own effigies, the body has *its* own effigy (the lut — see Figure 3), and spirit is represented in the idol of the Buddha, sitting on the wrist of the hand that contains the entire altar of the ritual (see Figure 4).

Now the religious view of the proper relationship between spirit, body, and demons may be seen as just the inverse of the lay view. The lay view, as discussed above, involves fear of physical weakening, in turn creating the condition for departure of spirit, and hence leaving the self prey to the attacks of demons from without. From the religious view, however, spirit *must* be able to dissociate itself (metaphorically) from body; insofar as it too closely identifies itself with the body and its fate, it fears destruction because the body is destructible.

And as for the demons, spirit must come to realize that they are within one. Detachment from concern over bodily destruction is the condition for realizing this, and for thus being able to "defeat" the demons. Where the lay attempt is to strengthen the spirit/body connection and hence keep out the demons ("run them out of town"), the religious attempt is to weaken the spirit/body connection (as it did in the funeral) hence in fact strengthening spirit, and creating the condition for "defeating" the demons by realizing their integration with the self. It is in light of these points that the gyepshi exorcism (following upon the do dzongup) may now be interpreted.

It will be recalled that the gyepshi involves the construction of an effigy of the sponsor of the ritual, the lut effigy, as well as effigies of the demon grouping to which the rite is directed. The lut is decorated with and surrounded by finery, and during the course of the ritual the onlookers shower it with flower petals and grain. Both flower petals and grain are appropriate offerings to gods. Sprinkling grain skyward is part of the opening act of every offering ritual, while flower petals, like all sweet-smelling things, have special godly associations — in some accounts of the heavens gods are said to eat nothing but sweet smells. But after all this high treatment, the lut is set out to be eaten by the demons. Further, the lut had been surrounded on the altar by concentric rings of four types of offerings, and the four demon effigies are taken out with and fed these offerings as part of the conclusion of the ritual. And when all of the altar items have been cleared out, the Buddha idol that had been sitting beyond the outer ring of offerings is placed in the center, where the lut had been.

The purification sequence of the gyepshi, reduced to bare essentials, is thus quite simple. The construction of the lut separates the body from the consciousness or spiritual dimension of the sponsor. Showering the lut with flowers expresses a relationship between the people and the lut (as did loading the tiger with excrement), but it is a relationship of transcendence of spirit over body. The body is then fed to the demons, and at the end, the idol [ku = (respect) body] of the Buddha is placed on the tripod where the lut had stood. The proper psychic hierarchy is thus rather starkly established: Spirit is able to detach itself from and transcend body, and thereby reigns supreme at the end. The sponsor first identifies with and clings to his body, giving it fine offerings. But then he voluntarily relinquishes this attachment, generously — perhaps the best term for the Sherpa context is "hospitably" — offering it to the demons. Having done this he attains instead the eternal body of the Buddha, made not of soft and perishable material, but of indestructible metal.

Through this process, the sponsor is meant to experience a changed relationship to his body, specifically an experience of it as separate from, and not the true locus of, the self. If spirit can be voluntarily detached from and rise above physicality, literally flying above it in the flower petals and metaphorically rising above it in the ability to take a generous attitude toward the demons, then in fact one is able to keep one's body, and indeed to get a better one. While the lay view of strong psychic integration stresses a strong body as a condition for keeping a strong hold on spirit, the religious view stresses that a strong spirit is the condition for having a "strong" body, not in the brute sense, but in the sense of being impervious to demons. Both exorcisms attempt to reestablish a relationship between spirit and body, and thus to integrate the self, as the condition for defeating demons. But in the gyepshi the dominance of spirit over body is a matter of spirit truly transcending body and being able, as it were, to take it or leave it. And once this attitude is established, as we saw, one is allowed to have the body back on one's own (spiritual) terms, and not on its unreliable (because ultimately mortal) terms.

These points are further developed through another aspect of the ritual, although the data here are rather unclear. The four circles of offerings that surround the lut were explained by one lama as representing parts of the person: He said that the butter lamps represented mind, and the miniature lut represented body, but he claimed to have forgotten what the other two represented.[26] It is not clear whether Sherpas are aware that the four sets of offerings represent parts of the person, although they do know that the little lut are indeed substitute bodies just as the large lut is. And of course they know that the whole ceremony is an attempt to satisfy the demons by feeding them substitutes for human flesh and blood. In any case, when the four demons are carried out at the end of the ceremony, each is paired with a basketful of one of these sets of offerings, while the main lut is not in fact observably fed to any particular demon(s). The demons in other words get the parts, while the whole lut body is left intact and in fact treated with some respect. Thus not only do the participants get a Buddha-body to replace the perishable one they sacrifice; they do not even lose (the representation of) their fleshly bodies as well, or at least not very dramatically. The process is gentle and invisible.

The treatment of the demons over the course of the rituals is the inverse of the treatment of the body. The problem of the body, according to the religious analysis, is that it is too integrated with, indeed confused with, the self; the fear is that bodily disintegration necessarily entails self-disintegration. The ritual thus entails creating a sense of distance and detachment from the fate of one's body. The problem of the demons, on the other hand, is that they are (mistakenly, according to the religious analysis) experienced as preying upon one from without; the point both symbolizes and explains the feeling of their being out of control. Thus in the ritual the sequence of treatment of the demons involves, if not actually integrating them into the self, at least establishing a relationship with them. The demons are brought in and fed, given hospitality. Hospitality is not only a relationship but, as we have seen, a hierarchical relationship, a relationship of power and control. And through this again one experiences and manifests the ascendance of one's spiritual forces. One overcomes the loathing and destructive attitude vividly expressed in chopping them up. One at least theoretically comes to experience pity for them, symbolized by the food and flowers offered to them. And one is able to muster the self-control necessary to invite them into one's home, give them hospitality, and treat them in a civilized social manner.

The final statement, in the gyepshi, on the proper integration of the self thus not only portrays the proper hierarchical order of the elements of the self but, more fully than the tiger exorcism, dramatizes a recipe or program, based on a subtle religious theory, for reestablishing that hierarchy. At the outset the body is seen as inextricably attached to the self, dragging it down in inertia and ultimate decay, and the demons are seen as preying upon this body from without. The ritual carries one through a structure in which one experiences relative detachment from the body, and relative integration with the demons. The structure is that of the hospitality process, except that it is one's own body that becomes the food of the guests. Detachment from body and integration of demons are thus shown to be complementary aspects of a single transformation, which is exactly as it should be, because they produce a unitary outcome: purification.

Rich and poor: resynthesizing the social hierarchy

The issue of social hierarchy has, we have seen, run through the entire funeral process. Symbolically it is represented in the various aspects of status elevation of the deceased, followed by the feasts in which status relationships among the living are denied. The demons, in turn, require treatment following these feasts. On this point, as well as on the basis of symbolism within the exorcisms proper, demons and exorcisms are as concerned with social hierarchy as they are with psychic hierarchy.

Within the exorcisms, rich-and-poor symbolism appears in several ways. In the first place, there is always the question of the social status of the peshangba and the handlers of other ritual items. It seems that, in theory, all of these should be poor, low-status people, but there is, among the Sherpas, a great deal of inconsistency on this point. On the whole, the people who carried away the demons with their offerings in gyepshi rituals were in fact poor, lowly people, or at least outsiders to the community, perhaps affinal relatives of the deceased. The same was generally true of the tiger-carriers in do dzongup rites, and to some extent of the people who carried the corpse to the cremation (although the latter were always members of the community). The peshangba, on the other hand, who escort and chop up the tiger, show a different status pattern. Their Tibetan forerunners, the *glud'gong,* were of the servant class (Nebesky-Wojkowitz: 508), and in the Khumjung village Dumji the peshangba figure (called the *gemaka*) was a poor Tibetan immigrant (von Fürer-Haimendorf, 1964: 202). But in Dzemu the peshangba were almost invariably played by middle-status, unmarried young males of the village, perhaps in keeping with the exegesis that the peshangba are "guards" or "soldiers," although I will argue that this fact may have greater significance.

More directly to the point is the costuming and decoration of the peshangba, on the one hand, and the lut, the effigy of the sponsor, on the other. The two figures manifest polarized symbolism of poverty and wealth. The peshangba are explicitly said to be dressed in poor or "bad" clothes, and seem to be caricatures of the poorest possible appearance, with their basket hats and rough animal robes. And while the Sherpa peshangba are explained as "guards," etc., the Tibetan scapegoats from whom they derive played the role that the lut plays in the Sherpa rituals: They were given rich gifts and sent out of town to be fed to the demons. Indeed, for a period prior to their final explusion, the Tibetan scapegoats were permitted to roam through the streets of Lhasa, "helping themselves freely to everything that attracts their attention, as it is an old established custom that every smaller object on which the glud'gong puts his hand becomes his property. He usually pays a compensation for the things he takes — but in worthless paper currency" (Nebesky-Wojkowitz: 508). On the day of expulsion of the glud'gong, "beggars and corpse-cutters appear from a side-street, carrying gifts presented to the glud'gong by the government as well as by rich merchants" (ibid.: 509).

While the function of the peshangba has changed, they still dress in the poverty costume of their ritual ancestors. On the other hand, the lut performing the scape-goat functions in the second exorcism are figures of wealth. They are clothed in finery; their features should be made of precious gems; they stand on a platform with gifts of money, food, and gems; and they are showered with godly offerings. They are specifically idealizations of the sponsor, made to be better, more beautiful, and even wealthier than himself.

It is clear that the unitary scapegoat figure in the Tibetan case has been polarized into two figures: the peshangba, middle-status people but poorly dressed, and actually performing a powerful role (killing the demons in the tiger) as agents of the community; and the dough lut, the effigy of the sponsor(s), richly dressed, laden with wealth directly from the sponsor, and further showered with high offerings by the assembled community, but then fed to the demons.[27] The treatment of the lut parallels the Tibetan ritual quite closely, even to the point of recruiting, if possible, lowly people to carry the gifts to the demons, but with one crucial difference — the lut is dressed in finery, while the Tibetan scapegoats were dressed in poor clothing. (See Figure 6 for the relationship between the glud'gong, peshangba, and lut.)

I turn now to the sequence of action, to follow the development and resolution of rich-and-poor symbolism in the rites. I remarked above that the people seemed to identify strongly with the peshangba in the first exorcism, and I shall begin by asking what the basis of this identification might be.

In the first place, the peshangba are simply human. They are played by real human beings, while all the other ritual items are inert objects. Further, they wear black-and-white makeup, and in other contexts a Sherpa metaphor for ordinary human mortals is the "white–black ones," stressing the various dualities of human nature.

But the most significant aspect of the peshangba in this context, I would argue, is the fact that they are middle-status people dressed in poor clothes. At this point we must recall the analysis of the tendency of the karmic system to be weighted in favor of downward mobility. Virtuous acts, to be recorded as meritorious, must be performed with conscious intent, while sinful acts are recorded as sins whether one was conscious of performing them or not. More immediately pertinent is the point that it is difficult for the poor to lead virtuous lives, and to perform great acts of merit making. The result is a general downward tendency in the system, at least partly recognized in the relativism with which the Sherpas apply the "big" and "small" social categories. On the one hand they distinguish "big people" (the very rich and high), "small people" (the very poor and low), and everyone else, "not-rich-not poor." But on the other hand everyone is "small" compared to the "big people," because there are really only two possible directions to go: In the working out of the system over time, middle status will almost always tend toward smallness. The peshangba seem powerfully to summarize this point; simultaneously of middle and low status, the peshangba are simply the people.

What then does the sende — the construction composed of a tiger ridden, led, and driven by anthropomorphic figures, and ultimately destroyed by the peshangba — represent? I submit that it represents the rich, the big people. Two sorts of lines may be developed in support of this contention. First, the ritual as a whole is fairly clearly a rite of reversal. The peshangba's costuming contains what might be called "flipping" symbolism — the black-and-white makeup, the suggestions, sometimes quite explicit, of androgyny. And if this is a rite of reversal, and the peshangba are poorly dressed, then there is a prima facie logic to the suggestion that what they chop up symbolizes the rich.

Second, and more specific, is the symbolism of the sende construction itself. For, as an assemblage including an anthropomorphic figure riding a wild animal, it closely resembles many representations of gods. Virtually every god has some manifestation in which he is depicted riding upon an animal vehicle, and generally a wild animal at that. The image of gods riding wild animal vehicles is known to all Sherpas from painted scrolls and temple frescoes, and the tiger construction may quite plausibly be interpreted as a sculptured version of this same image. Now, we have already noted the relative ease with which the gods can be seen as "reflections" of the rich, just as the demons can be seen as "reflections" of the poor, at least in one interpretation of the supernatural hierarchy. Thus the syllogism is simple: sende = gods; gods = rich; sende = rich.

If these points are accepted, then the interpretation of the tiger exorcism is as simple and crude as the execution of the rite itself: The small people chop up the big people, and get quite a kick out of it too. In a sense the tiger exorcism may be said to carry to its logical conclusion the antiestablishment theme of the gyowa feast. In the gyowa, status distinctions were leveled; in the tiger exorcism they are actually inverted with a vengeance.

But can this interpretation, which rests on seeing the sende as a representation of gods, be justified in light of the overt cultural claim that the peshangba are ritually destroying demons? The best justification can be derived from pointing to the disapproval of the high religious community on this point. Recall the lama — in fact the head of a monastery — saying that the people are *not supposed to* chop up the tiger (he charitably attributed their doing so not to their malice but to their ignorance). And recall the fact that monks will not, and indeed are not allowed to, participate in or even attend these rituals. And recall the close social and symbolic connections between the big people and the high religious community. Clearly people are performing, in the do dzongup, a forbidden act. And clearly they are not going to tell anyone (and probably do not even consciously conceptualize) that they are symbolically chopping up their gods and their monks and the highest members of their community. But the analysis indicates that, in all probability, this is exactly what they are doing. And if this is the case, then it is no surprise at all, and indeed it is a confirmation of the analysis, that yet another exorcism is called for to get things back in proper order at last. And so we find the solemn orthodox gyepshi superseding the lively, comic, violent — and very popular — do dzongup.[28]

Turning to the gyepshi, then, this ritual can be seen quite simply to restore the proper hierarchical order of social relations, with a bit of a moral lesson thrown in for those who would challenge it. In the gyepshi, the representative of the people is now the lut, the dough effigy of the sponsor of the rite that functions as an offering to the demons in place of the sponsor's flesh and blood. While the lut is specifically an effigy of the sponsor, it is more generally a scapegoat for the community as a whole — everyone knows that the lut represents "us," "people." It is an anthropomorphic figure, or sometimes two figures, male and female, dressed in finery and laden with luxurious offerings, all to attract and please the demons. Its richness and beauty, however, further heighten the willingness of the audience to identify with this figure, and they express/experience this identification in showering it with flower petals and grain over a long period of textual reading and music.

Finally, at the end of the reading, a series of ritual actions happen in quick succession. The rich lut, with which the people have identified, is taken out with all its finery and offered to the demons. The demon effigies, to emphasize the point, are carried out behind it, each with a basket of offerings, including a basket of small lut. And the representative of the gods behind the ritual, the valuable bronze Buddha idol that had been sitting unattended at the edge of the altar, is moved to the center tripod where the lut had been standing. The gods, in other words, triumph in the end.

Now if the lut was "the people," that is, the ordinary folk, and the Buddha idol, as a god, represents the rich, then it is clear that in this sequence the social hierarchy, inverted in the first exorcism, has now been restored to its proper order in the second. And as a participant, one not only experiences a simple re-reversal. For if one has really identified with the lut, as the rite encourages, then one experiences retribution for the previous reversal — one is fed to the demons. In the first exorcism, identifying with the peshangba, one had overturned the social hierarchy and chopped up the rich. And in the second exorcism, one had illegitimately pretended to high status oneself, by identifying with the rich lut. Now at the end one experiences what happens to ordinary people who have chopped up the rich in the previous ritual and promoted themselves to high status in this one — one is fed to the demons.

Thus the entire funeral sequence, *including* the first exorcism, is corrected by the second. In the funeral sequence there was illegitimate status elevation of the deceased, and status denial among the living. This sequence culminated in the first exorcism with full status inversion of the living: Representatives of the ordinary people destroyed a representation of the rich. But in the second exorcism, the orthodox one, illegitimate status elevation of the people, in the form of the richly decorated lut, is followed by the lut's destruction and by restoration of the social hierarchy. The correct downward slope of the system is reestablished for the people (who are fed to the demons), while the rich (= the gods, in the form of the expensive Buddha idol) are restored to supremacy at the end.

It is possible, however, to move one step beyond this relatively straightforward and indeed rather predictable interpretation. For we must ask why the Sherpas continue to perform the orthodox gyepshi, and with a sense of involvement almost as strong as that exhibited in the first exorcism. Why do they cooperate in the symbolic restoration of social hierarchy that they at first so gleefully destroyed? Clearly they have something invested in the gyepshi that has not been captured by the interpretation thus far.

This elusive factor may be grasped by recalling that the Sherpas are operating with the assumption of reincarnation after death. I would argue that the first exorcism, the do dzongup, speaks to the realm of the present, while the second, the gyepshi, looks to the realm of the future. That is, the Sherpas clearly wish to vent spleen upon the here-and-now, on-the-ground social hierarchy. But at the same time, on the chance, just the chance, that the karmic process might ultimately work out to the advantage of "small people," they are willing or persuaded to preserve the *principle* of social hierarchy for the future. This it seems is the meaning of being willing to shift one's enthusiasm from the tiger exorcism to the gyepshi, even though the gyepshi reestablishes the status quo.

It is even possible to locate the symbolic dynamic that generates, or at least facilitates, that shift: It lies in the relationship between the peshangba and the lut. As already discussed, the poor peshangba of the tiger exorcism and the rich lut of the gyepshi are polarized aspects of what was historically a single ritual figure. The Sherpas are dimly aware of the connection between these two figures, although we do not need to invoke the historical connection to make the point; we need simply note that the people attending the rituals in fact identify first with the peshangba and then with the lut. The sequence itself to some extent shows the present/future shift: poor now (as peshangba), rich after (as lut). More subtly, however, we can see that the shift is tied to reincarnation, since the peshangba in a sense die after they perform their functions; they strip off their costumes immediately and cease to exist, but they (i.e., the locus of the onlookers' identification) arise again in the form of the lut.

In shifting one's identification from peshangba to lut, in other words, one acknowledges that although one may wish to destroy the hierarchy of wealth and privilege in the present world, one would like to preserve its principle for the future. Through the karmic process of rebirth one may get to be high in some future life, and therefore the principle of hierarchy must not be destroyed. Of course one must, for these purposes, ignore the fact that the rich lut who rises, as it were, from the ashes of the peshangba ultimately gets fed to the demons. But we saw that the ritual action facilitates ignoring this, because the lut is not actually destroyed (as was the tiger), nor is it paired with a demon figure when it is set out. The demons instead are given sets of smaller and rather meaningless offerings, and the lut survives. Indeed, at the conclusion of the gyepshi in the Dumji festival, the lut was placed upon a ledge of the village shrine and apparently treated with respect. The lamas danced around it, allegedly expressing joy over the triumph over the demons, but at least visually celebrating the survival and triumph of the richly decorated lut, for the future.

Self and social order: dilemma

In the funeral, as we have seen, both self and social order undergo "disintegration." I have interpreted the exorcisms as responses to this situation, but they do not in fact deal with it in the same way. What, then, is the relationship between the two exorcisms, and what is the relationship between the psychological and sociological interpretations of their significance? Briefly (I shall elaborate below), the answer to these questions may be summarized as follows: The first exorcism, heterodox and "popular," attempts to reintegrate the self on the one hand, but to continue the process, begun in the funeral, of disintegration of the social order on the other. The first exorcism, in other words, attempts to have things both ways. The second exorcism, on the other hand, orthodox and "high," seduces the involvement and commitment of the congregation by offering a better mode of integration of the self than the first, but in such a way that when the self is reintegrated in this one, so too is the social hierarchy reestablished. Stated most starkly, the combined exorcisms in effect make adequate integration of the self contingent upon reintegration of the social order.

The Sherpas, as noted above, do not always perform the second exorcism, although it is felt that really they should. They are often content with the first, and we must therefore assume that the first accomplishes adequately enough the solution to their felt problem of psychic threat and disequilibrium (both "pollution" and demonic attacks). They patch themselves together in the form of the peshangba and in so doing gain the strength to drive the demons out of town. Although the peshangba may not be very fully integrated creatures, they do ultimately comprise an integration of the three elements of the self — spiritual, physical, and demonic. The integration achieved in the first exorcism favors the demonic element over the other two — the peshangba win by overpowering the demons with violence. But we have seen that if one is going to be polluted, one would prefer to be on the demonic rather than the physical side, aggressive and powerful rather than passive and defenseless. The peshangba solution of self-integration is clearly in response to the specific threat posed by death, the threat of sliding toward the physical (passive, defenseless) end of the pollution spectrum as the deceased has done. Further, the peshangba do not completely lack a spiritual component. I noted that the spiritual (control) component may be analytically located as initially outside them, in the text and music of the ritual that control their actions. I said that they may be seen as having broken away from this spiritual control, for in the end they take the cymbals away from the lamas and bring the music to climax themselves. But the point may also be read as their having now actively *appropriated* spiritual control, and having made it a part of their own integration.[29] The peshangba may thus be seen as constructing their role over time, beginning with strong physical connotations (the lewdness and fur robes), adding a spiritual component (the instruments), and thereby gaining the demonic strength exhibited when they chop up the demons.

Thus the "popular" solution to the pollution threat — primarily, from ego's point of view, the threat of moving toward the "physical" — is to compensate by leaning toward the "demonic," with a bit of spiritual control fed in to keep the whole thing together. But it is clear that, within the larger orthodox perspective, people could be persuaded to recognize the inadequacy of this solution. Violence in oneself may be relatively less disturbing than defenselessness, but only relatively so, for one will not always be strong enough physically (one will inevitably grow old and decay toward the "physical" side) to defend against the violence of others. We now gain further understanding of why the peshangba are generally played by adolescent males, because the stress is on strength and youth and vigor; only in this condition does one dare to be, and really have the capacity to be, violent. But the specter of old age and death, as all have just vividly observed in the funeral, makes violence clearly only a temporarily effective mode of functioning. On these grounds, then, the orthodox view can quite successfully compete with the lay view, in arguing that the first exorcism will not really do the trick, or not very effectively, and not for all, and not for long. For physical strength will ultimately fail one, whereas if one adopts the orthodox view one learns that physical strength is irrelevant. All that matters is the strength of one's spirit, which can operate independently of, and survive far beyond, the strength of one's body.

Thus people can easily be persuaded of the long-range value of the orthodox over the popular exorcism, of the religious view of integration of the self over the lay view, particularly after a funeral when people have witnessed physical death. The Sherpas themselves say that religion becomes more of a force in one's life as one grows old, that people in the prime of youth and vigor don't care about it very much, and that, in essence, religion's primary (subjective) relevance comes in the problem of facing death. Buddhism quite clearly has something to offer people on this score. The catch is, however, that its solution to this problem, its power as a psychological theory, is inextricably related to its social theory: The endurance of spirit as a psychologically comforting notion is linked to a moral system in which some spirits endure (are reincarnated) in better forms (social positions) than others. In order to avail oneself of the orthodox solution to the problem of the fear of death, then, in order to achieve transcendence of the fear of physical weakness, defenselessness, and ultimate mortality, one must also bow before the justness of unequal distribution of wealth and privilege. It is this "catch" that underlies the orthodox gyepshi, and that illuminates the relationship between the gyepshi and the do dzongup.

In the gyepshi one does, if it has worked, experience the transcendence of fear of bodily destruction. One separates one's self (one's true self, one's spirit) from one's body, the lut. And one experiences one's own spiritual survival and endurance despite one's body having been fed to the demons. And as the conclusion of, indeed in reward for, this sacrifice, one attains the indestructible Buddha-body instead. The message of the gyepshi could not be more orthodox (and if truly experienced, more comforting) on this score.

But the sociology of the gyepshi symbolism, equally orthodox, may be viewed as another sort of sacrifice, a sacrifice of the momentary liberation from social hierarchy attained in the tiger exorcism. In the tiger exorcism representatives of the lower orders symbolically triumphed over a well-disguised representative of the higher orders. The gyepshi turns this process on its head. The explicit representative of "the people" is the lut figure which, because it must be made attractive to demons and must be used to tempt and satisfy them, is decorated as richly as possible. The people thus identify with a luxurious figure which, however, must be sacrificed because it is also the offering of body, of flesh and blood to the demons. In order to experience, then, the transcendence of fear of bodily destruction, one must also experience a relinquishing of presumption of status elevation (the richness of the lut) and one must witness and accede to the reestablishment of the god figure to supremacy in the end, as the Buddha idol is placed where the lut, the representative of the people, had stood. Indeed, one must not only witness but experience the rightness of this resolution, for it represents the attainment of bodily indestructibility. But it also represents, as the hegemony of the gods represents, the triumph of the big people and the reestablishment of the social hierarchy. The transcendence of spirit over body, the highness of the big people, and the triumph of the gods are all rendered homologous. Divine protection, personal immortality — and social inequality — are all experienced as part of the same package.

We now move on to the final analytic chapter. Religion has been seen to play an ambivalent role in Sherpa experience, and I shall now argue that the Sherpas confront this problem directly, in the process of offering gifts to, and attempting to gain control over, their gods.

6. Offering rituals: problems of religion, anger, and social cooperation

Theoretically, Buddhism rejects the world, and validates no part of it. But analytically we have seen that Buddhism validates the world all too well, contributing to the reproduction of the two most pervasive and discomfiting dimensions of Sherpa experience — social atomism and social hierarchy. The discomfiture of social atomism has several aspects — economic insecurity, family conflict, personal isolation. And the discomfiture of social hierarchy also has several aspects — social insecurity, social resentment. The religion, in aligning itself with these pervasive social tendencies, can itself be shown, as we shall discuss in this chapter, to be resented. Theoretically part of the solution, it is really part of the problem.

Yet the Sherpas assume, in an ongoing way, the absolute indispensability of their religion. Village life is regularly punctuated by religious rituals that seek the protection and support of the gods. The religious ideals may sometimes be a sort of cultural burden, but the religion is also conceived of as having brought civilization to the Sherpas' ancestors, and as having made and continuing to make true society and culture possible.

This view is couched in myths and stories concerning the establishment of Buddhism in Tibet: The myth (recounted in Chapter 4) of the building of Samyang monastery is perhaps the classic example. All of them detail some situation in which people were trying to accomplish some task, or simply trying to go about their business, but were harassed by demons and then were saved by the intervention of a religious figure. In the Samyang tale, the problem is solved by the Guru Rimpoche teaching the Sherpas' ancestors how to make offerings to the gods to gain their protection. It is these rituals of offerings that constitute the ongoing core of Sherpa village religious practice, to be analyzed in this chapter.

Three strands of meaning will be isolated. First, I will examine symbolism of "the body" in the ritual, and relate this to the problem of the monastic sector, whose most distinctive features are celibacy and asceticism, rejection of the body. The monastic sector in turn is taken to symbolize the religion as a whole, and the problems the religion poses to the Sherpas, particularly its contribution to the

The reincarnate lama of Thami monastery

atomistic tendencies of the society.[1] Second, I will isolate symbolism of moods, of anger and "bliss," and discuss ways in which these are problematic to Sherpas in the context of a variety of social structural and cultural factors. And third, I will examine the fact that the offering rituals are couched in an idiom of social hospitality, particularly in the yangdzi or "persuasion" mode. Hospitality, the basic form of lay sociality, becomes in the ritual the structure of mediation between lay and religious perspectives. In forcing their gods to accept hospitality, the Sherpas get their religion to work for rather than against them.

The ritual calendar and the rite of offerings

First, a brief summary of the ritual calendar:

In February there are rites pertaining to the New Year. The offerings to the temple guardian are renewed, and various households hold *kangsur* rites, in which the local guardian gods and spirits are given offerings so that they will renew their protection of the village. At the conclusion of this period, a large all-village tso rite is held in the temple, directed to the high gods of the religion. Tso are explained simply as joyous parties of communion with the high gods, and they conclude every specific ritual performance as well as every full ritual cycle. They celebrate the renewal of well-being brought about by the rituals that preceded them.

In April there is the great Dumji festival. Dumji is explicitly an exorcism; it utilizes the above-mentioned kangsur texts in which the guardians are mobilized against the demons, but in addition it involves the lamas enacting, through costumed and masked dances, the actual divine encounters with and triumph over the demons. It goes on for five pressure- and excitement-packed days, and concludes again with a large all-village tso.

In May comes Nyungne, which also concludes with an all-village tso. Nyungne stands out from the rest of the ritual calendar in being concerned with other-worldy salvation rather than this-worldly successes, and in being addressed directly to the high gods rather than operating through the intermediaries of the local guardian gods (all of whom, however, are ultimately reflexes of the high gods).

From June through August there are again a series of household-sponsored kangsur rites, for the local, lower, guardian gods. There is a large all-village tso in July, marking the midyear. The various household kangsur may be seen as clustering around this event, although some may come before it and some after it.

In September there were, when I was in the field, a number of privately sponsored tso, held to gain merit for deceased parents of the sponsoring households, and in October there was a large temple tso on the occasion of the Nepalese holiday of *Dasain*. Dasain involves the sacrificial slaughter of animals, and the Sherpas hold tso on that day to make merit and counteract the sin brought upon the world by the Nepalese rites.

In November or thereabouts the village shrines are repainted, and in December come the great monastery festivals of Mani-Rimdu. (See Jerstad, 1969; Paul, 1972.) Mani-Rimdu parallels Dumji in being a full-scale exorcism, complete with masked impersonation of the gods and enactment of defeat of the demons. But the Mani-Rimdu festivals are held in monasteries rather than in villages, and the lay people gather at the monasteries and form a highly responsive audience for the rites.

From this brief sketch we can see that, apart from Nyungne, there are really only two kinds of rituals in which the Sherpas commune with their gods – the kangsur rituals (including the big exorcism festivals based on, though including more than, the kangsur texts), and the tso rituals. The former are directed to ferocious guardian gods, and specifically demand their protection from the demons, while the latter are directed toward the high gods of the religion, and are conceived as rites of communion with them, involving no specific demands. However, except for cases in which the point is simply to make merit (as in memorial-tso, or on Dasain), tso are never performed alone. They are always part of a cycle that includes the negotiations with the guardian gods for protection. Every single kangsur performance (indeed, every ritual performance of any kind, including Nyungne, funerals, and so forth) concludes with a tso – and every full cycle of privately sponsored kangsur concludes with a public tso. It is significant, too, that no new altar is constructed for the performance of tso at the conclusion of, say, a kangsur ritual. I stress these points in order to show that the high gods of the religion are behind, and assumed by, all rituals directed to lower deities, even though they are not directly addressed in those rituals. It is as if the distinction between kangsur and tso allows the high gods to keep their hands clean, and to enter the party only after their underlings have dealt with the messier issues.

The significance of these arguments will be clear in the course of the analysis. But it is important that they be established in a general way at the outset, to justify the fact that I will collapse the differences between the two kinds of offering rituals in the analysis that follows in this chapter. All such rituals have an unvarying minimal structure, or ordered set of events, and this structure in turn has essentially the same meaning, though not the same emphasis or importance, in every such ritual. Further, as the myth of the building of Samyang monastery indicates, whatever else the gods are asked (or not asked, in the case of tso) to do, the basic expectation of the outcome of these rites is that the gods will continue to protect the people and their endeavors from the onslaughts of the demons. Thus I will not, in this chapter, analyze any particular ritual, but rather the general structure within which, despite the variation of form and occasion, the Sherpas seek the help, and especially the protection, of their gods. And although this basic ritual form is also enacted by monks in monasteries, it will be viewed specifically from the point of view of the lay people, who see it, describe it, and intend it in terms appropriate to their own situation.

The structure may be summarized briefly. The first stage is always a purification rite, a sang, which itself may take many different forms, but which consists most commonly of offerings to the rather touchy and changeable local spirits to assure their good humor and benevolence, and hence to purify the area and the participants.[2] Following the sang, attention shifts to the main altar, upon which is arrayed a set of offerings freshly constructed and assembled by the lamas for the performance of the particular ceremony, and disassembled and disposed of at the end of the performance. The altar items are collectively referred to as *chepa*, "offerings," for everything that goes on the altar is casually said to represent some worldy category of gift for the gods.

The presentation of the offerings is guided by and synchronized with the reading of a text appropriate to the god and the occasion. At the opening of the service, the gods are invited to come and attend the feast being held for them. Loud music is played to attract their attention. Incense is flooded through the area, and grain and beer are sprinkled skyward, all as gestures of invitation and welcome. The *serkim,* or sprinkling of grain and beer, is also itself an act of offering for the lower spirits, the guardians of the guardians as it were.

Following the invitation and welcome, the gods are invited to be seated in the *torma*, molded dough objects that have been prepared to receive their presences. Then measures are taken to protect the ritual from the antireligious demons: The torma of the gods of the four directions is set outside the temple or the house as a receptacle for and an offering to them, so they will guard the boundaries of the precinct. And the special torma for the demons (the *gyek*) is thrown out as food for them, to satisfy temporarily their greedy desires and divert them from entering the temple and eating up the offerings. This is invariably a dramatic moment – the music slowly rises to a crescendo as the ritual assistant picks up, then holds aloft, the demons' torma; finally there is a cacaphonous crashing climax, accompanied by demoniac whistles, as the assistant dashes out the door and throws the torma hard and far from the precinct.

Next the gods are presented with all their offerings (the entire altar) and urged to eat fully and enjoy themselves. While they are partaking of the offerings, the lamas read "praises for the goodness and admirable qualities" of the gods, and recite the mantra appropriate to the chief god of the group. They then read "prayers for favors immediate and to come," and during the course of these readings representatives of the community approach the altar and perform prostrations, which signify apologies for past offenses and help cleanse one of sins.[3]

The ceremony always concludes with the tso, an offering to the high gods of cooked or otherwise immediately edible foods that have been laid out upon a bench at the foot of the altar. After being offered to the gods, the tso food is divided up among all the people present and eaten on the spot. The lamas read a brief benediction, and as they finish they allow their voices to trail off, suggesting the departure of the gods. The altar is dismantled, the butter lamps are allowed to burn themselves out, the lamas take away the raw grain, and the torma are given to children, taken home to sick or elderly persons, or fed to the village dogs.

Such is the elemental form of most Sherpa ritual performances. It all seems rather standard to anyone familiar with cross-cultural and historical religious data. The gods are contacted; they are given offerings; the people communally eat some of the offerings at the close of the ceremony. At least three things, however, make this a *Sherpa* ceremony of the genre, and give one entrée to its meaning in Sherpa culture. These are: (1) those peculiar items, the torma cakes; (2) the special kind of help or benefit sought from the gods – protection against the demons; and (3) the idiom through which the rite is formulated – that of social hospitality and the host–guest relationship. I will examine each of these elements as a way of arriving at some of the problems with which the ritual is dealing, and then return to the full sequence of ritual action to see how it in fact deals with them.

The problems of the ritual

Torma and the body problem

A torma is a dough figure, basically conical in form, ranging from several inches to several feet in height. The basic form may be elaborated upon by molding the figure itself, and by adding other dough elements. Some torma are left uncoated, while others must be colored red, black, or white, using melted butter colored with red vegetable dye or charcoal, or left undyed for white. Each torma is also decorated with bits of butter shaped into discs, dots, petals, flames, etc. All these variations in shape, color, and decoration have significance.

Although there are several different understandings concurrently held in the culture, and several different levels of meaning, the primary significance of the torma is as an abstract representation of, and a temporary "body" for, a god. Every god, from the lowliest locality spirit to the Buddha himself, has a prescribed torma; conversely, every torma has a name and identity from the god it represents. Whenever a god will be invoked in a religious service, a torma should be made for him beforehand. Then, when his name is called, he comes and enters the torma, where he remains through the reading, listening to people's petitions and receiving their homage. Because the Tibetan pantheon is enormous, there are literally hundreds of different torma forms, all achieved by performing transformations on the little conical cakes of dough (see Figure 7).

The second significance of torma is as food for the gods. This interpretation is held most often by laymen, either together with the body notion, or alone. But it was also explained by a lama that this is an orthodox interpretation in some of the other sects of Tibetan Buddhism. While a number of torma on the altar are designated specifically as food torma, in a general sense it is held that all the torma are food offerings for the gods to whom the ritual is directed.[4]

The same duality of meaning is expressed in exegesis on the decorations of the torma. When asked the meaning of the color coatings, lamas often replied offhandedly that red is like giving the god a monk's robe, which is red in Tibetan Buddhism. On the other hand, the orthodox meaning, also articulated by the lamas, is that red coating is for a god who eats flesh and drinks beer, while white coating represents a god who follows the so-called Brahmin-Chhetri purity rules, eating no meat and drinking no beer (and usually wearing white clothing). The two exegeses are, of course, contradictory, because monks, despite wearing red robes, observe the dietary purity rules: A red robe and a meat-and-beer diet simply do not go together. In orthodox point of fact, all red-coated torma are for ferocious, meat-eating gods, but if one asks lamas what red coating means, without reference to any particular torma, they will frequently say that it represents monks' clothing.

It is noteworthy, then, that while "gods' bodies" rather than "gods' food" is the more orthodox meaning of the torma as such, the more orthodox significance of the coating of torma refers to the diet of the god, rather than his clothes, his bodily covering. The food and body meanings are thus both ultimately embodied in orthodoxy.

Now, how a god appears in outward bodily appearance, and the diet that suits his taste, are related to one another as metonymic aspects of his mood or disposition. The interrelations between food, body, and mood will be important for subse-

Figure 7. Torma (from Nebesky-Wojkowitz: 351)

quent analysis. For the moment, however, let us focus on the issue of body, raised
exclusively by the torma and some of its immediately associated items on the altar.

Sherpa religion is ambivalent about the body. Their Mahayana heritage glorifies
the bodhisattva, who has achieved salvation but returned to the world in bodily
form to "help" others find the way. The bodhisattva concept has been institutionalized in Tibetan religion more literally than among any other Buddhist group,
in the figure of the *tulku* or reincarnate lama who is actually identified as a living
bodhisattva available to the direct acquaintance of the members of the community.
The image of the bodhisattva makes the point that the body is a good thing, insofar
(*but only insofar*) as it is a vehicle for practicing the religion — for learning, teaching, and exemplifying religious precepts, and for performing meritorious deeds. In

all other respects the body is a bad thing in that, according to teachings of classical Buddhism that have carried through into Sherpa religion, the body is the agency of desire for sensuous pleasure, which in turn leads humanity into sin.

The religious ambivalence concerning the body is nicely illustrated by some verses from a fourteenth-century Tibetan lama. They sum up Sherpa sentiment well:

> Now listen, you who would practise religion.
> When you obtain the advantages, so hard to obtain,
>   (of a well-endowed human body)
> It is best to accumulate merit
> By practising religion and so put all to good use.
> . . .
> Wine and women, these two
> Are the robbers who steal away your good conduct.
> Keeping far off from loved ones like poison
> Let this be your protective armour!
> . . .
> The best way to good rebirths and salvation
> Is purity of personal conduct.
> So never demean it. Hold to it
> As dearly as the apply of your eye!
>
>   (Snellgrove, 1967: 159–60)

Thus in this Mahayana tradition the body is considered valuable as a means of helping others, but the "help" is primarily by the example of "purity of personal conduct" and not by direct support of those with whom one is socially involved: "[Keep] far off from loved ones like poison . . ." Any other use of the body, any other appreciation of it for any other purpose, is bad, leading to sin, poor rebirth, and entrapment in the round of evil and suffering.

Other Sherpa beliefs, not derived from Buddhist orthodoxy, support the generally negative view of the body encouraged by Buddhism. Sherpa pollution beliefs stress the defiling propensity of the body, and its tendency to impair the mental (psychological, spiritual, moral, etc.) functions (Ortner, 1973a). Even Sherpa commonsense notions contribute the point that the body and its desires lead to children, who are felt to be a nuisance and who must be supported by hard labor. The body then, as a sum of all these points, is almost utterly negative in theory.

At the social level, the question refracts in a very important way through the major social category distinction of the culture: lay versus monastic. The only proper way out of the body problem, according to the religion, is to become a monk, that is, to practice celibacy and denial of sensuality while devoting all one's energies to the religion.[5] This remains a strong cultural ideal; most boys think about (or more accurately, toy with the idea of) becoming monks, although few do, while most older men wish they had. Yet despite (or possibly because of) this fact, there are indications of ambivalence on the part of the lay community vis-à-vis the monks. One strong piece of evidence for this is that the charity system of giving to monks is in disarray. Sherpa monks do not even try to sustain themselves by begging as, according to orthodoxy, they should; they are supported largely by their families, with supplemental support from endowments given to monasteries by a few wealthy people. A lama explained this by saying that in these evil times people think monks are lazy and so begrudge them food. The lama said it was to save the laity from the sin of their bad thoughts that Sherpa monks do not beg.

And the laity evidently do have such bad thoughts, although they are not often expressed. I recorded only one disparaging remark by a layman against religious personages, but it was a telling one. A nun had come begging for food, and after I gave her the standard offering, she began poking around the shelves of the house and asking for other things. After she left, a man who was present shook his head and remarked that although religious people were taught every day not to need and want many material things, yet they seemed to come out even greedier and more materialistic than everyone else. This is certainly an overstatement — monks as a group probably have about the same distribution of greed and materialism as the population at large, and there are a fair number of genuine saints among them who redeem the reputation of all the rest.

The impression of greater greed and materialism in monks is probably related to the fact that they do not work. Because they are forbidden to perform physical labor, and are supported by others, theirs is indeed any easy life compared to the rest of the population. Further, because they must largely be supported by their families, this means that they generally come from fairly well-to-do families in the first place. Thus it cannot be denied that, by and large, they constitute an elite group. On these points, however, the resentment of monks is not so much a religious issue as it is part of the problem of social privilege in lay society, as discussed in the preceding chapter.

As for the specifically religious issues involved in resentment of monks, however, when the lama said that lay people perceive monks as "lazy," he implied that it is because lay people are clouded with ignorance concerning the true value of their religious ideals. And the layman who said monks were greedy implied that the problem was one of individual religious actors not living up to those ideals. In either case, the ideals themselves are not questioned. Only one sector of the population, the noncelibate village lamas, actually questioned the monastic ideal per se, complaining of the injustice of the higher status of monks in the religious hierarchy. And their complaints strike at what seems to be the heart of the matter.

A village lama, they said, is constantly on call for the religious needs of the people. When there is a request for a religious ritual, he must drop whatever he is doing and respond to this request. A monk, on the other hand, does nothing but seek his own personal salvation; he does not respond to the needs of the people. It seems contradictory to the lamas, then, that monks are defined as more worthy of respect than lamas. Monks sit higher than lamas when both are participating in a single ritual, and monks gain infinitely more merit for their calling. The lamas in some of their bitter moments were obviously resentful of this state of affairs.[6]

The point that monks are only out for their own salvation, and do not have the needs of the lay people at heart, feeds directly back into the issue of conflict between lay interests, needs, and concerns, and the highest tenets of the religious ideology. Monks are only enacting what the religion has stated as the ideal. They are merely exemplifying the precepts of the religion, the ideal of nonattachment. If they are resented, then, it is not only because of their soft life and their elite social associations, but because they exemplify a system of norms and beliefs with which it is difficult for lay people, in the normal social process, to come to terms.[7] It is this conflict, in its various aspects, that we shall see to be at the heart of the offering rituals.

Gods, demons, and the problem of moods

The primary object of offering rituals is to get the gods to renew their primordial struggle against, and reenact their original triumph over, the demons and the forces of anarchy and violence. There are vast numbers, types, and grades of supernatural beings in the Sherpa universe, but I shall focus on the two extreme types — the high gods who preside over the system (and over every ritual), and the demons who pit themselves against the system (and against every ritual).[8]

The highest gods of the religion are defined as having achieved salvation and bliss. They are utterly fulfilled and self-contained; they "need nothing" and are basically not interested in worldly affairs. Their general disposition is said to be benevolent to and protective of humanity, but they are self-absorbed; unless people actively keep in touch with them through offerings, they will, as suggested by a number of myths, withdraw ever further and leave humanity at the mercy of the demons.

All gods designated as such (*hla*) have two mood aspects — *shiwa,* peaceful and benign, and *takbu,* fierce and violent.[9] The "same" god in his different aspects usually has different names; the benign form is considered more basic, while the fierce form is said to be adopted for the purpose of fighting demons. The appearances of the two dispositional aspects of gods are depicted with great realism and in great detail in scroll paintings and temple frescoes, both available in the villages for all to see. Gods in their benign aspects are usually shown in pastel colors, in calm postures, with relatively few limbs, and relatively pleasant expressions on their faces. Gods in their terrible aspects are depicted in dark and harsh colors, with snarling faces, in threatening postures, and usually with an excessive number of heads, eyes, teeth, arms, etc. A takbu god, further, is usually shown in sexual consort with a goddess, or he is at least depicted with an erect penis, while shiwa gods generally sit blissfully alone.

At the opposite extreme from the gods are the demons, all of whom are considered to be intrinsically evil, and aggressive against humanity. Not only threatening to individuals, they are also a menace to the religion in general. They try to tempt lamas and monks into sin, to eat temple offerings, and to undermine the religion however they can. Every Sherpa can recount tales of the struggles of gods and great lamas to subdue the demons and hence defend the faith. This dual aspect of the demons — enemies of the people, enemies of the faith — will be seen to be important to the successful symbolic outcome of the ritual.

The basic Sherpa rituals, then, ask for the help of the gods in combating the forces of evil. This involves making the high gods "happy," by feeding them, so that they will want to "help us" by engaging in the struggle against the randomly aggressive demons. Yet it would also seem to require, as we shall see in the analysis, making the high gods themselves a bit angry, so that they will be drawn down from their bliss long enough to engage in this struggle. The symbolism of the supernatural types, in short, seems in part to represent a complex commentary on the regulation of mood — the question of the optimum interrelationship between self-contained bliss, random aggression, appropriately focused anger, and active benevolence.

In what sense is regulation of mood problematic to Sherpas? While in day-to-day interaction they do not appear to manifest, like some other groups in the anthropological literature, rigid control of temperament — actually, they appear to a Western observer relatively spontaneous and open — nonetheless there are unmistakable indications that Sherpas experience chronic difficulty in dealing with anger and other bad moods.[10] There are, of course, all those demons to witness this point, and the fact that most of the gods with whom the Sherpas are most involved are ferocious takbu types. But one need not look beyond the human realm for such projection. The merest slight from a neighbor is taken to mean that he or she is angry with one, whereupon one immediately searches for some fault one may have committed. On the other hand, one's own bad moods (including lethargy as well as evil temper) are considered puzzling; one often puts them down to having encountered some pollution, rather than to an outside provocation. The feeling of the individual, in short, seems to be, "If my neighbor is in a bad mood, I must have done something wrong, and if I am in a bad mood I must have done something wrong."

All of this indicates a culturally engendered confusion, for the individual, about the locus, meaning, and sources of anger. Without attempting to postulate a single source of this problem, I shall here simply draw attention to some aspects of the culture and social structure that would tend to reinforce and regenerate it.

In the first place, there is a religious prohibition on violence — killing, fighting, angry words, and even angry thoughts are all considered highly sinful, bringing religious demerit to those who so indulge, and hence hampering their chances for a good rebirth and for salvation. These indulgences are also considered polluting, such that they may undermine one's physical and mental well-being in the present life as well. Now Sherpas are quite scrupulous about not killing, but as for the rest, fighting, angry words, and angry thoughts are relatively frequent and commonplace.

Thus the point is not that they do not have outlets for *expressing* anger – they do it all the time – but consistent with the cultural prohibition, there are no clear-cut models available for its expression in controlled and articulated ways. An angry Sherpa cannot challenge to a duel, mobilize his lineage for a vendetta, organize a war expedition, bring litigation, provoke a witch trial, participate in a collective confession, or in short have recourse to any socially organized mode through which he and others can get to objectify, comprehend, and systematically restructure disturbing feelings within a culturally sanctioned context. Only one secular form seems at least intended to provide such a structure – the institution of "joking" at parties which was discussed already in Chapter 4 – but it is often only partially successful.

Thus, when anger is expressed in the culture, in the absence of institutional forms for rendering it orderly, manageable, and comprehensible to both the angry party and the observers, if often takes the form of a tantrum. I witnessed several such outbursts, in which the individual (generally after drinking) simply went out of control and began to abuse and attack everyone in reach, ultimately to be dragged away, literally kicking and screaming, by kinsmen and friends.

The situation is strongly compounded by the peculiar fact of Sherpa social structure noted above – the highly diffuse authority structure of the society. Although there are, as noted, status differences in the society, the high-status people have no recognized powers of any sort. Among the Khumbu Sherpas, apparently, there are certain elected village officials (von Fürer-Haimendorf, 1964: 104) but even there it is acknowledged that

large spheres of social life lie outside the jurisdiction of these officials. The settlement of disputes relating to these spheres is left to private mediation, and the inability – or unwillingness – of the village community as a whole to assume authority in dealing with such matters, is one of the peculiar features of Sherpa social organization. (ibid.)

In the Solu village in which I worked, on the other hand, the situation is more extreme: There are no formal leadership roles, no elected "village officials." Currently, the villages are required to elect a representative to the district panchayat council, and in Dzemu one or another of the "big men" is generally "elected" to this post. But the post carries with it, at least at the time I was in the field, no formal powers that could be exercised within the village. Or again, there are two what might be termed "protopolitical" organs within the community, the temple committee and the school committee, each functioning to oversee the affairs of the respective institutions. These committees again are made up largely, but not entirely, of "big people," but they have no powers for dealing with disputes even concerning the school and the temple, no less in affairs not arising in connection with those institutions.

At the same time, the pattern of community "unwillingness" to deal with disputes in any systematic way holds true. I recounted above the Khumbu murder story, in which (as it is told) no one knew what to do about the murderer after the crime. He stayed in his home for two weeks while the villagers, though deeply upset, did nothing, and he finally ran away to Tibet. Two more examples from my own field experience will suffice. On one occasion, a big man from another village got drunk and disrupted the Dumji festival dancing. Even though, at Dumji, there are two ritual figures who are designated with authority to keep order during the festival, nobody interfered with this man, and he disrupted things for more than an hour. It was only when he went up into the temple balcony and began to lay about among the women with a stick that he was finally dragged away by some kinsmen and taken home. On another occasion, some young English trekkers came through the village and we secured lodging for them with the woman who lived next door. The next morning the woman came in and complained that they had stolen a valuable teacup. As they had not yet left the village, we went down and stopped them, but they claimed they had taken nothing. The villagers who had gathered around agreed with our suggestion that they should open their rucksacks and demonstrate that they did not have the cup. They sullenly opened their sacks, but said that they were not about to empty them out. At that point we tried to get our neighbor or anyone else to go through the sacks (we did not feel that we should ourselves be the prime actors in this drama) but neither the aggrieved woman nor anyone else would undertake this. Everyone stood around shifting from foot to foot, and finally the trekkers closed up and shouldered their packs and walked away. Although we and everyone else felt fairly certain that they had the cup, and although the woman was a respected member of the community, no one was willing to have a confrontation with them to defend the woman's interests.

As things now stand, then, Sherpa social structure does not provide channels for dealing systematically with socially disruptive behavior. Further, tendencies toward such behavior (as well as tendencies toward virtuous behavior) are thought to be inherited personality traits, to run as it were in the family, and hence not really to be amenable to change. The upshot of all this is general social paralysis in the face of socially threatening situations. There is a feeling — all things considered, a quite realistic feeling — that nothing can be done, or at least nothing effective.

Thus, aspects of social structure and cultural belief converge against the formulation of any models for the systematic comprehension and constructive transmutation of ill feeling. The angry gods and violent demons dealt with in the ritual signal the fact that the ritual is in some sense an attempt to deal with this problem. Part of the analysis, then, will be an attempt to show how the ritual works to help its participants achieve a particular subjective orientation, consonant with the realities postulated by and experienced in this culture. In particular, for the Sherpas, it is a matter of "correctly" understanding the nature and sources of one's moods and dispositions, and discovering appropriate, constructive, and comfortable forms and courses for them to take.

Hospitality, anger, and body

The Sherpas make the explicit analogy between the offering ritual and social hospitality. The people are the hosts, the gods are their guests. The people invite the gods to the human realm, make them comfortable, and give them food and drink, all of which is meant to give them pleasure, "to make them happy" so that they will want to "help" humanity by providing protection from the demons.

According to the native model, all of the business of the ritual in relation to the gods is accomplished by the same mechanisms whereby human cooperation is obtained in hospitality (and especially yangdzi) practices.[11] Thus the music, incense, and sprinkling of grain and beer with which the ceremony opens are described as "invitations" and "gestures of welcome" to the gods. The gods are then "seated" in their torma, and the assemblage of altar offerings is served as one serves the food and drink of a party for the sensuous enjoyment of the guests. Thus aroused, pleased, and gratified, the gods, like one's neighbors, will feel "happy" and kindly disposed toward the worshipers/hosts and any requests they might make.

Further, just as ordinary social hospitality assumes and accords a latent power of coercion to the host, so does the ritual. In social hospitality the invitation may take the form of a disguised command that it is virtually impossible to disobey (see Chapter 4); similarly, the invitation portion of the ritual text contains mantra that do not ask but actually conjure the gods into coming. And the invitation to the gods is coupled with various sensuous temptations (music, incense, food, and drink) that lure rather than merely invite the gods.

Second, the seating of a guest in ordinary hospitality has a culturally defined latent coerciveness — once he can be got into a seat, he must accept the proffered hospitality or risk gravely insulting the host. Once in the house and seated, in short, he has become a *guest* and must follow through in the appropriate ways. The coerciveness of the seat is also seen in funerals where, in order to make sure the soul does not wander off and miss the reading of the totul, a special seat is prepared for the soul with a mystic design in the center; the soul is conjured into sitting there and its presence is thus assured for the remainder of the reading. Similarly, then, the conjuring of the gods into their torma receptacles is a coercive gesture that controls their presence and their availability for being fed, pleased, and petitioned.

And, finally, just as feeding the guests is seen as intrinsically powerful and coercive in ordinary social hospitality, so the feeding of the gods is not only propitiatory but coercive in the ritual. In discussing the effectiveness of yangdzi, I stressed that food and drink are thought to have certain *natural effects* upon people, such that, having been wined and dined, they become more open, friendly, and receptive to oneself and one's wishes. (The converse holds too — not feeding others automatically makes them angry and uncooperative at the very least.) Drink in particular, through its intoxicating properties, is said to render the personality expansive and the resistance to various temptations and imprecations low. That analogous effects are expected to take place in the gods' dispositions is seen in the (already cited) passage from one of the ritual texts: "I am offering you [the gods] the things which you eat, now you must do whatever I demand." (Quoted in von Fürer-Haimendorf, 1964: 193). Thus, as in yangdzi, the guests (in this case the gods) are not only being given pleasure in the vague hope that they will be kindly disposed toward their host. The various pleasurable offerings mask mechanisms assumed to have intrinsic coerciveness.

The hospitality model is thus applied intact as the native gloss on the action and expectations of the ritual. And this extension makes perfect sense — a tried and more or less true procedure for gaining assistance in ordinary life is applied to an apparently similar situation in dealing with the gods. But how similar is the situation? The gods, unlike people, have no bodies and hence no sensuous desires; they are specifically said to "need nothing." If nothing else, then, this point serves to call into question the appropriateness and efficacy of the hospitality structure itself, which, perhaps, is exactly what is intended. In other words, it may be that social hospitality *is* a problem, and that the ritual, cast in the idiom of social hospitality, is at least in part a device for dealing with it.

At this point we must reexamine hospitality through different lenses. For present purposes, two problematic aspects of these events come to the fore: First, hospitality is one of the major contexts of village life in which the moral implications of "the body problem" are most sharply highlighted; and second, it is the matrix par excellence where the issue of confusion over anger and other moods is most seriously raised.

First, the body problem: Hospitality raises the issue of body not as an abstract concern with relevance only for one's ultimate salvation, but as a conflict between religious ideals and the pragmatic requirements of worldly social life. The religious ideal devalues the body, but social pragmatism indicates that sensuality is not only personally pleasurable but a socially constructive mechanism; it is the body with its weaknesses that renders others subject to social manipulation. The whole hospitality ethic dictates that it is a good and socially useful thing to give others sensuous pleasure, by providing them with food and drink, because when people are thus gratified they will, in a word that has great import in the culture, *help* one another. Without the hospitality procedures, the Sherpas feel that they would be virtually at a loss for means of gaining social cooperation, especially from higher-status figures who have no ongoing obligation to them. Virtually the only way to get people to do something in the culture is to make them *want* to do it, to generate in them some sense of obligation. Thus the whole hospitality system with which villagers are so much involved virtually all of their nonworking time, and upon which the whole integration of village social life is felt to depend, winds up putting people in direct conflict with the highest ideals (and even the lower-order beliefs concerning pollution and the like) of their culture and their religion.

The conflict between the religious devaluation of sensuality and the necessary social manipulation of sensuality finds much concrete expression. A cultural notion — fully borne out by experience — is that hostesses force one to eat and drink too much, making one drunk and lethargic, analogous if not equivalent to polluted states that signify an upsurge of the lower aspects of one's being. In particular, hostesses are said to tempt village lamas with too much food and drink, undercutting whatever minimal gestures toward asceticism these clerics, falling short of full-scale monkhood, try to make. I have even seen a drunken father trying to force his monk son to drink beer. And local villagers who try to swear off drinking are subject to the most intense sorts of pressures by hosts and hostesses to take a drink. All of this serves to point up the vital importance of sensuous susceptibility for the social workings of village life, and the conflict between that and the ideal of ascetic self-control stressed by the religion. Even the slightest gesture of asceticism, such as swearing off drink, is a threat to village social dynamics.

These points further illuminate some of the meaning of the villagers' ambivalence about monks: Rejection of sensuality, while good in terms of ultimate salvation, seems virtually immoral from the perspective of village life. Ascetic leanings represent social nonavailability; sensuous susceptibility is the basis for real social help and mutual support.

As for the problem of mood, the Sherpa party is meant to make people happy, and it does that quite often and sometimes quite intensely. It is meant to pacify anger and create mutual benevolence, and it often performs these functions as well. But it also generates plenty of anger, anxiety, and ill feeling. This is not to say that Sherpas do not experience the various moods in other contexts of their lives, but only that they seem to experience all of them most intensely, in the most complicated mixture, in a short period of time, and in a confined and rigidly structured social space, at a party.

We have already discussed, in Chapter 4, the notions of angry host and angry guest, and the mutually irritating and anxiety-provoking aspects of the host–guest relationship. And we have seen too the ways in which the long period of drinking and "joking" may produce a great deal of tension. The joking of course is not supposed to culminate in fighting — on the contrary, it is obviously meant to provide a nonviolent format for the articulation and resolution of ill-feeling. Yet it often becomes quite vicious, an intolerable provocation that culminates in a fight between the parties to the repartee. If the fight comes late in the event, the party may actually break up, leaving a residue of anger and bad feeling all around. Or if the fight breaks out, and some friends hustle the fighters off to their respective homes, the party will continue, but with the pall of the unresolved fight over it. Or a fight might not break out, but in that case at least some of the guests spend the rest of the evening sulking and smoldering with anger. All these outcomes are at least as probable as the ideal of the mass of happy and satisfied guests warmly in the host's debt at the end of the party.

Now it is not only true that some large-scale parties turn out exhilaratingly well, but also that there are many instances of smaller-scale visiting and inviting in which the chances of both high exhilaration and strongly provoked anger are low. But it is also true that when a host invites a few people to a small party he often wants some particular favor from them, and these parties thus turn more on the anxieties of the host–guest relationship described above — the host's anxiety about being able to bring off his persuasion, the guest's feeling of being pressured and coerced, the fear of each of angering the other. Either way — large parties with highs of good feeling and lows of surliness and resentment, small parties with their smaller pressures and anxieties — the Sherpa hospitality situation is a matter of the complex experiencing of a mixture of moods and feelings generated by sensuous stimuli and problematic social relationships.

Hospitality, then, is a situation in which the two problems outlined above — "body" and "anger" — are highlighted and intensified in various ways. It is fraught with contradiction. It is supposed to be a form for making people happy — stimulating the senses and feelings in positive ways, and soothing and pacifying aroused ill feelings — yet it often generates, or at least serves as the matrix within which is generated, as much ill feeling as good. And it is the situation par excellence that highlights the contradiction between the standard ethics of village social life, which value the sensuous susceptibility of the body as a means of gaining social aid and cooperation, and the ideals of the religion, which strongly oppose as inimical to salvation, any pandering to sensuality. The guest who doesn't eat, who leaves "with an empty mouth," may be such a charged figure precisely because he summarizes all these issues: not eating means anger, not eating means asceticism, both anger and asceticism mean (from different starting points) social noncooperation.[12]

The solutions of the ritual

Let us now return to the action of the ritual, to analyze the symbolic development and handling of each of the problematic issues outlined above. For the problems are not simply represented; they are dramatized in particular relationships to one another and modulated toward particular resolutions.

Social hospitality provides the metaphor, the outer form as it were, in which the ritual is encased. We saw above both the surface analogy — invitation, seating, feeding — and the hidden analogy — the command beneath the invitation, the entrapment underlying the seating, the intentional manipulativeness of the feeding. Yet it is clear that much more is going on in the ritual than this analogy allows us — and perhaps the participants — to see. Let us look more closely at the offerings and at the action surrounding them.

The structure of the altar platform is that of a series of steps. On the first or lowest step are placed the *chinche*, the "outside offerings" [also called, in Tibet, "the offerings to accomplish drawing near" (Ekvall: 166)]. These include the "eight basic offerings" — water for drinking, water for washing, a flower for good smell, incense for good smell, a butter lamp for light, water for cooling, a simple uncoated torma for food, and cymbals for music.

On the next step are arrayed the *nangche,* the "inside offerings." The nangche represent offerings *of* (not *to*) the six senses. There should be cloth, as clothing, signifying touch; a plain torma, as food, signifying taste; incense, signifying smell; cymbals, as music, signifying hearing; a mirror, signifying sight; and a sacred book, signifying the sixth sense, thought or spirit. The nangche level is often omitted in setting up simple altars, but it was stressed by the lama informant as conceptually important.[13]

The next two steps comprise the *sangche* or "secret offerings." On the lower of the two are the torma of the lesser gods of the constellation being worshiped, the "soldiers," "helpers," etc., of the high god. On the right-hand end of the row, as one faces the altar, stands the special torma that will be thrown out to the demons, somewhat separated from the others, usually with a butter lamp interposed. On the top row in the center stands the large main torma, for the focal god of the text being read on this occasion. This is called the *torma che,* the "senior" or "head" torma, or the *khil-khor torma.* Khil-khor (Skt., mandala) means a constellation of gods, of which the khil-khor torma represents the head god; it also means the palace and more generally the heavenly realm or abode of that god and his constellation. Khil-khor also refers to a diagram of this realm/palace/constellation, the minimal reduction of which is a complex geometric form combining in various ways circles and squares, each inside the other (see Ortner, 1966; Tucci; Snellgrove, 1957). A khil-khor diagram should be placed under the head torma.

The main torma is flanked by its two immediate guardian torma. To the gods' right goes the *dutsi*, a mixture ideally composed of all the foul ingredients of the world, said to signify semen, and usually represented by beer. The term dutsi literally means demon juice. To the gods' left goes *rakta*, ideally menstrual blood, usually represented by tea.[14]

In front of the completed altar a bench lower than the first level of offerings is set up. On this bench is placed the tso food, a set of cooked or otherwise immediately edible foods that will be offered to the gods at the end of the service and then eaten by the people (see Figure 8).

The offerings are said to be presented in order from the bottom to the top of the altar, from the "outside" to the "inside" to the "secret" offerings. One lama's exegesis presents the sequence as follows. The chinche or "outside" offerings are "for people" — the worshipers are transformed at the beginning of the action into (low-level) gods, and are propitiating themselves with the first-level offerings. Then the people/gods at the first level offer the nangche or "inside" offerings at the second level to the *chepi hlamu*, the offering goddesses. The nangche offerings, it will be recalled, are composed of symbolic representations of the six senses. The offering goddesses in turn offer the sangche or "secret" offerings of the top level to the gods of the ceremony, the secret offerings being the torma and the polluting liquids.

Following the presentation of the offerings, hymns of praise to the gods are read, prostrations are made by members of the congregation, and prayers of petition for favors are entered. Finally, the tso feast is offered, said to be a party in celebration

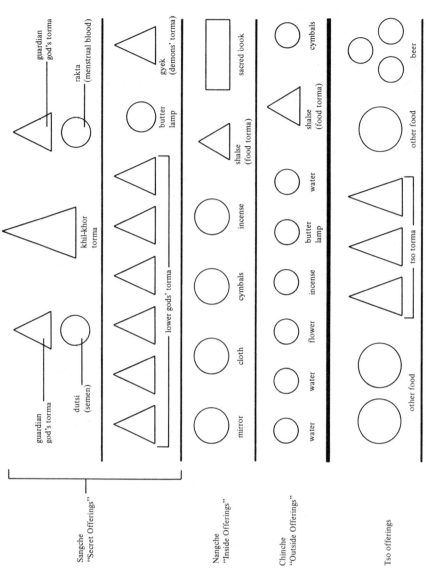

Figure 8. Schematic representation of an altar

of the positive effect the ceremony has wrought — the gods are said to be in good moods as a result of receiving their offerings, and they join the worshipers in a party in which they and then all assembled consume the tso foods.

Let us now try to construct, in our terms, the sense being constructed by the ritual action itself. I suggest, first, that the rite may be read as an extended and systematic pollution of the gods, through a double process of embodying and, contrary to the native model that says they are being "made happy," infuriating them, all strangely enough producing the positive outcome of triumph over evil. In the process, I will try to show, the participant is meant to experience a transformation of consciousness concerning both his body and his anger. And finally, all of this, by being encompassed within the hospitality framework, winds up reconciling the felt contradiction between pragmatic social life and religious values. We must now look to see how the trick is really done.

Bodying the gods

The rite can be read, first, as a series of symbolic acts and representations that encase the gods more and more tightly in more and more substantial forms, especially, though not exclusively, in bodies. If we turn the sequence of altar action upside down, and read from the top of the altar downwards, rather than from the bottom up, we see an interesting development of meaning. A justification for this analytic inversion is created — and perhaps the point is not lost on the worshipers either — by the hospitality structure of the ritual, which dictates that the first step of the action is the installation of the gods in their seats, the torma, which stand at the *top* of the altar. And the conclusion of the rite is always the offering of the tso, explicitly a party in the most festive sense, the tso foods standing at the *bottom,* actually below, the altar.

The very first move, then, in this reading, is to force the gods to take bodies at the "secret" level of the altar. The body itself, as discussed above, is a pollution to the spirit; it is also the source of semen and menstrual blood, both highly polluting, representations of which flank the senior torma on the highest level of the altar. Further, in the Sherpa view of human reproduction, the body is the *product* of semen and menstrual blood; conception occurs as a result of their being mixed. The torma body which the god is forced to adopt is thus, it may be inferred, both the source and product of its polluting companions on the altar. It seems clear, then, that these items are not here for the god to eat, but as the generators and sustainers of the bodily form that he has been forced to adopt. They set up a self-sustaining system, like the poles of a battery, which keeps his body powerfully charged, which in turn keeps him trapped inside it.

Beyond this, the torma have coatings of "clothing," as described above, developing further the gods' physical encasement. And the head torma at least, which summarizes all the others, is placed on his khil-khor, the geometric representation of

his palace and his realm. The khil-khor design depicts enclosures within enclosures —
squares inside circles, circles inside squares. Thus each of these elements stresses
ever heavier layers of physical encasement. The body encases the god's spiritual
essence, the clothing encases the body, the palace encloses the embodied god, and
the boundaries of the territory enclose the palace.

It is noteworthy that, according to various textual translations and exegeses, the
verbal material at this early stage stresses descriptions of the physical appearances
of the gods.[15] According to a summary of a text given to von Fürer-Haimendorf by
a Sherpa lama, the invocation is followed by "detailed descriptions of the gods"
(1964: 193). [The "informant thought that these were recited in order to prove
to the deities, believed to suspect their worshipers of being ignorant of their true
nature, that the lamas are well aware of their appearance and character" (ibid).]
A bit later, theoretically following the offering of the torma and the polluting
liquids, "the seat of the god is then described in detail" (194) — the seat presumably
being his heavenly realm and palace, as signified by the khil-khor upon which he is
also actually sitting. We also see, in a "hymn of praise" from a different text, translated by Waddell, careful attention to details of the deity's physical appearance —
face, hair, hand, foot — as well as his (actually "her"; the hymn in this case is to a
goddess) spiritual and magical powers (437). Thus there is great stress throughout
the textual material, which accompanies and directs the symbolic action, on the
outward physical forms the gods have taken.

Having boxed the poor fellow in, as it were, the second level provides those important entries — the senses — to the now shielded interior of his being. We saw that
the second-level offerings are representations of the senses, a point which is difficult
to comprehend except in the context of the present interpretation. So the ritual
action now gives him sight, hearing, smell, touch, etc., to render him susceptible to
the further machinations of the worshipers.

Finally, moving down to the third level, the outside offerings, the ritual action
stimulates and arouses the god with gentle sensuous offerings. His body is caressed
with cleansing and cooling waters, incense and flower scents are wafted before his
nose, softly glowing candles flicker before his eyes (the Sherpas explicitly think of
the light of butter lamps as a soft and gentle light), sweet music is sounded to his
ears, and he is fed a bit of delicately prepared food (the food torma) and drinking
water. At this point too, hymns in his praise are sung, caressing his pride as well.
Now, surely, he is at the worshipers' disposal.

For what has been done? He has been, it seems clear, turned into a human being,
trapped in a body and suffused with sensuous desires. And to prove it, he is now
invited to the tso feast, where the food is *real human food,* none of that torma and
incense business, but cooked rice and vegetables, sweet corn stalks and raw peas,
oranges and bananas, even packaged biscuits from the bazaar, and big jugs of beer.
The only indications of the divinity of the guest at this point are the fact that the
cooked rice is formed into the conical torma shape (and it is called a tso torma),
and the fact that the guest is courteously allowed to eat first.

The molding of anger

The demons, as we saw above, manifest and signify capricious and unpredictable anger and violence. The potential allies of humans in the struggle against the demons are the gods, but they are problematic too. The shiwa gods, in their state of blissful fulfillment, are utterly detached from the world, and indifferent to its affairs. The ferocious takbu gods, on the other hand, are the more logical allies of the people, because they are by definition engaged in the struggle with the demons — that is why they are ferocious. Yet if the takbu gods are already fighting the demons, why do people have to perform the ritual at all? To answer this we must recall that the takbu state is a special transformation on the shiwa state. *All* gods need nothing and are *fundamentally* fulfilled and blissful. Takbu gods are still gods; they presuppose and point to the fulfilled, self-contained state from which they came and to which they can return. The general tendency — the "pull," as it were — of the whole religious system is toward shiwa bliss; the implied threat of the takbu gods (and hence the precipitating factor of the ritual), is that they will abdicate their struggle, subside into bliss, and leave people at the mercy of the demons. According to one informant, discussing the seasonal offering rites performed by households, "If you don't do [these rites] the big gods will go away." And part of the refrain of this ritual, called out repeatedly by the householder at appointed moments in the lama's reading, means, according to the informant, "Please [gods] don't go away."

In short, the problem for the ritual is less to get rid of the demonic "enemies" (indeed, the exorcismic elements in these, compared to other Sherpa rituals, are marginal) than to stimulate the active support of the rather inert divine "allies." And this in turn, given the shiwa "pull" of the system, seems to be a matter not of making the gods "happy" (they are tending toward too much happiness already), but rather of making (or keeping) them angry. Indeed, as I will try to show in this section, we can observe over the course of the ritual a controlled and systematic arousal of — and, simultaneously, a particular shaping and formulation of — godly anger. I will return below to the difference between divine and demonic anger, to the doublethink of infuriating the gods while claiming to make them happy, and to the paradox of giving offerings to beings who "need nothing."

If we accept the notion that part of the problem is not only to combat capricious violence, but also to combat emotional detachment ("bliss"), then the whole first part of the ritual — in which the gods, contrary to their natures, are trapped in bodies, encased in heavy material forms, fed, and otherwise polluted — can be seen as an attempt to infuriate the gods, to rouse them to passionate reaction. We must recall the general attitude concerning the body in Buddhist and Sherpa thought — it is the agency of desire ("attachments"), which is the source of frustration, which is the source of anger. Thus bodying the gods, and providing various things to sustain and fortify their bodies (the semen and menstrual blood, the food) must be assumed to anger them, if the body → attachments → frustration → anger logic has any force. And following the offering of the altar to the gods, the worshipers perform prostrations, theoretically as apologies for past offenses, but conceivably as apologies for polluting and angering the gods within the ritual itself.

While the above points are somewhat speculative, or at least merely deductive, the arousal and shaping of godly anger can be seen quite clearly in the so-called Hymns of Praise, read while the gods are consuming their offerings. The one text I have at hand is actually to a shiwa (blissful) goddess, Drolma, the highest goddess of the pantheon and a deity of personal mercy rather than demon killing. Even so, in it we see clearly the verbal shaping of the deity's anger and its orientation against the proper foes. The hymn begins, as is appropriate to Drolma, with praises to her mercifulness: "Deliveress sublime," "Rich . . . in pity's store," "Soother of our woe," etc. But then it modulates into stronger dispositions, getting down to the business that people (at least the Sherpas, if not all Tibetan Buddhists) tend to be at least as interested in as mercy and pity: power and fury against the demons.

> Hail to thy *tut-tārā huṅ* [her mantra]
> Piercing realms of earth and sky
> Treading down the seven worlds,
> Bending prostrate everyone!
>
> Hail! adored by mighty gods
> Indra, Brāhma, Fire and Wind
> Ghostly hordes and Gandharvas
> All unite in praising Thee!
>
> Hail! with Thy dread *tre* and *phat*
> Thou destroyest all Thy foes:
> Striding out with Thy left foot
> Belching forth devouring fire!
>
> Hail! with fearful spell *tu-re*
> Banishing the bravest fiends
> By the mere frown of Thy brows
> Vanquishing whole hordes of foes![16]

The text may be read as a symbolic device for shaping and orienting the deity's anger, read after the offerings have strongly aroused it, while she is eating the offerings. Even in these brief verses we can see that the goddess is read through a series of very specific modulations of her mood, each then directed against the various fiends and foes. First her mantra is said to "pierce" evil — it is sharp; then she "treads down" heavily; then she "belches fire" — broadcasting rage; then — perhaps so focused and controlled now is her anger — she "merely frowns" and it is enough to "vanquish whole hordes of foes." While one would certainly need to look closely at a range of similar texts, presumably they all have the same general form and intent.

The meaning is carried not only by the words, but by the other media of the ritual — the physical manipulation of the altar items and other ritual instruments by the lamas, the prescribed hand gestures (*mudra*) made by the lamas as they read, and the music that weaves through the reading. The music is probably of paramount importance, and unfortunately here I am not competent to offer an analysis analogous to the one just suggested for the text. The pace and intonation of the chanting varies with different parts of the texts; in some places there are recognizable and repeated melodies with which the lay people often hum along. The percussion instruments — large drum and bells — sometimes accompany the chanting, and again people recognize and tap along with some of the rhythms. From time to time the full orchestra plays. The orchestral music is sometimes a series of extended chords, even in length and rhythm, and sometimes accelerating melodies that begin with long deep blasts upon the alpine horns, then build to a cymbal-clash climax. All of this, it may be argued, conveys to the worshipers the intent of the text concerning the moods of the gods and their readiness for encounters with the demons. Indeed, the music is probably the primary vehicle through which the unlettered layman may understand and experience the divine mood conversions taking place.

It does not take much imagination to suggest that what is being manipulated here are the moods of the worshipers themselves. I have already described the culturally engendered problems the Sherpas have in dealing with anger; given the general prohibition upon its expression, there are few structures within which a Sherpa learns to comprehend and order his unruly feelings. The ritual lays out these moods in pure archetypal forms — the absolute detachment and self-contained bliss of the gods, the absolute violence of the demons. It then proceeds to transform bliss itself into anger or violence, but of a controlled and focused sort that can triumph over the uncontrolled violence of the demons. The rite is hence both a "model of" a complex emotional state — let us call it positive anger, or an anger of commitment — for which few models are provided in ordinary Sherpa life (or perhaps in any life), and a "model for" achieving such a state.

It is important to be clear on this point: I am not saying that the rite simply provides some sort of symbolic outlet or catharsis for repressed anger that has no avenues of expression in the culture. What I am saying is that, as indicated above, although the Sherpas experience much anger, and in fact express it (or explode with it) not infrequently, they have very few resources for understanding or dealing with it in any systematic way. Both their own and others' bad moods, not to mention rages, are largely mysterious to themselves. The rite provides a symbolic vehicle not only for the expression of those moods, but for their structuring: One participates in a sequence over the course of which one's feelings are sorted, as it were, into the elements of a morally approved pattern, and the achievement of this patterning is the resolution of the "problem of anger." If this discussion is accepted, it would explain why the rite seems more concerned with *building* anger (in the gods) than with *destroying* it (in the demons). For it is at least as important, given this thesis, to experience how and of what one's mood is constructed, as to dissipate it; indeed, that is the condition for overcoming it.[17]

But this is not all that the ritual is about. It would distort it as much to reduce it solely to this "subjective function" of providing a template for the structuring of emotional states, as it would to reduce it to the social function of dramatizing (say) the proper relationship between monk and laity, although as suggested above, it might also be doing some of the latter. We must not lose sight of the fact that this is a religious ritual; its religious import remains to be delineated.

Hospitality: mediating religion and the social order

Religion can be minimally defined as a metasystem that solves problems of meaning (or Problems of Meaning) generated in large part (though not entirely) by the social order, by grounding that order within a theoretically ultimate reality within which those problems will "make sense." At the same time it must be realized that religion, by virtue of being a metasystem that is separate from and yet addressed to the social order, itself engenders paradox, contradiction, and conflict. When one says that religion is an autonomous element of a sociocultural system, one is not saying that it floats free of a social base; one is simply saying that while it is responding to (both "reflecting" and attempting to solve) some problems, it is creating others.

By making offerings to their gods in the idiom of social hospitality, the Sherpas are saying something about both their social order and their religious order. Sherpa hospitality, as we have seen, is a vital element of the Sherpa social process, yet it is also fraught with problems. It is a locus, for the participants, of complex feelings and moods that are disturbing in other areas of life, and disastrous in this particular context — a context intended to be pleasing, soothing, and productive of social cooperation. Further, hospitality has the problem of being implicitly denigrated by the religious devaluation of sensuality, a point that ultimately calls into question the entire morality of secular existence. At the same time, from that secular perspective, hospitality opens a serious question concerning the morality of the *religious* world view and ethos, for it is hospitality that, according to the culture, renders people cooperative and mutually supportive, as opposed to a religious orientation in which it is every man for himself, pursuing his own salvation.

Actually, the religious critique of the social order, specifically of hospitality practices, and the social critique of the religious order, have more subtle and detailed dimensions. Let us look a bit more closely at both.

Even if we grant, as certain defenders of Sherpa religion might well argue, that the religion does not utterly devalue sociality as such, it can at least be argued to take the following stance: The trouble with the social order, as it is normally lived, is that people treat it as an end in itself. Entertaining, feeding, helping one's neighbors are not ipso facto wrong or irreligious, but they become so when used primarily as means to personal self-enrichment and self-aggrandizement, and this is how they are normally used. What the religion might claim to be criticizing is only a certain *mode* of sociality, namely, "interested" as opposed to "disinterested" giving. One should live the social order, enact its forms, in the name of some higher good; the ideal is to give with no thought of material gain, to give as a meritorious act. One's own merit will not only improve one's fate, but also increase the general

store of merit in the world and thus contribute to world salvation. The right kind of
sociality, "disinterested" benevolence, reestablishes one's contact with this higher
moral order, regrounds one in the religious cosmos, and ennobles all one's words,
thoughts, and deeds.

These points of the religious critique of the Sherpa social order clarify a number
of issues about gods and demons. In the first place we can see that, among other
things, the demons are bad because they represent the worst form of the wrong
kind of sociality: They make demands upon others (by making people sick and
demanding ransom for the patient's health) for their own trivial, personal ends —
the pure pleasure of food and other rewards. Second, we can see why divine takbu
anger is "good" while demonic anger is "bad": takbu anger by definition is directed
against the demons in their role of enemies of the moral system, while demonic
anger represents petty rage at personal frustration. Takbu anger is universalistic,
concerned with a relatively disinterested defense of the system; demonic anger is
particularistic, because even their enmity toward the religion is based on the fact
that the religion limits their activities and frustrates their desires. (The problem
from the other point of view is that the takbu gods' anger, though more social and
"engaged" than the shiwa gods' bliss, is still too abstract; takbu gods defend the
system but not the people. I will return to this in a moment.)

Finally, the distinction between interested and disinterested giving helps solve
the central paradox of the ritual: We can understand how Sherpas could reconcile
or at least rationalize giving offerings to beings who "need nothing." When one
feeds people who are needy, one is potentially playing upon their need, and banking
(almost literally) on their gratitude as insurance for future favors. When one feeds
beings who need nothing,[18] one's aims are theoretically purer. One's gift is humble
in relation to their wealth, it is more literally a sacrifice, and effaces rather than
aggrandizes oneself. In fact, of course, this is not the spirit in which the ritual is
conceptualized by the lay people, but technically it can be used, and was used by
lama informants, to rationalize the paradox of offering material things to totally
fulfilled gods.

From the secular point of view, on the other hand, the fine distinctions between
good and bad — interested and disinterested — sociality that the religion might be
claiming to make are probably largely lost. While secular criticism of the religion is,
as was noted, very rarely heard, it seems clear from all our discussions that the
religion may appear to the lay perspective extremely antisocial, and hence virtually
immoral. It appears to devalue all those social forms that render people cooperative
and helpful among themselves, and that in fact make Sherpa social life possible. If
people and demons are too "interested," the gods are too "disinterested." The gods
from this point of view thus represent all the tendencies of Sherpa religion that
encourage the pursuit of one's own salvation while ignoring the needs of others, a
salvation which, moreover, itself consists of utterly self-contained, asocial bliss.
They represent everything from the doctrine itself, to the monks who live its tenets,
to the villager who seems unresponsive to social forms and does not fulfill his social

responsibilities. In theory, the only "help" for people that the religion sanctions is help-by-example, the showing of the way to salvation by reincarnate bodhisattvas and monks. The ritual says that this is not enough. The gods must be actively engaged on behalf of humanity, and if it takes a bit of magic and manipulativeness — a judiciously chanted coercive mantra, a dose of pollution, some well-phrased flattery — so be it.

The Sherpa ritual of making offerings to the gods, cast in the idiom of social hospitality, is an attempt to deal with all these problems. The symbolism of the ritual catches up and reworks the issues so as to render a different judgment upon each. Through the symbolic process of the ritual, as I will try to indicate in this final section, religion in the most general sense is made to be less selfishly oriented than it, in pure dogmatic form, appears to be, while secular life is made to be less sinful, self-interested, and mired in sensuality for its own sake than it, from the religious perspective, appears to be. The application of worldly forms — bodies, food, hospitality — to divine processes — engaging the gods to fight the demons — results in simultaneously rendering the religion more moral, and providing ultimate moral sanction for those worldly forms. The gods are rendered socially "engaged" rather than self-absorbed, while the forms of human existence are shown to contribute to the preservation of cosmic order, by functioning as the stimuli and vehicles for defeating those enemies of cosmic order, the demons.

The essence of this process would seem to lie in the relationships of encapsulation between the various levels of a symbol-work in the ritual. The core of the ritual, the central dynamic, is the transformation of the gods' mood from abstract bliss (present in takbu rites as a tendency, and by implication) through abstract anger (defending the system) to a final state which has the dual properties of anger against the demons and (and also because of) active benevolence toward humanity. That this emotional transformation is culturally, and not just analytically, the essential dynamic of the ritual, is evidenced partly by the fact that when one asks Sherpas why they do these rituals, the first answer is almost invariably "to make the gods happy." For a long time I treated this as an almost phatic statement, but I came to understand that the mood changes of the gods form the premises upon which everything else depends.

The whole system of mood states and transformations in the ritual, in turn, is carried by (encapsulated in, represented by, and often engendered by) the body symbolism. The lama molds the torma from formless dough to represent appropriate bodies for each of the gods of the ritual, and the formal elements of the torma (shape, color, decorations) are the major loci of visual representation of the shiwa/takbu mood distinction. Further, the differential treatment of the gods' and demons' torma exhibits the difference between godly and demonic anger, and deals differently with the two types: The demons' torma is thrown out of the temple and smashed, a gesture that both portrays their indiscriminate and scattershot violence, and wards it off by forcing them to scatter and chase the crumbs; the gods, on the other hand, are invited into their torma, a move which portrays the more focused and responsive nature of their dispositions, and which actually (as we saw) begins the transformation of their mood. Finally, and most importantly, through the sequence of first enticing the gods into the torma "bodies," then endowing them with organs of the senses, then stimulating those senses with the delicate "outside" offerings, the active anger of the gods is aroused. This anger thus becomes available for shaping in line with human modes of emotional response, and in relation to ends with which humans are concerned. In short, most of the visual development of the mood process of the ritual is carried by the treatment of the torma, that is, by the treatment of the body symbolism. And by having this critical symbolic role in effecting the success of the ritual, the body itself receives strong validation as a vehicle for moral action.

But the process is not complete. By endowing the gods with body, they are rendered human, but only in a very crude sense. They are still lacking that final critical dimension of humanity, sociality. The final transformation, then, is effected in two ways. In the first place, the tso is performed as the conclusion to the ritual. It is at the point of the tso that the gods have been symbolically brought as far as possible to the human state of corporeality and sensuousness, for here they are feasted with real human food as opposed to the divine foods of torma, incense, and the like. And the tso foods stand beyond and below the outer offerings of the altar, again indicating the point that the gods have been almost fully brought to the human state. But the critical point is that the tso feast is actually shared with the gods by the human worshipers, whereas the other altar items are not made part of any social feasting. In the tso, in other words, with its most explicit social hospitality ("party") format, the gods have finally become social allies. Only now can it truly be said that they have been humanized.

But the point of interest here is that, only at the point of the tso, when the gods have been as fully "humanized" as possible, are they finally asserted to be "happy." The tso is always said to be joyous, an expression and celebration of the final transformation of the gods to a positive, benevolent, and expansive mood, ready and eager to help humanity by doing battle with the demons. This conclusion to the ritual thus dramatizes the point that the human bodily state is, ideally, also a state of active benevolence vis-à-vis others, and, further, that both of these conditions — bodiness and benevolence — find their fullest and best means of expression in the context of a party, the context of social hospitality.

But if the only representation of hospitality in the ritual were in the tso, the moral attitude of the ritual toward hospitality would remain ambiguous. If the transformation of the gods to a state of sociality and active alliance with human concerns were merely the closing act of the body-and-mood-manipulation drama of the central part of the ritual, then hospitality would merely be the last in a string of clever tricks. The whole system of problems revolving around hospitality — its immorality from the religious point of view, and its challenge in turn to the ascetic ethic — would stand unreconstructed. But in fact the entire sequence of ritual action, from beginning to end, is encapsulated in an idiom of hospitality. The gods are cast as guests from the very outset of the ritual, and the development of their alliance with humans by the end is the product not (only) of cheap manipulation, but (also) of working through a full social event, from the manipulative invitation at the beginning to the establishment of mutual respect and at least temporary mutual trust by the point of parting. And the torma are not just bodies, trapping, irritating, and manipulating the moods of the gods; they are also food, tokens of social exchange in the creation of bonds of higher mutual interest.

With this, the full statement of the ritual on the problems with which it is concerned can be articulated. The thrust of the ritual, through its many layers, is simply to make the gods "human" — to make them corporeal, to make them susceptible to sensuous pleasure, to make them angry, to render them socially engaged, to get them to "help." The significance of this point is twofold: to validate the human modes of being and operating in the world, by showing their contribution to the preservation of cosmic order and not just to individual self-interest; and to "humanize" the religious order, that is, to counteract its essentially antisocial bias, by literally turning the gods into human beings and forcing them to become agents of direct social help and support. Put in other words, the ritual figuratively humanizes the religion, by literally humanizing the gods, while at the same time sacralizing the apparently irreligious and sinful social forms by having them serve as vehicles for a collective moral struggle.

In the process of this double movement, however, the various aspects of humanness that play a role in the ritual are themselves transformed and restructured. Anger in the ritual is developed and then transcended in a controlled and satisfying way. It achieves a complex structure that is neither the frustrated rage of the demons nor the abstract moralistic hostility of the gods toward the enemies of the faith. It becomes an anger of social commitment, generated by identifying one's own needs with the needs of one's social allies, and hence moving to a more universalistic (but still not totally abstract) mode of emotional response. As for the body, the sequence of ritual action shows a similar movement from treating it as an instrument of personal pleasure, to celebrating it as a vehicle of collective triumph over the forces of evil. And finally, the fact that the gods respond to the hospitality procedures, despite needing nothing and having no use at all for paltry human offerings, provides a model of the way in which hospitality should ideally be treated and responded to: in a spirit of essentially disinterested benevolence. The gods enter into social partnership with the people not because they needed all that food and felt obligated for having been satisfied by it, but in recognition of the goodness of the act of giving itself.

In sum, the religious ideal of "help" (as an abstract exemplification of The Way) is transformed downward by being integrated into a system of practical social alliance, while the lay social forms are transformed upward and brought into line with the religious ideal by being rendered more universalistic and stripped of simple self-interest. In these rituals, in other words, religion and society may be said to reach a compromise. But the great fragility of this compromise is attested to by the frequency with which it must be constructed and reconstructed, over and over, in the religious life of Sherpa villagers.

7. Conclusions: Buddhism and society

It seems fairly safe to say that orthodox, canonical Buddhism was a religion of and for individuals — or, to slant the point somewhat more strongly, a religion of anti-social individualism. In focusing its critique of the world on egotism, Buddhism highlighted and gave additional form, weight, and meaning to the very phenomenon it attacked. At the same time, all its solutions to the problem, while designed ultimately to eradicate the sense of personal ego, entailed further isolation of and attention to the individual. One who would be saved must renounce all ties of family, marriage, and wider social reciprocity. The quest for salvation is a matter of private mental exercises, and no one can help another in this quest. Further, the quest entails discovering that all the problems that seemed externally caused are really within one. Social life and social bonds are thus doubly devalued — they are trivialized (not the real causes of one's problems), and yet seen as insidiously destructive in enmeshing and blinding one, blocking awareness of truth.

There is, then, an a priori logic to the argument that Buddhism, given its premises, will be antagonistic to social life and will thus be problematic for lay people operating in religion's shadow. The Sherpa case seems to manifest this logic. Sherpa Buddhism, which in many respects can hardly be called orthodox, nonetheless retains the central Buddhist tendency to isolate and atomize the individual, and devalue social bonding and social reciprocity. Indeed it is hard to imagine how Buddhism could be Buddhism without retaining this bias. A Buddhism of social bonding and communal solidarity seems a contradiction in terms. And yet — such is the refractoriness of the empirical world in refusing to conform to our theoretical expectations — much of Southeast Asia has developed, in contrast to the Sherpas, precisely such a social, communal Buddhism. It is all the more ironic, again more from the theoretical point of view than from the people's own, that Sherpa Buddhism is part of the Mahayana tradition, supposedly a more socially concerned, "compassionate" form of the religion, while the Southeast Asian groups are within the Theravada tradition, supposedly more austerely focused on individual salvation.

In order to highlight the particularities of the Sherpa case, I will contrast it with a case from Thailand (documented by Tambiah). The comparison will not only demonstrate (if it still needs demonstrating) the weakness of a simple a priori argument, but will also generate an important question: If Buddhist societies need not sustain the individualistic bias of orthodox Buddhism, why then does Sherpa society do so? But first, the cases.

In the community of Baan Phraan Muan in northeast Thailand, the *wat* or monastery complex is located in the village, and lay people and monks are conceived to have close ties and reciprocal relations with one another. The lay villagers feed the monks daily, and the monks in turn make themselves available for regular and frequent merit-making ceremonies for the laity. There is a wat committee composed of the abbot of the wat and senior lay villagers. The villagers think of the wat as "our wat" and may hold ceremonies to honor and thank a respected monk for his services. Most of the monks are actually from the village.[1]

Among the Sherpas, on the other hand, monasteries are built in high and inaccessible places. They draw their recruits from many villages and have no established ties with any single one. Lay people and monks do not systematically interact. Monks are invited to the villages only for funerals, or for special meritorious activities such as a complete reading of the sacred canon, and the latter sort of event is quite rare and expensive. In both cases they are invited and paid by the individual family concerned. Lay people usually go to the monasteries only for major festivals. They may also go, as individuals or representatives of their families, to give donations and thus earn merit, but again this is relatively rare, and very much a matter of individual piety.

The contrast extends to the nature of the monastic calling in the two groups. In Thailand, monasticism is not expected to be a lifetime commitment. Virtually every young man receives ordination as a monk, but very few remain as lifetime monks. The vast majority leave the monastery after a few seasons, return to lay life, and get married. No stigma is attached to leaving the orders. Among the Sherpas, every one of these statements may be inverted. Few men take vows, but they are expected to stay a lifetime. To leave the monastery and get married after completing the vows incurs great sin for the monk, and a monk who has broken his vows brings pollution to the community. Monks and nuns who break their vows generally flee the area.

The contrast may also be drawn in terms of the emphases and forms of ritual action in the two areas. In the Thai case, Buddhist action is almost entirely preoccupied with merit making, and especially with feeding and giving gifts to monks. Above and beyond the daily feeding of monks, merit-making rituals are public and collective, and one of the most important of these is sponsoring and celebrating the collective ordination of village young men as monks in the village wat. Further, there is a systematic practice of transfer of merit, such that when one acquires merit one passes some of it on to family, to the dead, and to gods and evil spirits. Strict observation of Buddhist renunciations is not considered a powerful way of making merit for lay people.

The whole tone of Sherpa religious action is different.[2] Most lay religious energies go into attending, and sometimes sponsoring, the temple rituals of offering and exorcism, as well as the highly elaborate and lengthy funerals. A concern for active merit making is not pervasive, although it is always considered a good thing to make merit whenever one gets a chance. Monks are rarely fed or given alms by villagers, and are in fact supported by their families, although the Sherpas recognize this as a compensatory and unorthodox practice. Insofar as Sherpas do work actively at merit making in daily life, they do so in a distinctly unsocial way, through various forms of mechanical repetition, which may be performed entirely by the individual — spinning a prayer wheel, circumambulating a religious edifice, endlessly repeating a mantra — or by no agent at all — prayer mills turned by water and prayer flags blown by wind. Beyond these methods, the dominant model for merit making derives from the lives of monks, and involves observation of the Buddhist precepts of abstention from and prevention of sin. Thus the Sherpas have Nyungne, the holiday of atonement, on which individuals observe rules of fasting and silence, thus attaining the most merit possible within lay life.[3] And finally, the Sherpas do not systematically practice the transfer of merit; whatever merit one accrues, one keeps.[4]

One last contrasting point: It seems that the only major classical Buddhist deity with whom the Thai concern themselves is Maitreya, the loving savior who will eventually come and bring collective salvation. The Sherpas are much more theistic than the Thai, but they are quite uninterested in Maitreya, and in fact are quite uninterested in collective salvation.

Several things emerge from this brief comparison. The Thai case, which is quite representative of (though not of course identical with) large areas of Southeast Asia, demonstrates a relatively successful transformation of Buddhism into a rather social — exchanging, communal, solidarity-sustaining — religion. The a priori argument, predicting conflict between Buddhism and society from the antisocial premises of the doctrine, simply does not hold.[5] The comparison also highlights the relative orthodoxy of Sherpa Buddhism in a variety of practices, and more generally in the overall unsocial — nonexchanging, private, individualistic — bias that pervades all these practices. And finally, of course, the comparison strongly indicates that the relative orthodoxy of Sherpa Buddhism must itself be explained.

Part of the explanation must be located in historical facts. In Tibet, where the Sherpas originated and where their religion took the form that it retains for the most part today, the religion was supported by the theocratic state. State support of religion, in turn, allowed the monastic community to cut itself off from society more completely, because it was not directly dependent on the laity for support. Thus although Tibetan Buddhism absorbed a great many elements of popular religious practice and belief, it did not get involved in popular social life as such, as Thai Buddhism evidently had to do to survive. When the Sherpas, several centuries out of Tibet, became prosperous enough to begin to build monasteries, they continued the Tibetan model of establishing them outside society, without in fact having the political structure (centralized taxation) necessary to support them. This in turn has involved the Sherpas in the contradictory practice of having individual families support their monk sons, a contradiction the Sherpas themselves recognize, and the consequences of which remain to be seen.

Yet the historical explanation is not in itself adequate. About 300 years elapsed between the Sherpas' exodus from Tibet and the founding of the first Sherpa monasteries. While the Sherpas were in continuous contact with Tibet, commercially and religiously, during that period, surely even such contact would not have sustained the orthodoxy of Sherpa–Tibetan Buddhism if Sherpa society itself had not evolved structures within which these religious forms still seemed meaningful. A relatively orthodox, individualistic Buddhism, in other words, is sustained by the Sherpas not only for historical reasons, but because it remains experientially apt for them in relation to the contemporary structures of their world: The Sherpa social world, I have argued throughout the book, is itself quite atomized and individualistic. The explanation of Sherpa "orthodoxy", then, lies in those aspects of secular life that both express and produce these tendencies toward atomization and individualism, which I will now briefly recapitulate.

Beginning with the individual (as the Sherpas would probably begin), the view of human nature as basically stingy, greedy, materialistic, and almost exclusively self-interested is quite well established.[6] While these characteristics are considered near-universal (though of course lamentable), particular individuals may exhibit them to a particularly high degree. Stingy, mean-spirited, antisocial individuals, living and dead, are gossiped about: X who never entertains others at hospitality, Y who never contributes to temple events, Z who "never helped anyone," who "never gave anybody anything." Similarly, generous, good-hearted people are admired, discussed, and remembered, although the sense is that they are exceptional in kind, while the mean ones are exceptional only in degree. Yet there is some ambiguity about the factors that precipitate notable individual cases. Often a hereditary explanation is given — that a bad person is a product of much demerit in a past life, or, in a less religious vein, a product of what we would call bad blood. Sometimes, however, there is a social explanation — that a good person has experienced suffering as a child and so understands the necessity of compassion for others. In any case, however, the stories of selfish and generous individuals both highlight the cultural concern with individualistic/egotistical characteristics, and focus on individual natures as the primary location of these tendencies.

At the social structural level, the significant unit of exchange or nonexchange within the community is the private-property-holding nuclear family household. Families as units may be characterized as particularly generous or stingy, like individuals, and gossip about actual or remembered antisocial families plays a significant role in sustaining such a view. More important, however, is a whole series of cultural devices and social practices that both reflect and reproduce the tendency toward closure of the family/property unit. Beliefs about "bad-luck days," on which the family must not engage in exchange at all, and beliefs and practices about family "luck" that may drain away, and that should be periodically shored up and revitalized through ritual, reinforce the sense that families should be and will be relatively closed and cautious about social exchange and social bonding. Further, families are slow to give up their children in marriage, taking time to get together the son's inheritance or the daughter's dowry, and gaining cultural support for such foot dragging from the fact that the marriage process may entail five or six distinct — and expensive — phases. Eventually, of course, marriages are made and new families formed, although there are cases in which the parents never formally give their children the economic and ritual independence of marriage.

If individuals and families tend toward social closure and resistance to exchange, the dominant exchange strategy in lay society both reflects and reproduces these tendencies. The strategy is yangdzi, which entails softening up the hardness of others through gifts — traditionally beer — to gain their cooperation. Yangdzi is based on the assumption that the other will be resistant to one's request, and unmovable by purely moral/social appeals; hence the need for the gift. Further, it has the form of a finite contract such that there are no residual ties or bonds between the parties once the terms of the transaction have been fulfilled. Yangdzi operates at the level of individuals, overcoming their presumed closure to one's appeals for goods or assistance, and it also operates at the level of families: The marriage process may be described as a sort of giant extended yangdzi, as the groom's group brings the bride's group increasingly elaborate gifts of beer and food to persuade them to part with their daughter. And just as yangdzi leaves individuals independent after the fulfillment of the contract, so it does with families, where once the new couple has finally been established, there are no residual bonds between their respective groups. While there are in fact long-term mutual-aid groups in Sherpa society, the mutual-aid idiom has a restricted application, and is not extended to other sorts of relationships. The gods, as we have seen, are dealt with in the yangdzi mode, rather than being invoked as mutual-aid partners. Thus yangdzi — finite contractual reciprocity between independent units — has ideological and practical hegemony over other forms of exchange.[7]

The notion, often borne out in practice, that individuals tend to be selfish; the culturally encouraged closure and idealized autonomy of the private-property-based nuclear family; and the dominance of short-term exchange contracts over enduring reciprocity relations; these, very briefly, sketch the dimensions of individualism or social atomism in secular Sherpa society. Thus the individualistic bias of Sherpa Buddhist orthodoxy is grounded in the structures of the Sherpa social world.

Yet Buddhism claims to be opposed to all the structures of worldly social life, and I have suggested that the Sherpas perceive the religion as antagonistic, and struggle against it in their rituals. It now seems possible to say, however, that the Sherpas' "struggle" with their religion is partly a struggle with those aspects of their own society that in fact make them such good Buddhists. From this point of view religion is merely functioning as a lightning rod for ills of the social order itself. The real threat to the fabric of Sherpa society is not, as religion would have it, some form of violent demonic anarchy, but the tendencies toward isolation and atomization, generated largely by the family/property structure, and imaged not by the demons but by the gods. Individualism permeates social life, and insofar as religion merely reflects and objectifies this problem in its images, rituals, and cosmology, it merely operates as a focus of discontent, and provides a language through which to restructure experience of these socially based problems.

But we have seen quite clearly that religion is more than merely a symbolic language for social problems: It is itself a force in generating and/or sustaining those problems, and as such it too comes under attack. Buddhism both describes certain stresses of Sherpa society and prescribes for them in ways that do little to undermine and indeed much to reinforce the structures that generate them. Its emphasis on the spiritual virtues of individual isolation, its psychologistic interpretations of causes, its symbolic idealization of the family, its bias against reciprocity and sustained social bonding – all these are not, for the Sherpas, abstract or esoteric doctrines, but are experienced as powerful confirmations of the world in which they find themselves. Departing from social actuality, the Buddhist vision of the world does what, analytically, we assume religion to do: It completes it.

Secular Sherpa life, while premised on culturally defined and structurally induced tendencies toward individual selfishness and family insularity, nonetheless must and does overcome these tendencies by social means. The Buddhist ideal, on the other hand, involves intensification and idealization of the isolation of individuals. Given this, I have argued that the struggle in ritual is not merely against social problems through a medium of religious symbols that reflect those problems, but against religion itself as a force in hardening the overall structure of the Sherpa world.

The Buddhist ideal is enacted by the self-involved monastic community, and the Sherpas' ambivalence about monks is expressed in the lay people's lack of enthusiasm for alms giving, and their failure adequately to support their monasteries. But the monks are largely out of sight and even out of mind; the primary agents of high religious ideology within lay life are actually the rituals. Here the individualistic ideology is rarely overtly preached, but rather is structured into the imagery and the symbolic progressions in ways that are experienced, over the course of hundreds of participations, rather than directly perceived. In this way, the Buddhist modes of seeing, feeling, interpreting, categorizing, and so forth, all of which assume/demand a highly private, highly psychologized, antisocial self, are constantly and systematically fed into lay experience.

But if the rituals are the primary conduits of high ideology, they are also the primary arenas for symbolically confronting that ideology, and rendering it more compatible with lay life. To conclude this book, then, I return to the set of rituals already analyzed, to highlight the subtleties of both sides of this process.

The ritual mechanism

It has been argued, at least since Weber's (1964, 1958a) studies of the sociological implications of world religions, that what is involved in popular sacrifices and the like is mediation between the "other-worldly" focus of orthodoxy and the "this-worldly" needs of the people, a mediation between what might be called "later" and "now." But this formulation is somewhat misleading. In the case of Sherpa Buddhism, both orthodox and lay perspectives share the perception that suffering derives from egotism/individualism. They diverge, however, both in their diagnoses of the causes of the problem, and in their formulations of the solution. Where the religion sees the causes as subsocial (in human nature) and the solutions as extra-social (literally, moving out of society), the lay perspective may be said to retain at least a suspicion that the problem has social roots, and in any case a rather strong conviction that it can and must be overcome by social means. It is thus not a matter of short-term ritual stopgaps handling immediate problems that religion is too lofty and future-oriented to bother with, but rather a matter of ongoing nego-tiation, as it were, between two visions of the relationship between social and spiritual life.

We may begin by recalling the classic Buddhist stance on the sources of personal suffering. Suffering derives in the first instance from what are seen as natural pro-cesses — physical needs, sensuous desires, and the natural tendency to develop "attachments" to things and persons that gratify those needs and desires. It is denied that social relations are the root causes of the problems of human existence. Yet the religiously prescribed means of overcoming "natural" egotistical tendencies in fact require changing one's social relations, thus suggesting that society has some-thing to do with it after all. The lurking contradiction is handled by arguing that social problems — with family, with superiors and inferiors, with neighbors — while not causal, strongly complicate matters by blinding one, in their immediacy, to the deeper inner causes. Thus the religious point is to get beyond or beneath the social, and social symbolism seems to be present in some Sherpa rituals precisely to be transcended, superseded by more "profound" categories of perception and awareness.

The point can be glossed by saying that the ideological thrust of Buddhism is to "desocialize" all human problems — to render them through a radical shift of per-spective as generically natural, aspects of the normal, unilluminated, existential condition. This thrust is in sharp contrast to many premodern societies, where the ideological and ritual thrust seems to run in the direction of rendering, as far as possible, even the most intractable existential problems as social. The most drama-tic case in point is the cultural construal of illness and even death in such societies as entirely socially caused — proximately if not ultimately — through witchcraft, sorcery, and the like. It is not insignificant that Sherpas hold such "primitive" notions, but they are not validated by Sherpa Buddhist ideology. According to the lamas (who are not always consistent on this point), witches, ghosts, and the like only plague those with low religious consciousness, and Sherpa monks, by their own statements, are not bothered by such illness-causing beings, who only operate down in the villages.

There are several ways in which largely social problems are reinterpreted in wholly nonsocial terms. Natural physical aspects may be stressed, as when the problem of old age is seen in terms of physical weakness and/or approaching death, rather than in terms of social abandonment and economic insecurity. Or the problem may be seen as generated by lowly aspects of psychological "human nature" – greed and the like – rather than by social structures that engender competitiveness and materialism. And in both cases, the solution is essentially to raise one's spiritual consciousness, rather than to reorder social relations. I shall, for convenience, label all these modes of nonsocial interpretation and prescription – the physical, the psychological, and the spiritual – as "existential" stances, collectively opposed to a social stance. And, as noted, these are the stances of Buddhist orthodoxy.

It is in light of these points that we may understand the major sense in which the corpus of village rituals "mediate" between orthodox views and secular experience: Each of the rituals constructs a different permutation of the relationship between the social and the existential as both causes of and solutions to one's ills. Specifically, in Nyungne (Chapter 3) the Buddhist "pull" toward desocializing and existentializing actors' problems most fully prevails, with the appropriate psycho/spiritual solution. Exorcisms (Chapter 5) are more complicated, but as we have seen, the orthodox perspective prevails in the end. Offering rituals (Chapter 6), on the other hand, go the other way: The pull is from the existential to the social. We must now reexamine the rituals as a set, to highlight these progressions in the rites themselves.

It may be noted first that people participate in Sherpa rituals as individuals, rather than as members of particular groups, or representatives of particular social categories.[8] Thus social phenomena – institutional structures, roles, relationships – are not *in* the rituals, except via two mediations: They are alluded to by ritual symbolism in various ways, and they are embodied in the structures and contents of consciousness with which actors arrive at the rituals.

The first ritual complex analyzed was Nyungne, the days of atonement on which individuals, generally old people, retire to the temple, observe rules of fasting and silence, and concentrate on achieving identification with the all-compassionate god Cherenzi. Nyungne is the most orthodox of the lay rituals, and its structure embodies the ideal Buddhist progression of consciousness, whereby one is moved from an experience of social embeddedness to a sense of one's problems as purely existentially generated and hence spiritually soluble. Nyungne is designed to produce true Buddhist individuals, socially detached, expecting nothing from others and giving nothing to others.

I analyzed Nyungne in terms of the social problems of late adulthood in Sherpa society, a situation of perceived, and often virtual, abandonment of parents by children. These problems of family betrayal and generalized lack of social support are initially refocused, however, by the very rules of observance of the ritual, in terms of the individual's lamentable physicality, one's lowly animal needs for food and drink. Natural biological weakness is immediately foregrounded as a major dimension of the problem, the solution to which becomes, according to the ritual, a matter of private spiritual will, the ability to control one's urges through fasting.

At the same time the ritual recognizes, in its symbolism, that one's problems at least have social accessories. The social allusions of Nyungne symbolism are to the family, in the prescribed prostrations to the parental god Konjok, and in the aim of identification with the parental god Cherenzi. The point however is to get beyond these, in Buddhist terms, mediate sources, to transcend them and arrive at a higher consciousness and understanding. And the mechanism for achieving this transcendence is built into the structural development of the ritual itself, in a form of dialectical progression. That is, the participant is guided by the narrative sequence into identifying successively with *both sides* of the problematic relationship, thus finally identifying with neither and transcending the whole struggle. The participant enters as (real) parent. He or she is then recast, through prayer and obligatory prostrations, as dependent worshiper/child vis-à-vis a parent-figure god. And finally, he or she achieves identification with the transcendental deity, the personification of the attitude of great religious compassion. By forcing actors to take both perspectives of a given social-structural antagonism (in this case parent–child), the ritual succeeds in divesting them of interest in either side, placing them beyond the social, as it were, in the universalistic, indiscriminate compassion of the gods.

Nyungne is entirely a vehicle of orthodox ideology, bearing the orthodox interpretation of and solution to one's woes in its rules of observance and its final apotheosis. Its focal deity Cherenzi (Avalokiteśvara) is one of the Sherpa trinity of high Buddhist deities, along with Ongpame (Amitabha) and Guru Rimpoche (Padma Sambhava). Cherenzi is the only one of the trinity directly worshiped in the entire ritual calendar, and achieving identification with him thus signifies an utter identification with the high orthodox perspective. But the orthodcxy of the rite is also encoded in its "existentializing" progression, a progression that brings about a deinvestment in the problematic social relationship, transcendence of "petty" social antagonisms, and movement into a diffuse religious state of consciousness that is neither generated by specific others nor directed to specific others.

The second ritual complex analyzed was the extended set of exorcism rites that follows a funeral, and that also forms part of the major annual festivals of both village temples and monasteries. The problem for the ritual(s) is to cleanse pollution that has accumulated in the form of greedy cannibalistic demons. In the first stage, clown figures dressed in "poor clothes" run an effigy containing the trapped demons out of town, and the effigy is hacked to pieces. This ritual is highly popular, but is considered somewhat unorthodox, or at least "low." The lamas say that it is wrong to chop up the effigy because one can't really kill demons anyway, one can only placate them. Thus there is almost always a second stage to the exorcism, in which a more orthodox (Tibetan Buddhist) format is used. In this, effigies of human beings are constructed and dressed in jewels and finery, and eventually set out as food offerings to the demons, in place of the human flesh and blood they were seeking.

Taking the cue from the poor clothing of the clowns and the rich finery of the food effigies, I analyzed the rituals in part as dealing with problems of economic inequity in the community, conceptualized by the Sherpas as the distinction between the big people and the small. From this analytic point of departure, it is possible to see in the ritual a dynamic similar to that in Nyungne, a process of desocializing and existentializing actors' experience of the problem, in this case the problem of rich and poor. The onlookers first identify with the clowns, that is, with figures of poverty who are nonetheless powerful against the demons. In the second phase, however, the locus of identification shifts to the richly dressed anthropomorphic effigies, explicitly representing the people. Thus here again the ritual progression moves one's identification from one to the other element of a problematic social structure, in this case from the poor to the rich. The effect is to divest one of interest in either status, especially because the locus of one's second identification, the rich effigy, gets fed to the demons. Feeding the effigy to the demons in turn represents one's ability to rise above a clinging to one's own body and one's own material attachments, and to achieve a stance of pure spirituality, above "petty" concerns with mortality and worldly goods.

Again, then, the ritual carries an orthodox structural progression from the social to the existential, from an "interested," particularistic perspective within the social structure, to a disinterested transcendental perspective chiefly concerned with the purity and survival of one's soul. In addition, the final act of the second exorcism entails placing an idol of a god where the effigy of mortal humans had stood, the effigy now having been fed to the demons. Thus the final moment is implicitly one in which the people, having transcended their attachments to physicality and materialism, now "become" gods. As in Nyungne, then, people come to identify with the gods at the end, although the point is less stressed.

In both the movement toward identification with the gods, and in the structural progression from the social to the existential plane, exorcisms, like Nyungne, embody what we may call the orthodox "pull." Even though, unlike Nyungne, these rites are not concerned with salvation but are primarily oriented toward "this-worldly" protection of lay people from demons, the Buddhist dynamic operates. Partly this is explicable by the linkage of exorcisms with death, and the particular power and appeal of Buddhist orthodoxy in the context of death. People are vulnerable to its message about the necessity for deinvesting in the material world in preparation for their own postdeath fates.

Yet while we can see these orthodox tendencies in the exorcisms, we can see at the same time a certain infusion of lay interests, a certain pull against orthodoxy toward a more social perspective. In the first exorcism the point is quite overt: The people try to defeat the demons directly, rather than through the agency of the gods. But because the people use violence, they scarcely rise above the level of the demons themselves, and the rite does not (according to some lamas) succeed. Thus there is a second, more orthodox, exorcism, which I analyzed as a corrective to the first. If it were consistent with highest orthodox theory, it would express the view that the demons are really projections of the psyche, to be conquered metaphorically and spiritually rather than literally and materially. This view, however, is known only to the highest adepts, and so the rite merely stresses that people must feel compassion for the demons rather than hate, and therefore must feed them to get them to depart.

Here then the ritual employs a social mode for solving the problem, although because one feeds the demons a representation of one's own body, the apparently social act has a spiritual meaning: transcendence of physical attachments and of concern for mortality. Yet because one feeds the demons as social others, because they remain external and are not treated as psychological entities to be transcended through meditation, the act remains a significant compromise with the lay social perspective.

Finally, I analyzed the generalized rites of offering to the gods, held to insure their continued protection of the community against the demons. In these rites, the gods are conjured into "bodies," represented by conical dough figurines (torma), and are then fed and praised and petitioned for their ongoing support. While the gods are theoretically guardians of the people and the community, their tendency is toward a certain inertia, such that they will not engage in demon fighting unless prodded to do so by human ritual efforts. I argued that the gods could be taken to symbolize the socially disengaged monastic community, and more generally the entire religious ethic in its stress on personal disentanglement from social bonds and obligations. And because these rituals, through a socially defined hospitality process of feeding and pleasuring the gods, succeed in fact in engaging them in at least temporary alliance with people, the offering rites may be seen as most thoroughly pulling the system in the direction of lay interests and experience. Where the movement in the other rites is toward an unsocial, transcendental stance, here the movement is in the opposite direction, hitching the gods and the religion to the social process, and doing so by means of the most standard mode of sociality in the culture.

The thoroughness of the imposition of the lay perspective in these rites may be seen in many aspects. First, not only is hospitality used to solve the ritual problem, but it is used not on the demons but on the gods themselves. Because demons are already "social," albeit in the worst — predatory — way, feeding them does not introduce a radical new dimension into their beings. For the unsocial gods, however, it actually pulls them into a whole new mode of intercourse, and establishes the appropriateness of social practice directly against the orthodox ideal of social withdrawal.

Second, we can perhaps see within the symbolism a progression from the existential plane to the social, rather than the other way around. The point hinges on the relationship between the food meanings and the body meanings of the offerings. In exorcisms the dough effigies fed to the demons signify the human body, but feeding them to the demons has a higher meaning of transcendence of attachment to mortal life: *Food* signifies *body*, and the sacrifice of body signifies *human transcendence.* In offering rituals, on the other hand, the tormas' initial significance is as bodies that trap the gods in physicality, but then as the rite progresses their significance as food in a hospitality process becomes dominant: *Body* becomes *food,* and the gods' consumption of food signifies *divine debasement.*

Finally there is the point that, where in Nyungne and exorcisms the people end up identifying with the gods, in offering rituals the gods wind up identifying with the people. The final stage of the offering rites is always the tso, a feast shared by both gods and human community. The tso consists of inviting the gods to feast on ordinary human foods – rice, chips, fruit, vegetables, biscuits, beer – after they have consumed their more divine offerings, and these ordinary foods are then distributed equally among all the worshipers. Where in Nyungne the people, like the gods, show that they need no material sustenance, in offering rituals the gods, like the people, eat a hearty human meal, including the ritually essential beer with all its meanings of social contract and social exchange.[9]

The three rituals thus manifest three possible articulations between orthodox and secular perspectives. In Nyungne, an observance oriented toward salvation, in which the people become "like monks," orthodoxy prevails in its interpretation of the causes of suffering, and in its solutions to it. It is not irrelevant that this is the most poorly attended of village rituals. In offering rituals, on the other hand, the secular perspective most fully prevails. Social hospitality is the mechanism for solving the problems the ritual deals with, and the gods are made to identify with the people. Exorcisms, finally, most fully manifest the struggle between the two perspectives, although the orthodox perspective, for reasons discussed, prevails in the end.

Exorcisms are the most distinctive rites of the Sherpas' Nyingmawa sect, and both monasteries and villages stage annual full-scale exorcisms in which the roles of the gods conquering the demons are danced and enacted. I have not analyzed these full-scale festivals, but their theme is the reenactment of the original struggle and triumph of the religion against the demons, in the conversion of the Sherpas' ancestors to Buddhism. When Sherpas first explained these rites to me in these terms, saying that they were celebrating the long-ago triumph of the religion, I tended to discount the explanation and search for more contemporary issues to which the rites could be seen to be addressed. It was not at all clear why the ancient success of Buddhism, now apparently so firmly established, needed to be celebrated or legitimated in any way. Yet if the analyses and arguments of this book are accepted, we must now take the Sherpas' primary explanation of their greatest festivals more seriously. Buddhist orthodoxy is indeed regularly challenged by "demons" – by the "low consciousness" of lay people who do not enthusiastically support their monks, and by the ritual practices that "socialize" the gods into worldly forms and concerns. And the rites really *are* about the struggle and would-be triumph of Buddhism against these demons, not long ago, but today. The religion must annually reassert its claims to people's allegiance and dependence, reconquer its "foes," and reestablish its hegemony. At the climax of the Mani-Rimdu festival, when the monks (as gods) stab the quite anthropomorphic demon effigy in a hell-shaped triangular box, the crowd roars the traditional cry, *"Hler gyaló!*, May the gods triumph!"* And each year they do, but not without a challenge.

Notes

1. Introduction: some notes on ritual

1 Of course there are other relevant approaches that I pass over here. A major variant of the approach through cultural performance is an approach through a key text, as in Weber's (1958b) use of a long excerpt from Benjamin Franklin's diary to launch a discussion of the spirit of capitalism. Another rather different method entails the ethnographer's selection of "key symbols," which are then "unpacked" for the complex of meanings they condense, and which are shown to underlie, organize, and illuminate a variety of social and cultural structures and processes. (See Ortner, 1973b; Schneider, 1968; V. Turner, 1967.)

2 Closely relevant works include: Lévi-Strauss (1963a), V. Turner (1967, 1969), Geertz (especially 1957a, 1972), Munn (1969, 1971), T. Turner, Warner, and Myerhoff. Yalman's (1964, 1966, 1969) more structuralist approach to ritual is analogous to, but not identical with, the approach utilized here. Kenneth Burke's work in "dramatistic" analysis of literature (e.g., 1957, 1968) is an indispensable source outside of anthropology.

3 Geertz is more interested in what might be called convergence, rather than narrative, processes — the ways in which the whole complex of elements within, say, a ritual, combine to create a certain quality of perception, feeling, and understanding.

2. The surface contours of the Sherpa world

1 All historical data from Oppitz.

2 The Nepalese government has also recently completed a 90-mile road running westward from Kathmandu to Pokhara, and the Chinese are currently contributing, as part of their foreign aid to neutral Nepal, to the construction of another large road segment.

3 The *Encyclopaedia Britannica* (1974) puts the number of Sherpas at 85,000, which is way off the mark. It is probably based on regional (rather than ethnic) breakdowns in the Nepalese census.

4 The use or nonuse of terracing seems also culturally, and not just ecologically, determined.

5 All of the so-called Hillary schools have now (1976) been taken over by the Nepalese government. Unfortunately, the quality of education provided in them seems to have declined, as the government has less resources for their support (or has chosen to devote less resources to their support).

6 There has been an expansion of vegetable cropping in both Solu and Pharak.

More field area is now (1976) devoted to it, and new varieties — especially cabbage and cauliflower — are being grown.

7 James Fisher, returning from Khumbu in 1974, told me that Khumbu men earning much cash in mountaineering work are now hiring Solu men to come north and work their fields for cash wages (personal communication). This pattern, if it becomes widespread, could have far-reaching effects on the political–economic structure of Sherpa society.

8 See Goldstein, 1971a, 1971b, 1973, for discussion of various aspects of the structure.

9 In Khumbu in 1976 I witnessed a marriage between a man of a Sherpa clan and a woman of a well-off "Khamba" family. Nobody seemed at all bothered by this, and indeed the bride's family insisted on being referred to as Khambas in the wedding speeches because, as they said, "We have a country." Normally they were called by a term referring to the fact that they used to herd yaks for other families, whereas "Khamba" at least has a descent connotation, as a clan name does.

10 Consistent with the marriage norms, the cousin terminology is "Omaha" in type: One's father's brother's daughter and one's own sister are called by the same term, one's father's sister's daughter and one's sister's daughter are called by the same term, and one's mother's brother's daughter and one's mother's sister are called by the same term.

11 Oppitz reports a Dzemu case where the big people of the village made a *maksu* so uncomfortable that he gave up and went back home (91).

12 I was told, however, that there used to be a rule of groom service, for three years, three months, and three days.

13 See Miller, and Aziz (n.d.), for descriptions of the structure and functions of mutual-aid groups among Tibetans.

14 See note 5, this chapter.

15 The village as a collectivity theoretically has the power to exile people who commit serious polluting crimes, because the pollution could spread to the rest of the community. However, in all the cases I heard about, the offenders ran away out of shame before such a sanction could come into play.

16 Nonetheless, it might be noted that the central government has a somewhat negative attitude toward the Sherpas. They seem to resent the fame achieved by Sherpas in mountaineering and the Sherpas' popularity with Westerners who find them so congenial and romantic.

17 Barbara Aziz, returning from Solu in 1973, reported that the nunneries seemed to be enjoying some growth, and that the new head of Takshindo monastery was taking the unprecedented step of sending nuns along with monks to perform funerals in villages (personal communication). If these points indicate a genuine trend, it could have most interesting effects on the situation of women in Sherpa society.

3. Nyungne: problems of marriage, family, and asceticism

1 This description derives from observation of the ritual in Dzemu. There may be considerable local variation.

2 See Ortner, 1973a. The complete observance of Nyungne has the same generalized structure described below for all offering rituals: *sang*; invocation of the gods into their ritual bodies; presentation of the altar as offerings to the gods; paying respect to the gods and articulating the requests specific to the ritual, in this case

redemption from sin; and a *tso* party for gods and congregation at the end. But in Nyungne, although all the stages are gone through, the first three are minimized.

3 Von-Fürer-Haimendorf notes that all the Nyungne participants in Khumjung were barefoot (1964: 183). I also noticed that most village men had their hair cut (shaved off – the normal hair cut) just before the holiday.

4 Tib., *sPyan-ras-gzigs*. This is normally transcribed as Chenrezi, and apparently pronounced as such by Tibetans, but the Sherpas shift the nasalization as they do with many Tibetan words and names.

5 Some funerals use texts of shiwa gods, and some tso texts are to shiwa gods.

6 Saving any life is, of course, highly meritorious, and I do not mean to imply that Sherpas would make more of an effort to save a goat than a fellow human being. My point is simply that, when one asks people for examples of meritorious deeds, they often spontaneously first mention saving an animal that was going to be killed.

7 Culturally recognized variants include polyandrous families, which are nonetheless often functionally nuclear, as the husbands arrange to be alternatively absent (5%; polyandry is now illegal in Nepal); polygynous families, which again tend to be functionally nuclear, as each wife has a separate house, often in a separate village, with the husband visiting each alternately (3%); and the three-generation household – old parents, their youngest son and his wife, and the younger couple's children, which arrangements are not as common as they normatively should be, because the old parents tend to move out. (Statistics from Oppitz: 122.)

8 Compare with this passage from a Mahayana sutra: "There are four kinds of gratitude: (1) to the parents, (2) to other beings, (3) to rulers, (4) to the Three Treasures [i.e., the Triple Gem or Konjok Sum]" (Suzuki: 132).

9 On the derivation of Konjok: On the one hand there is the *Konjok Sum*, the "Triple Gem" of orthodox Buddhism: Buddha, Dharma, and Sangha, that is, the Buddha, the Doctrine, and "the Community." The last is now specified as the monastic community, although originally it referred to the entire community of adherents to the Doctrine. Because the basic and constantly recited vow of commitment to the faith is known as "taking refuge in the Triple Gem," the suggestion is conveyed that the Triple Gem (Konjok Sum) is a source of help and protection, a "refuge" in the bosom of which (or "of whom") one is sheltered and cared for. The idea that the Triple Gem is "a god," and in fact the ultimate god, has a long history in its own right in Tibet (see Ekvall: 65), but among the Sherpas it seems to draw sustenance from being confused with another triadic conception, the "Three Bodies" scheme (see below, note 14). Because the "Triple Gem" and the "Three Bodies" are both three-part schemes, the first a locus of "refuge," and the second an evolutionary scheme of emanations from a supreme creator, these seem to have merged in Sherpa thought as a divinity named Konjok with parental connotations.

10 The household among the Sherpas tends to be coterminous with the nuclear family, as noted, although Aziz (1974) points out that the household as a unit should be conceptually distinguished from the family in analysis of Tibetan social structure.

11 Saturday was the bad day in Rinzing's household, but because it was bazaar day, and a member of the family often needed to go shopping on Saturdays, Rinzing's mother would put the shopping money outside the house the night before. Saturday was also the bad day for Kamiu's household, and Kamiu would never sell me milk on those days. One Saturday, however, he was seen going to bazaar to sell a tin of butter, and sure enough, his horse broke its leg on the way and had to be killed.

12 It would be interesting to see whether luck-shoring ceremonies tended to be commissioned after a child got married — the major event of "drain" upon the family. (In Khumbu in 1976 I discovered, as this note had "predicted," a great deal of ritual business at weddings concerned with keeping the luck of the bride's household inside when she is departing for her husband's household.)

13 Sometimes such families get their comeuppance. Tsering's family lived in an isolated house up the hill from the village, and participated little in village social life. Their failure to volunteer to support temple rituals for as long as anyone could remember was always a good topic of gossip. One night Tsering's animal shed, attached to his house, caught fire. It was perfectly clear to the villagers that this was karmic retribution for the family's isolationist, antisocial history, although everyone of course rushed up the hill to put out the fire and save the house, which, amazingly enough, they succeeded in doing. Tsering was subsequently seen doing a lot of sheepish visiting and gift giving. People felt smugly satisfied that he had learned his lesson.

14 Skt., *trikaya*; Sherpa, *choku-lungku-tulku sum*. Cherenzi is the *lungku* of the system, the creator: "Three world cycles have passed; we live in the fourth cycle, of which Amitabha [Sherpa, Ongpame] was the author. The actual creator was Avalokiteśvara [Sherpa, Cherenzi], and the Sakyamuni, the historical Gautama Siddhartha, was the . . . Mortal Teacher." (Gordon: 30) The Sherpas as Nyingmawa-sect Tibetan Buddhists use the Guru Rimpoche, who converted Tibet to Buddhism, as the "Mortal Teacher," the *tulku*, in place of Gautama Buddha.

15 See Beyer for a discussion of Drolma worship in Tibet. It is extremely interesting to note that in East Asia Cherenzi is a female deity, Kwan-yin in China, Kwan-non in Japan. But in Tibetan Buddhism, as in classical Indian Buddhism, he retains his anomalous nature of being a male god with female attributes. He thus qualifies well for mediating a variety of oppositions. In the Tibetan system he is reincarnated in the Dalai Lama, the pope-king, mediator of the religious and secular realms.

16 Daughters are to her (and to the father) ultimately less important because they will leave, and indeed the mother–daughter relationship is not given much cultural significance, although no doubt many mothers and daughters develop close relationships.

17 One writer on the significance of Nyungne in Tibet stresses the fasting as almost the exclusive focus of the ritual (Schlagintweit: 240–2), and the name of the holiday actually simply means "fast" (*smung-gnas,* Jaeschke: 428).

18 There apparently was, at least in Solu, a tradition of groom service, which persists today not as a rule but as a matter of etiquette: The groom should help out from time to time on his in-laws' estate, as long as his wife is still living in her parents' home. Even if the groom has been given his inheritance and the bride has gone to live with him, she is still obligated to help her parents if they call her, until certain wedding rites (varying between Solu and Khumbu) have been completed. And it is her parents who will (or will not, as the case may be) set the dates for these rites, because they must pay for them.

19 Unless the couple is willing to go off and seek its fortune in the cities.

20 There are differences between Solu and Khumbu in the stage structures of weddings.

21 One body of data on resistance is the symbolism of the marriage rites themselves; most of the symbolism expresses the bride's family's reluctance to part with its daughter. There is also a great deal of antagonism at weddings, both symbolic and real. But a discussion of Sherpa weddings is beyond the scope of the present work.

22 It is perhaps not surprising that several of Hlakpu's sons became monks, for ultimately if parents are tenacious enough, and powerful enough personalities, a child may come to see the truth of the radical religious analysis of the problems of family structure, and take the full step of asceticism as its solution (Paul, 1970: passim).

23 One piece of evidence for the cultural encouragement of parents locating their identities in their children may perhaps be seen in the growing popularity of teknonymy. The practice seems relatively new, and is only prevalent among the Solu Sherpas who are said, by Khumbu Sherpas, to have borrowed it from the Nepalese. But it would seem to indicate a trend in the direction of further strengthening the patterns discussed here.

24 Far from developing naturally in individuals, however, it would seem that the rites of marriage are partly structured in such a way as to foster this transformation for the individual. Unfortunately, again, analysis of weddings is beyond the scope of the present discussion.

25 This woman had a five-year-old son and an infant, and her husband was out of town. She really could not observe the holiday, as it would leave her children untended for four days. The baby was still breast feeding, and while someone theoretically could have taken care of the boy, in general Sherpas do not take care of children from other families, and it is not common for Sherpa parents to free themselves from child care by farming out children in this way for any period of time. It is clear that if parents have only small children, it would be virtually impossible for them both to observe Nyungne, and for a mother with a nursing infant it is quite impossible. Thus the point (taken up in the next section) that younger parents would not feel a need to observe Nyungne because they have not yet begun to experience "abandonment" by children is reinforced by the practical difficulties of leaving small children untended in a system where child care is almost exclusively the responsibility of the nuclear family. This exclusiveness of child care, in turn, would tend to reinforce the tight parent–child bond early in life.

26 Because the value of altruism theoretically applies to everyone, the rite is open to people of all ages and stages of life (except children). But because the rite is de facto observed largely by postparents, it may be speculated that it is only after, or in the process of, severing the particularistic ties with one's own children, that one may begin to be truly capable of, or driven to, universalizing those sentiments vis-á-vis the larger social world.

27 E.g., Guenther: 32, 107.

28 Perhaps some individuals do charitable acts of some sort after Nyungne on an ad hoc basis. I have no data on this, but at any rate there is no explicit tradition or norm for it.

29 In Dzemu the "Gelungma Palma" text is read on Nyungne. Von Fürer-Haimendorf notes that the Gelungma Palma text is read in the Kunde and Khumjung village Nyungne observances (182), but does not cite the legend. One of my lama informants on the other hand seemed to think the use of this text was confined to Dzemu and one other Solu village, and further that it was being replaced by the Tuchi Chumbu text favored by the powerful Tibetan refugee lama who had established himself as the highest religious authority in the area. Tuchi Chumbu is a takbu (fierce) manifestation of Cherenzi.

30 In the classic rite of passage the participants are, as noted, "segregated" from normal social relations, and the ensuing liminal phase further classically involves engendering in the participants some sort of asociality or antisociality (van Gennep; V. Turner). But these elements are normally interpreted as part of the death-and-rebirth scenario: The initiates are symbolically reduced to such a state in order to

be reborn into a new status and in order to be open to the attitudes and orientations consistent with that new status. In the Sherpa case, however, and perhaps in all Buddhist cases, this antisociality is to a large extent an end in itself. At the extreme, one who underwent such rites and experienced their full effect might become a solitary hermit like Milarepa, or, more likely for these particular people, mendicant religious widow(er)s (*genchu*). And while hermithood or genchu are clearly "new roles" themselves, they are roles of permanent liminality or marginality.

31 Prostrations are part of every ritual performance (see above, note 9). Konjok is not specifically invoked during Nyungne, but then neither is he specifically invoked during any other ritual. His presence seems simply to be assumed, and evoked by the act of shawa (prostration) itself.

Just who or what Konjok is, to the Sherpa mind, seems very hazy, but suffice it to say that he (or it) is thought of as the ultimate ground of the universe, from which all levels of being derive, as well as a creator god in a more material sense, responsible in an ongoing way for the specific sensible forms of the animate world. And it is he/it to whom one prays for help in situations of grave danger or distress. And every time one performs prostrations and recites the refuge formula, one takes refuge in Konjok, that is, in the Konjok Sum or Triple Gem of the religion.

Because Konjok both created and helps humanity, humanity is both indebted to him and dependent upon him. His name also appears in the parental proverb concerning the hierarchy of forces of aid in the universe: (from lowest to highest) father, mother, lama. On all of these counts, then, Konjok, like Cherenzi, is a divinity with parental connotations, and also like Cherenzi, he seems to be a composite parent. While he is not as overtly androgynous as Cherenzi, his gender is ambiguous (or nonexistent) and the proverb relates him to both father and mother.

32 Once again the proverb – "Father konjok lowest, mother konjok higher, lama konjok highest" – takes on new significance. We can now see that this is not just a description of the hierarchy of forces of aid in the cosmos, although it is presented as such. It is also a paradigm of movement or progression, from family (father and mother) to religion as the ultimate refuge and resting place.

33 Especially in view of the Sherpas' rather sparse sex life – see Paul, 1970: 445–50.

34 Theoretically it is possible to decide to become a monk after marriage, although one must have the wife's permission. But such cases rarely arise.

35 Neither men nor women are expected to be virgins at marriage, but both are expected to be sexually faithful afterwards. Adultery is a heavy sin.

36 An orphan will generally be taken over by a sibling of the deceased father, but its fate is very variable. In some cases it might be treated as no more than a servant, and no other group or collectivity has the power or feels the responsibility to intervene. For solitary old people the situation may be even more extreme. They may literally have no place to go, and these are in fact the primary people who become genchu, religious mendicants. Such people are virtually the only beggars one sees in Sherpa society. They adopt religious trappings (and indeed perhaps make a serious commitment to the religion; they have good enough reason to do so), lodge in monasteries or temples, and go about begging for food.

Begging, in turn, is thus almost synonymous with not having a family. People who have families, even if desperately poor, would never beg. They might work for wages, occasionally steal, or most likely move to a city to find work. Monks and nuns on the other hand are enjoined to beg, and this signifies among other things their having symbolically cut their family ties.

37 It is possible to argue that tight family structure, particularly tight mother-son bonds, may *directly* reproduce ascetic practice, through sons who find the

parental bond so difficult to break that they choose monasticism rather than marriage (Paul, 1970: 557–8). I will not pursue this line of analysis here.

38 There is an added incentive in modern times, if an individual is earning cash
through outside labor (e.g., from mountaineering). Any income of any member is
theoretically available to all members of the family, as long as the income-earning
member has not been formally separated from the family by the rites of marriage.
Thus a person cannot refuse money to parents or siblings, and further cannot consider it as a loan to be repaid. Once one has completed the rites of marriage, however, these norms no longer prevail; while people continue to find it difficult to say
no to a parent's or sibling's request for money, it may (especially in the case of a
sibling) be counted as a loan with an expectation of repayment.

4. Hospitality: problems of exchange, status, and authority

1 The status hierarchy of females is undoubtedly more interesting and complex
than is known. While in general it simply parallels that of the males, the women's
husbands and fathers, this is not entirely the case. Thus when, early in my stay, I
asked someone who was the richest man in town, the informant named a woman
who was the wife of one of the lower "big people," and it seemed that her seating
status among the women at parties was higher than that of her husband among the
men. Indeed her husband was often away on business, a point that may be both
cause and effect of his wife's status. On the one hand, his extended absences were
probably one of the conditions that allowed his wife's economic skills to flourish,
yet on the other hand he may have been staying away from local affairs because he
was somewhat embarrassed by his wife's energy and success.

2 Three major types of transaction are not conducted within a hospitality
format: sale, wage, and alms giving. In all three cases the point seems to be that, in
engaging in these transactions, one is not "being social." All three types symbolically stand outside the ongoing social life of the community.

3 All these statements were spontaneously volunteered. Each of the interviews
with shamans was private, and none heard the others' statements.

4 Perhaps the pleasures of sex are also implied, although erotic pleasure is never
specifically evoked in the heavenly images of great sensuous enjoyment.

5 The highly sinful status of theft is significant in a private-property society.

6 The verb "eat" is also used to mean "inherit," and here the usage is morally
neutral in tone. But the general notion that one "eats" wealth does not simply
mean "consume" in an abstract way. The eating metaphor is still a live metaphor,
and people make eating gestures with their hands when they use the word "eat" in
the context of money or property rather than food.

7 Elsewhere, I have recounted this myth in more detail and offered a fuller
analysis of it (Ortner, 1973a).

8 For a fuller discussion of these points, again see Ortner, 1973a.

9 While beer is said to be sinful rather than polluting, its effects, in cultural
theory, are identical to the subjective effects of pollution. This is seen in the bit of
folklore that recounts the invention of beer by the Guru Rimpoche. He included
among its many wonderful ingredients owl's eye and tiger's heart, and this explains
why, when people get drunk, some get sleepy while others get belligerent. The two
types of drunkenness parallel exactly the two types of polluted states, the one in
which one is dull and lethargic, the other in which one is emotionally agitated
and aroused.

10 Apparently there are some elected officials with authority to enforce certain

regulations in some other Sherpa communities (von Fürer-Haimendorf, 1964: 104), but this was not the case in the village in which I worked, nor, as far as I know, throughout most of the southern Sherpa region of Solu in which Dzemu is located. For the record, among the Sherpas the village lamas are not political figures.

11 It should be noted that some Sherpas do act as absentee feudal-type land-lords in other tribal areas. They own tracts of land, have it farmed by a tenant farmer who must give up half the produce, and can even occasionally call upon these tenants (*pishingba*) for free labor in the landlord's home fields, and in his house for major hospitality events when extra hands are needed. But I am aware of no instances of such feudal relationships within the Sherpas' home territory of Solu-Khumbu, relationships *between* Sherpas as landlord and tenant.

12 In addition to these structural factors, sheer age will eventually raise an individual's status, other factors being equal. A reasonably respected old man will sit quite high up in the line at a party, but this fact plays little role in the system as such. His children and descendants will be accorded seats on the basis of their "real" status.

13 These attitudes may well be changing. See note 7, Chapter 2.

14 "Big" status may of course turn into real power. Big people nowadays get elected to the district panchayat council, and panchayat representatives in turn may tend to become agents of the Nepalese government, rather than representatives of the people. But the panchayat system, at least out in the hills at the time I was in the field, was still in an embryonic stage of development.

15 The pun is between *kha tongba* ("mouth empty") and *kha tong(up)* (call, invite, literally "mouth send").

16 The Sherpas, by the way, think Westerners fart too much. It is of course difficult to get objective comparative data on this, but it may be a matter of Western stomachs not being geared to Sherpa hospitality.

17 This pattern continues into adulthood. People do not like to convey one person's excuses to another. They will generally only report an abbreviated and unenthusiastic version of them, perhaps only the refusal itself, without the reasons that were given.

18 It should be noted that monks never protest gifts, never act out the forms of secular hospitality etiquette. A monk is supposed to help people make merit by accepting their alms, and perhaps he would be betraying his duty if he even *seemed* to refuse such an act. Yet it also seems relevant that a monk, by definition, never materially reciprocates a gift (this would negate the meritoriousness of the giver's act), and thus need not express, even symbolically, a fear of being placed under personal obligation by accepting it. (The monk's unprotesting acceptance of any-thing given him may fuel, at some unperceived level, the Sherpas' occasionally expressed notion that monks are even greedier than lay people.)

19 These points apply to spheres of action outside the workings of the mutal-aid system. It is precisely the distinctive feature of the mutual-aid system that exchange may be taken for granted. But the mutual-aid system only operates in very restricted contexts — see Chapter 2.

20 Such joking in American adolescent culture also has status implications. It is (or used to be) called "ranking" or "ranking out," at least in Newark, New Jersey, where I grew up. In more modern parlance, we also speak of "putting down," and refer to a well-aimed piece of antagonistic wit as a "put-down."

21 To some extent, the seating string is also deployed at rituals in the temple.

22 Ideally, if this suggestion has any force, the food is probably delayed long enough to let the joking work out as much as possible of the content and feeling it is dealing with. While again this would not be deliberate on the part of the host, it

does seem significant that the food is almost never served until quite late in the party.

23 This is the term (*lawa*) that von Fürer-Haimendorf found used in Khumbu (1964). I used the term, following his usage, when I first arrived in Dzemu, and it was accepted and understood. But eventually someone told me that lawa, though not incorrect, was not really "nice," and the term current in Dzemu for ritual sponsors was *chiwa*. I do not know what, if any, literal meaning this term may have.

5. Exorcisms: problems of wealth, pollution, and reincarnation

1 In the broadest sense, kurim could be glossed as "rites of protection" (in this-worldly endeavors). Thus one informant included in the kurim category the *tse-uong* rite, in which people consume specially consecrated dough pellets and beer for the purpose of strengthening the life force. Kurim would also include a variety of recitations, without enactment of either offerings to gods or confrontations with demons, for the protection of households and the curing of sick people. The only rituals that are probably not categorized as kurim are those enacted almost entirely for merit making, whose focus, in other words, is other worldly.

2 There are further problems in defining the category for analysis. Shamans, village lamas, and monks all do exorcistic rituals, that is, rituals involving direct confrontation and struggle with evil forces. Shamans and lamas do similar curing rituals, with very similar structures, but shaman work is not classified as *choa*, religious work, and shaman exorcisms, no matter how similar they appear to lama exorcisms, are not called kurim. Even further, exorcisms performed in villages for lay people, by shamans *or* lamas, are specifically considered lower "lay people's" religion work and must not be attended by monks. The only lay village rituals in which monks participate at all are funerals, and the monks dramatically troop out at the end of the funeral proper, leaving the village lamas to conduct the exorcism with which every funeral concludes. Yet every monastery has an annual exorcism (Mani-Rimdu) that is very similar to the annual village-temple exorcism (Dumji) in form and content. Villagers attend the monastery festivals, while monks do not attend the village festivals. In sum, Sherpa religion as an *analytic* category is consistent throughout its modes in stressing rites of exorcism. But the *cultural* category of "religion" excludes some of these practices, and further subdivides and sub-classifies others. These exclusions and classifications are primarily related to different categories of practitioners and will not be discussed further here.

3 Thread crosses (*mdos*) are much used in Tibetan and Sikkimese exorcisms. The demons are said to be trapped or ensnared in them, and then the whole thing is destroyed (see Waddell, Nebesky-Wojkowitz, Gorer). But in Sherpa exorcisms the thread crosses seem to have lost this meaning, and the term mdos (which I transcribe as *do*) seems to have been generalized to mean the ritual item, of what-ever form, into which the evil beings are lured in order to be got rid of. Hence the tiger exorcism is called a *do dzongup* (getting rid of the do), but "do" seems to refer to the entire effigy complex, including tiger, human figures, thread crosses, banners, etc. The tiger effigy alone, which is the specific receptacle for the demons, is called a *sende* (= "dough demon"?).

4 It should be noted that there is virtually no representation of giving pleasing offerings to the demons in the do dzongup. In this respect, all three Sherpa perfor-mances I witnessed differ from the only description I have found of this rite in the literature, in which it is noted that pleasing offerings are strewn around the tiger on his tray: "morsels of every kind of eatables, grains, fruits, spices, including raw meat

and wine; also a few small coins of silver and copper" (Waddell: 495n). Waddell also provides a few lines of the lamas' incantations leading up to the disposal of the tiger: "O death-demon do thou now leave this house and go and oppress our enemies. We have given you food, fine clothes and money. Now be off far from here! Begone to the country of our enemies!!! Begone!!!" (ibid.)

5   The two are also performed together at the annual Dumji village temple exorcism. It seems however, at least in the context of funerals, that the do dzongup may be performed without the gyepshi, but not vice versa.

6   The ceremony may be reduced by a factor of four — twenty-five of each offering.

7   By the same token, it gets much more treatment in the literature of Tibetan Buddhism. See Nebesky-Wojkowitz.

8   It is not at all clear where the *dü* have come from in relation to the funeral. The performance of the gyepshi is the first they have been heard of in the entire proceedings. The dü seem to be a more general type of demon, who vie with *de* in the Sherpa system to be the generic demons of the system. Some people actually said that de were a special kind of dü, but the de seem to have more of a role in the popular imagination, while the dü seem to represent a Buddhist attempt to supersede the de with a higher and more general type, whose main attribute is that they can be dealt with (read: are created by) Buddhist myth and ritual. While both de and dü are greedy, vicious, cannibalistic, and antireligious (as any proper demon must be), dü show up mainly in tales and rituals as being defeated by lamas, while de perform more specific and immediate antisocial and antipersonal acts (especially attacking hospitality events) and can be combated by lay people and local lamas without the help of higher representatitives of the religion.

9   For a fuller development of these points, see Ortner (n.d.a).

10   Not, however, sex. The demons by and large do not have sexual connotations.

11   We culturally distinguish social greed as envy. The Sherpas have this distinction, and the envious evil spirits are called *pem*. Pem cause individual illness and are treated in individual curing exorcisms. The stress on greed rather than envy in the collective orthodox rites seems part of the general religious tendency to desocialize all affective problems, to see them as matters of individual private urges having nothing to do with social relations. The point is analogous to the stress on sex rather than marriage as the focus of asceticism, as discussed in Chapter 3. (See Ortner, n.d.b.)

12   Two types of people are culturally said to be greedier than others: monastics, and women (not necessarily in that order, or in the same breath). I will discuss the problem of monks in the next chapter. Women are unfortunately beyond the scope of this book.

A case may also be made for the category of high-status outsiders as referents of the greedy predatory demons. The high-status outside world is slowly but surely encroaching on Sherpa society in a systematic way. The Nepalese state, for example, is becoming every "hungrier" and "greedier" to the Sherpas, as it applies and extends its taxation system more efficiently, and as it begins to enforce a land-reform law that could, if fully carried out, greatly alter the face of Sherpa society. During the annual Dumji exorcism festival, a wealthy and high-status man from another village interrupted the dancing with a long drunken monologue. He vented resentment of the king and government of Nepal, which threatened to make particular inroads into his life. Because he was wealthy and had large landholdings, he would be taxed more heavily, and might even lose some of his land. Again this line of analysis — demons as symbols of the high-status outside world — leads beyond the scope of the present discussion.

13 This point will be significant in light of the discussion in the next chapter, where we shall see that nondrinking is considered an antisocial gesture. Because the chief mode of "persuading" someone to cooperate (yangdzi) involves plying him with drink, the nondrinker is less accessible to being manipulated into cooperation. The point will be used with reference to monks, and to the ascetic ethic generally, as being antisocial, but we can see that if the Sherpa "big people" do not drink as part of their process of "Brahminization," then they would fall into the same category. In other words, there is a convergence of symbolism (not drinking) here for two different groups from two different sources (religious ideals, secular status mobility) which nonetheless winds up expressing and regenerating the same point – social inaccessibility.

14 For a full development of these points, see Ortner, 1973a.

15 It should perhaps be stressed here that sex in the Sherpa system tends to go on the "physical" side, not just because it is a physical bodily function, but because it is associated ultimately with dullness rather than with the violent passions. As one lama said, in a statement I have cited elsewhere: "People who indulge frequently in sexual intercourse, or who eat a lot or sleep a lot, are like animals, and will be animals in the next life. These things distract from study. Monks should keep their eyes 'on the path,' on their books, and not be distracted. The more indulged in, the more these things dull the senses."

16 But the notion that any given person "contains" both tendencies, and thus the analytic point that the deceased should also be seen as "releasing" and not just "attracting" demons, is not totally unexpressed in the funeral and the conceptions surrounding death. For in fact there is a popular fear that the deceased will turn into a greedy predatory ghost (nerpa), if he is not given a proper funeral and does not achieve, through the funeral process, appropriate detachment from the world of the living and movement into a new state of being. The demonic aspects of the person of the deceased thus are in fact given recognition, since the process of "helping" the deceased achieve a good incarnation is also explained as defending the living against his return as a nerpa. Nerpa, like demons, are polluting (and dangerous), and the fear of nerpa may be interpreted as supporting the view that the person *contains* demonic as well as physical tendencies, and releases them when he disintegrates.

17 The term generally used for the nonmaterial element that leaves the body at death, and to which all the readings are addressed, is the *namshi*, which refers to the aggregate of the perceptual and cognitive faculties. The Sherpas consider that there are six "senses," the *"namshi tuk"* (tuk = six), the five perceptions of sight, hearing, taste, smell, and touch, as well as what we would call mind, *sem*. The situation is actually more complex than this, as there are other nonmaterial aspects of the person, but a consideration of these would be beyond the scope of the present discussion. For purposes of simplification, I will refer to the nonmaterial element of the person dealt with by the funeral rites as the spirit or soul of the deceased. The namshi is generally translated in Buddhist literature as the "knower," emphasizing that this is the part of the self that is cognitive.

18 Although I shall not analyze the cremation itself, it might simply be noted that its exorcismic aspect consists of calling, attracting, and inviting the demons, and actively feeding them the corpse.

19 The Sherpas do not use the term "karma" but it is a standard term in Buddhist literature, and I shall use it for convenience. In Sherpa the term for Buddhist retribution, the cosmic principle of cause and effect, is *le*.

20 See Matsunaga and Matsunaga for even more vivid examples.

21 There are certain restrictions on this point. People who were very good in

their past lives are born with good spiritual tendencies and are the ones who become monks; monks in turn have the best chance to achieve salvation. Women, on the other hand, have no direct chance for salvation; they can only hope to be reborn as men and from that position aim for higher things. The point that no one is intrinsically better or worse off in his opportunity to strive for salvation applies primarily to normal males within the normal social scale.

22 Obviously these built-in tendencies of the reincarnation system parallel the actual economic advantages of wealth, and the disadvantages of poverty, discussed at the beginning of the chapter.

23 And this morning there was an event (the *kungsang*) at which all the people in the host's reciprocity network brought him gifts of food, money, and beer, and everyone, by tradition, got utterly drunk. Drunkenness is culturally considered to be a state of psychic disintegration, contributing further (from an analytic point of view) to the pollution that the exorcisms will be rectifying.

24 The cremation, as noted, is also an exorcism, and it follows a sequence of psychic and social disintegration that has precisely the same structure as the sequence of events leading up to the final grand exorcisms.

25 Tibetans also had gyepshi and other rituals with dough scapegoats as well.

26 This particular lama had a phenomenal knowledge of ritual and doctrinal detail, and generally when he "forgot" something it was of a sexual or otherwise esoteric nature.

27 To avoid confusion, it should be noted again that the Tibetans had both gyepshi exorcisms with dough lut, and the human scapegoat ceremony. The Sherpas have combined the gyepshi, which they use in quite orthodox form, with the do dzongup, an apparently heterodox ritual in which the key figures, the peshangba, are nonetheless quite clearly modeled on the Tibetan human scapegoats.

28 The suggestion that the highly orthodox gyepshi runs contrary to the popular will expressed in the tiger exorcism may explain why the Sherpas, who are usually reasonably forthcoming with exegesis on their own rituals, were unable to come up with anything beyond "feeding the demons" in explaining the gyepshi. I made many attempts to get people to explain what was going on in gyepshi, what the various items signified, and so forth, but virtually to no avail.

29 In light of the point that this ritual is recognized to be somewhat defiant of orthodoxy, it may not be insignificant that the peshangba, representing the ordinary lay people, take the cymbals away *from the lamas,* and complete the ritual on their own terms and in fact in a way that lamas say is technically incorrect (attempting to kill the demons outright).

6. Offering rituals: problems of religion, anger, and social cooperation

1 One could also, as in the preceding chapter, relate the monastic sector to the rich, and to the problem of social hierarchy; here a different aspect of the problem is being brought into focus.

2 For a discussion of some aspects of the sang ritual, see Ortner, 1973a.

3 Quotations from Waddell: 431.

4 The torma also has phallic connotations. These are not orthodox, but are nonetheless fairly overt in the culture (Paul, 1970: 352). This connotation will not be incorporated into the analysis, although it would not, I think, be contrary to it.

5 In the history of Tibetan Buddhism, celibate monasticism did not become a generally accepted ideal until the fifteenth century, when there was a successful reform movement that called for a return to a purer Buddhism and that became

institutionalized as the Gelugpa sect. The Nyingmawa sect resisted this reform for a long time, and continued to permit its lamas to marry and remain in the villages serving the lay people's religious needs. Later, however, this sect (still in Tibet) began to mimic the politically and religiously dominant Gelugpa sect's monastic system, while retaining the institution of married lamas (*banzin*). The whole thing has not fully sorted itself out even today, among the Sherpas. Some Sherpa monasteries were celibate from their founding; some were "married monasteries," communities composed of "monks" and their families; and there were and are married lamas in the villages. One "married monastery" started a reform toward celibacy within the present generation. It now only accepts celibate candidates, and although the married monks have not actually been purged, they cannot sit on the same row of seats in the temple as the celibate monks.

6 For a discussion of the difficult and contradictory role of village lamas vis-à-vis monks on the one hand and lay people on the other, see Paul, 1970: 582–8.

7 There may be at least one other (symbolic) basis for lay ambivalence about monks. The only times monks systematically come into villages and homes are for funerals. Monks thus not only cut themselves off from lay life; they are associated largely with death. To meet a monk in a dream is a bad omen, suggesting a funeral.

8 For an extended discussion of the Sherpa system of supernatural beings, see Ortner, n.d.a.

9 Actually there are four mood aspects: *shiwa* (ZHi Ba) − "mild"; *gyewa* (rGyas Pa) − "increasing or expansive"; *'ong* (dBang) − "powerful"; and *takbu* or *towu* (Drags Po) − "fierce" (Ekvall: 169). But the Sherpas largely operate with the shiwa/ takbu opposition. As a general rule, the high gods have both benign and fierce aspects, while the lower guardian gods (*sungma*) have only fierce aspects for the Sherpas.

10 For a discussion of this issue from another point of view, see Paul n.d.a.

11 While the general model is hospitality, the context makes clear the assumption that this is yangdzi, or "persuasion" hospitality, in which the guests are entertained as a prelude to making some demand of them. The tso at the conclusion of the ritual is also referred to as a party, but it is distinct from the body of the ritual, and as we shall see, it is more in the nature of generalized, celebratory, and non-instrumental hospitality.

12 See note 13, Chapter 5.

13 Beyer calls these offerings "sense gratifications," and his entire discussion assumes that these are offerings *to* (not *of*) the senses of a god (157). But each offering is presented with a recitation of a verse, and the texts of these verses seem to me ambiguous on the of/to question. For example:

> The most excellent of sounds
> in all the worldly realms of the ten directions
> (all that is melodious to the hearing of the Conquerors)
> are emanated as hosts of the Lady Diamond Sound;
> and these we offer up to the hosts of glorious gurus.

There is no explanation of why the line, "all that is melodious to the hearing . . ." is in parentheses, and it may represent a later addition that distorts the original meaning in the direction of "gratification *to* the senses." At the same time, "emanated as hosts of the Lady Diamond Sound" strikes me as implying that the offering is an aspect *of* the deity, rather than *to* her, or at least that it can be read either way. I am fairly certain, however, that I understood my Sherpa lama informant correctly, and if he gave an idiosyncratic/unorthodox interpretation, it still seems significant that he came up with this particular one. It should be noted that there is actually an offering torma used in certain rites that is a quite realistic (and rather gruesome) dough composite complex of sense organs — ears, nose, tongue, etc. Here there is no question that the offering is an offering *of* the human senses to the gods.

14 Shiwa gods, benign and pure, theoretically eschew these delicacies. Yet my notes show these items on altars of shiwa rituals. Possibly their presence could be explained as offerings to the ferocious guardians of the shiwa gods. In any case, most Sherpa rituals are directed toward the takbu divinities, who demand this sort of fare.

15 The orthodox function of this is to facilitate the process of visualization of the god for the ritual practitioner.

16 *Tre* and *phat* are "mystic spells used by wizards — *phat* means break or smash!" The hymn is translated by Waddell (437). He ends with "etc., etc., etc., etc." — obviously there is much more in the same vein. For a different translation, see Beyer: 211ff. Beyer's translation, which is quite beautiful, downplays the sharpness and anger evident in Waddell's.

17 It should be noted that Tibetan Buddhism, being highly psychologically sophisticated, does not miss this point in its esoteric practices. High-level meditation consists of mentally constructing, bit by bit, detailed mandalas, which in turn become the source of mystical comprehension of cosmic unity. "The mandala born, thus, of an interior impulse became, in its turn, a support for meditation, an external instrument to provoke and procure such visions in quiet concentration and meditation. *The intuitions which, at first, shone capricious and unpredictable are projected outside the mystic who, by concentrating his mind upon them, rediscovers the way to reach his secret reality*" (Tucci: 37, emphasis added).

18 Not just gods; the best, most meritorious objects of charitable giving are high reincarnate lamas, who are the objects of so much donation that they are generally quite rich.

7. Conclusions: Buddhism and society

1 All statements about the Thai case, above and following, are from Tambiah, passim.

2 It is actually more comparable in many respects to the Sinhalese case. See Yalman, 1964, 1969, and Gombrich.

3 Spiro (192) states that expiation or atonement is "foreign to Buddhist thought." In the strictest sense these are Judeo-Christian concepts that are probably not found in any other religions. But Nyungne comes close to being a Buddhist rite of atonement.

4 Except in funerals, where the living kin make merit for the deceased. The Sherpa funeral resembles the Thai funeral quite closely, and Tambiah remarks on the impressive consistency of funeral rites across the various Buddhist societies (192).

5 This is not to say that orthodox Buddhist doctrine has no impact, even problematic impact, upon Thai society, but only that it has been integrated differently than it has been among the Sherpas.

6 See Ortner, n.d.a., for a discussion of the Sherpa view of human nature.

7 It is noteworthy that, among the Thai, gods are not propitiated for assistance, but rather receive merit transfers along with members of the family and ancestors (Tambiah: 140).

8 The exception to this point is the funeral, where the family of the deceased has some specialized role qua family of the deceased.

9 To repeat, *all* rituals, including Nyungne and exorcisms, are framed within the structure of the generalized offering ritual — that is, the gods are conjured into torma at the beginning, the specific business of the ritual is then conducted, and there is a tso at the end. Thus in some sense each rite is a microcosm of the overall ritual calendar, constraining the orthodox perspective within the secular.

Bibliography

Aziz, Barbara. 1974. "Some Notes about Descent and Residence in Tibetan
Societies," in C. von Fürer-Haimendorf (ed.), *Contributions to the Anthropology of Nepal.* Warminster, Wilts.: Aris and Phillips.
n.d. "Social Cohesion and Reciprocation in a Tibetan Community in Nepal,"
forthcoming in James Fisher (ed.)., *Himalayan Anthropology: The Indo-
Tibetan Interface.* World Anthropology Series. The Hague: Mouton.
Beyer, Stephan. 1973. *The Cult of Tara.* Berkeley: University of California Press.
Burke, Kenneth. 1957. *The Philosophy of Literary Form,* New York: Vintage.
1968. *Language as Symbolic Action.* Berkeley: University of California Press.
Clarke, Sir Humphrey. 1958. *The Message of Milarepa.* London: John Murray.
Ekvall, Robert B. 1964. *Religious Observances in Tibet.* Chicago: University of
Chicago Press.
Evans-Wentz, W. Y. (ed.). 1957. *The Tibetan Book of the Dead.* London: Oxford
University Press.
Funke, Friedrich W. 1969. *Religiöses Leben der Sherpa.* Innsbruck and Munich:
Universitäts Verlag Wagner.
Geertz, Clifford. 1957a., "Ethos, World-View, and the Analysis of Sacred Symbols."
Antioch Review 17: 421–37.
1957b. "Ritual and Social Change: A Javanese Example," *American Anthro-
pologist* 59: 32–54.
1966. "Religion as a Cultural System," in M. Banton, ed., *Anthropological
Approaches to the Study of Religion.* London: Tavistock.
1972. "Deep Play: Notes on the Balinese Cockfight." *Daedalus,* winter 1972:
1–37.
1973. *The Interpretation of Cultures.* New York: Basic Books.
Goldstein, Melvyn C. 1971a. "Taxation and the Structure of a Tibetan Village."
Central Asiatic Journal 15(1): 1–27.
1971b. "Serfdom and Mobility: An Examination of the Institution of 'Human
Lease' in Traditional Tibetan Society." *Journal of Asian Studies* 30(3): 521–34.
1973. "The Circulation of Estates in Tibet: Reincarnation, Land and Politics."
Journal of Asian Studies 32(3): 445–55.
Gombrich, Richard F. 1971. *Precept and Practice: Traditional Buddhism in the
Rural Highlands of Ceylon.* Oxford: Clarendon Press.
Gordon, Antoinette. 1959. *The Iconography of Tibetan Lamaism.* Tokyo and
Rutland, Vt.: Charles E. Tuttle.
Gorer, Geoffrey. 1967. *Himalayan Village.* New York: Basic Books.
Guenther, Herbert. 1966. *Tibetan Buddhism without Mystification.* Leiden: E. J.
Brill.

Jaeschke, H. A. (ed.). 1965. *A Tibetan–English Dictionary*. New York: Ungar.
Jerstad, Luther G. 1969. *Mani-Rimdu, Sherpa Dance Drama*. Seattle: University of Washington Press.
Lévi-Strauss, Claude. 1963a. "The Effectiveness of Symbols," in *Structural Anthropology*. Tr. C. Jacobson and B. G. Schoepf. New York: Basic Books.
    1963b. *Totemism*. Tr. Rodney Needham. Boston: Beacon.
    1966. *The Savage Mind*. Tr. anon. Chicago: University of Chicago Press.
Lienhardt, Godfrey. 1961. *Divinity and Experience: The Religion of the Dinka*. Oxford: Clarendon Press.
Matsunaga, Daigan, and Alicia Matsunaga. 1971. *The Buddhist Concept of Hell*. New York: Philosophical Library.
Mauss, Marcel. 1954. *The Gift*. Tr. Ian Cunnison. New York: Free Press.
Miller, Beatrice D. 1956. "Ganye and Kidu: Two Formalized Systems of Mutual Aid among the Tibetans." *Southwestern Journal of Anthropology* 12: 157–70.
Munn, Nancy. 1969. "The Effectiveness of Symbols in Murngin Rite and Myth," in Robert F. Spencer (ed.), *Forms of Symbolic Action*. Proceedings of the Annual Spring Meeting, American Ethnological Society. Seattle: University of Washington Press.
    1971. "The Transformation of Subjects into Objects in Walbiri and Pitjantjatjara Myth," in R. Berndt (ed.), *Australian Aboriginal Anthropology*. Nedlands: University of Western Australia Press.
Myerhoff, Barbara. 1974. *Peyote Hunt*. Ithaca, N.Y.: Cornell University Press.
Nash, Manning (ed.). 1966. *Anthropological Studies in Theravada Buddhism*. Cultural Report Series No. 13. New Haven: Yale University Southeast Asia Studies.
Nebesky-Wojkowitz, Réné de. 1956. *Oracles and Demons of Tibet*. The Hague: Mouton.
Oppitz, Michael. 1968. *Geschichte und Sozialordnung der Sherpa*. Innsbruck and Munich: Universitäts Verlag Wagner.
Ortner, Sherry B. 1966. (Sherry Ortner Paul.) "Tibetan Circles: An Essay in Symbolic Analysis." Unpublished Master's thesis. Department of Anthropology, University of Chicago.
    1970. (Sherry Ortner Paul.) "Food for Thought: A Key Symbol in Sherpa Culture." Unpublished Doctoral dissertation. Department of Anthropology, University of Chicago.
    1973a. "Sherpa Purity." *American Anthropologist* 75: 49–63.
    1973b. "On Key Symbols." *American Anthropologist* 75: 1338–46.
    n.d.a. "The White-Black Ones: The Sherpa View of Human Nature," forthcoming in James Fisher (ed.), *Himalayan Anthropology: The Indo-Tibetan Interface*. World Anthropology Series. The Hague: Mouton.
    n.d.b. "Religion and the Decline of Sherpa Shamanism." Ms.
Paul, Robert A. 1970. "Sherpas and their Religion." Unpublished Doctoral dissertation. Department of Anthropology, University of Chicago.
    1972. "The Thirteenth Dance of Mani Rimdu." Paper delivered at symposium, "Structuralism Today," Sarah Lawrence College. Ms.
    n.d.a. "Instinctive Aggression in Man." Ms.
    n.d.b. *Sherpa Monasticism: The Dynamics of Religious Role Choice*, Ms.
    n.d.c. "A Mantra and its Meanings," forthcoming in *The Psychoanalytic Study of Society*.
Ricoeur, Paul. 1969. *The Symbolism of Evil*. Tr. Emerson Buchanan. Boston: Beacon.

Rosen, Lawrence. n.d. "The Rope of Satan: Social Relations and Reality Bargaining among Moroccan Men and Women." Ms.

Schlagintweit, Emil. 1863. *Buddhism in Tibet.* London: Trübner.

Schneider, David M. 1968. *American Kinship: A Cultural Account.* Englewood Cliffs, N.J.: Prentice-Hall.

Singer, Milton. 1958. "The Great Tradition in a Metropolitan Center: Madras," in M. Singer (ed.), *Traditional India.* Philadelphia: American Folklore Society.

Snellgrove, David L. 1957. *Buddhist Himalaya.* New York: Philosophical Library.

1967. (ed.) *Four Lamas of Dolpo.* Cambridge, Mass.: Harvard University Press.

Spiro, Melford E. 1970. *Buddhism and Society.* New York: Harper & Row.

Suzuki, Beatrice Lane. 1963. *Mahayana Buddhism.* New York: Collier.

Tambiah, Stanley J. 1970. *Buddhism and the Spirit Cults in Northeast Thailand.* New York: Cambridge University Press.

Tucci, Giuseppe. 1961. *The Theory and Practice of the Mandala.* Tr. A. H. Brodrick. London: Rider.

Turner, Terence. 1969. "Oedipus: Time and Structure in Narrative Form." in Robert F. Spencer (ed.), *Forms of Symbolic Action.* Proceedings of the Annual Spring Meeting, American Ethnological Society. Seattle: University of Washington Press.

Turner, Victor. 1967. *The Forest of Symbols.* Ithaca, N.Y.: Cornell University Press.

1969. *The Ritual Process.* Chicago: Aldine.

Van Gennep, Arnold. 1960. *The Rites of Passage.* Chicago: University of Chicago Press.

Von Fürer-Haimendorf, Christoph. 1964. *The Sherpas of Nepal.* Berkeley: University of California Press.

1974 (ed.) *Contributions to the Anthropology of Nepal.* Warminster, Wilts.: Aris & Phillips.

1975. *Himalayan Traders.* New York: St. Martin's Press.

Waddell, L. Austine. 1895. *The Buddhism of Tibet, or Lamaism.* London: W. H. Allen.

Warner, W. Lloyd. 1961. *The Family of God.* New Haven: Yale University Press.

Weber, Max. 1958a. *The Religion of India.* Tr. and ed., H. H. Gerth and D. Martindale. New York: Free Press.

1958b. *The Protestant Ethic and the Spirit of Capitalism.* Tr. Talcott Parsons. New York: Scribner.

1964. *The Sociology of Religion.* Tr. E. Fischoff. Boston: Beacon.

Willis, Janice Dean. 1972. *The Diamond Light of the Eastern Dawn.* New York: Simon and Schuster.

Yalman, Nur. 1964. "The Structure of Sinhalese Healing Rituals," in E. Harper (ed.), *Religion in South Asia.* Seattle: University of Washington Press.

1966. "Dual Organization in Central Ceylon," in Manning Nash (ed.), *Anthropological Studies in Theravada Buddhism.* Cultural Report Series No. 13. New Haven: Yale University Southeast Asia Studies.

1969. "On the Meaning of Food Offerings in Ceylon," in Robert F. Spencer (ed.), *Forms of Symbolic Action.* Proceedings of the Annual Spring Meeting, American Ethnological Society. Seattle: University of Washington Press.

Index

accommodation, in ritual, 4
age, and participation in Nyungne ritual, 58–60
aged parents, prospects for, 46–7
aggregation, in Nyungne ritual, 54–5
agriculture, 13–15
altar
    gyepshi ritual, 96, 97
    offering rituals, 144–7
altruism, and Nyungne, 48–52
anger
    body, hospitality, and, 141–4
    molding, in offering ritual, 149–52
    and regulation of mood, 137–40
animal herds, 16–17
antidrainage symbolism, 40
antirelationalism, religious bias toward, 38–9
ascetic ideology
    and crisis of children's marriages, 43–8
    and family structure, 55–60
atonement, rite of, 3
authority and hospitality, 77–8
autonomy, religious bias toward, 38–9

bazaar, Dorphu, 14
beer
    and hospitality, 81
    and offering ritual, 86
    sinfulness of, 73
body, hospitality, and anger, 141–4
body problem and torma in offering rituals, 132–7
bodying of gods, in offering rituals, 147–8
borrowing and indebtedness, 67–8
Brahmin (Bahun) caste, 27
Burke, Kenneth, 1, 8

cash, ways of earning, 17–18
celibate monasticism, 30–1
celibate monks (tawa), 30
charity, acts of (gyewa-zhinba), 37–8
chepa (offerings), 131
chepi hlamu (offering goddesses), 145
Cherenzi (god), 36, 41, 165
    identification with, 50–1

Chhetri caste, 27
children
    exclusion from Nyungne ritual, 35–6, 53
    inheritance, 20–1
    marriage, as family crisis, 45–8
    and parents, Nyungne symbolism, 41–3
chinche (outside offerings), 144
Chiwong monastery, 31
clan
    lineage, 20
    named, exogamous patrilineal, 18–19
    nuclear family, 20–1
    in regulating marriage, 18–19
closure, family, Nyungne in reinforcing, 57–8
coercion
    civilized, and reproduction of hosts, 85–90
    latent power in ritual, 141
compassion, and mother–child metaphor, 42–3
consciousness, ritual in shaping of, 5
constraints, inner, 26–7
courts, Nepalese, intrusion of, 27–8
crime, ways of handling, 27–8
crops, 14–15
cross-cousin marriage, 19
cultural performances, rituals, 1–3
cultural pluralism, 28–30
culture, defined, 7

Dasain (holiday), 130
daughter, marriage, 20–1
death, pollution of, 106–7
    see also dzongup
demchang (first wedding event), 21
demons
    and gods and problem of moods in offering rituals, 137–40
    greed, social predation, and, 98–103
    in gyepshi exorcism, 118, 119–20
dewa (happiness), 64
dirnmu (demoness), 73
disintegration of self, pollution, and subversion of social order, 103–9
disputes, settlement of, 26–7

191

Divinity and Experience (Lienhardt), 6
divorce rate, 21, 46
do dzongup (exorcism ritual), 93–5
  and dilemma of self and social order, 127
  interpretation of, 122–3
  as purification, 114–17
dowry, 20, 21
drink and hospitality, 68–71
  see also beer
Drolma (goddess), 41–2
  Hymn of Praise to, 150
Dumji festival, 96, 130
dungal (suffering), 64
  and reincarnation, 111
Durkheim, Emile, 65
dutsi (demon juice), 145

economy, 14–18
empty mouth principle and hospitality, 78–82
engagements, broken, 46
environment and origins, Sherpas, 10–14
exorcism rituals, 3, 92–3, 165–7
  and dilemma of self and social order, 125–7
  do dzongup, 93–5
  gyepshi, 94, 95–8
  problem of demons, greed, and social
    predation, 98–103
  problem of pollution, disintegration of
    self, and subversion of social order,
    103–9
  problem of reincarnation theory and social
    order, 110–13
  as purification, 109, 114–20
  and purity/pollution beliefs, 103–9
  solutions of, 113–27
  and status hierarchy, 3
experience
  reorganized, ritual as, 6–7
  ritual in control of, 5

family, 20–1, 22
  as atom of society, 39–41
  and ceremonial life of temple, 24
  closure, Nyungne in reinforcing, 57–8
  corruptive aspects, and religious monasti-
    cism, 44–5
  and crisis of children's marriages, 45–8
  and mutual-aid groups, 22–3
  one-to-one interactions, 23
  structure, and ascetic ideology, 55–60
  subsistence economy, 16
fasting, Nyungne, 35
food
  distribution after religious services, 31
  and hospitality, 64
  power of, 68–74
four dü (demon grouping), 96
functionalism and ritual, 4

funeral feasts (gyowa), 38, 63, 108–9
funeral rituals, 106–9
  see also do dzongup

Geertz, Clifford, 1, 5, 7, 8
Gelungma Palma myth, 51
genchu (religious mendicant widows), 35, 47
generosity
  and status, 76–7
  value of, 65–6
giving and receiving
  etiquette of, 78–82
  problem of, 65–8
glud'gong and peshangba, 120, 121
gods
  bodying, in offering rituals, 147–8
  and demons and problem of moods in
    offering rituals, 137–40
  offering rituals as parties for, 86–7
  and parents and social sentiments as prob-
    lem of Nyungne ritual, 41–3
Gordza clan, 19
grazing stations, 17
greed, 66–7
  demons, social predation, and, 98–103
  and power of food, 72–3
gyepshi (exorcism ritual), 94, 95–8
  and dilemma of self and social order, 127
  as purification, 117–20
  in restoring social hierarchy, 123–5
gyewa-zhinba (acts of charity), 37–8
gyowa (funeral feasts), 38, 63, 108–9

health and food, 70
Hillary, Sir Edmund, 14, 23
hlabeu (curing seance), 63
hlermu (fun), 81
hospitality
  anger, body, and, 141–4
  civilized coercion and reproduction of
    hosts, 85–90
  empty mouth principle and etiquette of
    giving and receiving, 78–82
  mediating religion and social order in
    offering rituals, 152–6
  party, 61–4
  problem of giving and receiving, 65–8
  problem of power of food, 68–74
  seating and joking, 82–5
  and social exchange, 65–8
  status, power, and authority problems,
    74–8
hosts, reproduction, and civilized coercion,
    85–90
household religious ceremonies, 31–2
human nature, individual and family view of,
    160–2
hymn of praise in offering ritual, 148, 150

illness and shamanism, 32
indebtedness and borrowing, 67–8
inheritance
    land, 15–16
    sons, 20–1
inheritance system, and crisis of children's
    marriages, 45

joking
    and seating, 82–5
    and tension, 143

kangsur rites in ritual calendar, 129–30
Khambas (Tibetan immigrant clan), 19
khil-khor torma (senior torma), 145
killing, 27
    as sin, 71–2
kinship and mutual-aid group, 22–3
kirmu (bliss), 71
Konjok, 39, 165
    and prostrations in Nyungne ritual, 53–4
konjok sum, 39
kurim (ritual category), 92–3

Lama clan, 19
lamas vs. monks, 136–7
land inheritance patterns, 15–16
land reform, 28
Lévi-Strauss, Claude, 65
Lienhardt, Godfrey, 5
    on Dinka rituals, 6–7
liminality in Nyungne ritual, 53–4
lineage
    clan, 20
    segmentation, and mutual-aid group seg-
        mentation, 23
    in status hierarchy, 24
luck (yang), 40
lut (dough effigy), 95–6
    in gyepshi exorcism, 118–19
    in restoring social hierarchy, 123–5
    vs. scapegoat and peshangba, 116–17

Mani-Rimdu festival, 63–4, 130, 169
marriage, 19–22
    of children, and ascetic ideology, 43–8
    as extended yangdzi, 161
    and parents' grip on children, 59
    stages, 21–2
married monasteries, 30
Marx, Karl, 65
matrilateral cross-cousin marriage, 19
mediation, in ritual, 4
merit (payin) and sin (dikpa), 36–7
merit making
    Sherpa vs. Thai, 158
    and social atomism as Nyungne problem,
        35–41
models, symbolic, 7–8

monasteries, 30
    Sherpa vs. Thai, 158–9
monasticism
    and corruptive aspects of family, 44–5
    Sherpa vs. Thai, 158
monks vs. lamas, 136–7
monogamy, 21
moods problem, and gods and demons in
        offering rituals, 137–40
moral corruption and power of food, 71–3
mother–son relationship, 42–3
mudra (hand gestures), 150
mutual-aid group (tsenga tsali), 20, 22–3
    and weddings, 56

nangche (inside offerings), 144–5
nerpa (ghost), 66
nuclear family, *see* family
nyingje (compassion)
    imagery surrounding, 50–1
    and mother–son relationship, 42–3
Nyingmawa Tibetan Buddhist sect, 30–1
Nyungne ritual, 34–6, 164–6
    ascetic ideology and family structure,
        55–60
    and fostering of altruism, 48–52
    and parent/child symbolism, 41–3
    as passage to postparenthood, 52–5
    problem of ascetic ideology and crisis of
        children's marriages, 43–8
    problem of gods, parents, and social senti-
        ments, 41–3
    problem of merit making and social
        atomism, 35–41
    in ritual calendar, 129–30
    solutions of ritual, 48

offering rituals, 167–8
    bodying the gods in, 147–8
    gods, demons, and problem of moods in,
        137–40
    hospitality in mediating religion and social
        order, 152–6
    as kurim, 93
    molding of anger in, 149–52
    as parties for gods, 86–7
    and problem of hospitality, anger, and
        body, 141–4
    and ritual calendar, 129–30
    solutions of problems, 144–7
    torma and body problem in, 132–7
old age, prospects for parents in, 46–7
Ongpame, 165
Oppitz, Michael, 46
orientation, transformation in ritual, 6
orthodoxy, Sherpa vs. Thai Buddhism, 158–60

pak (dough lumps), 93

Panchayat council, 27–8
parent/child symbolism, Nyungne, 41–3
parental prospects in old age, 46–7
party, 61-4
    for gods, offering rituals as, 86–7
    as politics, 82–5
patrilateral cross-cousin marriage, 19
Pawa Cherenzi (god), 36, 41, 165
pem (witch), 79
peshangba (ritual clowns), 93–4, 115–16
    and dilemma of self and social order, 126
    symbolism, in resynthesizing social hier-
        archy, 120–2
piety and status, 25
political structure, village, 25–6
politics, party as, 82–5
pollution
    disintegration of self, subversion of social
        order, and, 103–9
    and power of food, 73-4
polyandry, 20
polygyny, 21
population, 12
postparenthood, Nyungne as passage to, 52–5
power of food, 68–74
    and hospitality, 77
prostrations (shawa) in Nyungne ritual, 35,
    53–4
psychic hierarchy, exorcisms in reconstitut-
    ing, 114–20
purification, exorcism as, 109, 114–20
purity/pollution beliefs and exorcisms, 103–9

rakta (menstrual blood), 145
reality bargaining and breakdown of ritual, 1
receiving and giving
    etiquette of, 78–82
    problem of, 65–8
reciprocity relationships with village people,
    23–4
reconciliation in ritual, 4
Refuge formula, 50, 51
reincarnation theory and social order, 110–13
religion, 11, 30–2
    and social order, mediating in offering
        rituals, 152–6
    solution to body problem, 135–6
    as system of meanings, 4–5
religious action, Sherpa vs. Thai, 158–9
religious services
    privately sponsored, 32
    at village temple, 31–2
rich-and-poor symbolism in exorcism, 120–5
Ricoeur, Paul, 74
Rimpoche, Guru, 68–9, 85–6, 165
ritual
    departures from, 3

mechanism, 163–9
Nyungne, 34–6
restructuring of meaning in, 5–6
ritual calendar and offering rituals, 129–32
ritualism of hospitality, 62–3

Samyang monastery, 85–6, 128
sang (purification rite), 35, 131–2
sangche (secret offerings), 145
Sang-ngak texts of Tibetan Buddhism, 30
scapegoats, peshangba as, 115–16
seating
    and joking, 82–5
    and status, 74–5
segmentation, lineage and mutual-aid group,
    22
segregation, in Nyungne ritual, 53
self
    disintegration, and subversion of social
        order, 103–9
    eradication of, 37
    and social order, dilemma of, 125–7
self-regulation, communal, and status, 88–9
sende symbolism, in resynthesizing social
    hierarchy, 122–3
sensual greed and food, 72–3
sensuality, religious devaluation vs. social
    manipulation, 142–3
serkim, 131
shamanism, 32
    and hospitality, 63
shiwa gods, 137
    in offering rituals, 149
sin (dikpa) and merit (payin), 36–7
Singer, Milton, 1
social atomism and merit making as Nyungne
    problem, 35–41
social closure and orthodoxy, 160–1
social control mechanisms, 26
social exchange and hospitality, 65–8
social hierarchy
    gyepshi in restoring, 123–5
    peshangba symbolism in resynthesizing,
        120–2
social order
    and reincarnation theory, 110–13
    and religion, mediating in offering rituals,
        152–6
    and self, dilemma of, 125–7
    subversion, and pollution and disintegra-
        tion of self, 103–9
social organization, 18–30
social predation, demons, and greed, 98–103
social sentiments and gods and parents, as
    problem of Nyungne ritual, 41–3
socioeconomic hierarchy, demons, and greed,
    101–3
Solu-Khumbu, 12–14

son-in-law, resident (maksu), 21
sons, inheritance, 20–1
status
    and communal self-regulation, 88–9
    hierarchy, 24–6
    and hospitality, 74–6
    ranking at secular parties, 3
stinginess, 65–6
subsistence economy, 16

takbu gods, 137
    in offering ritual, 149
Takshindo monastery, 31
tawa (celibate monks), 30
Tengboche monastery, 31
Thami monastery, 31
Tibet, Sherpa link with, 10–11
Tibetan Buddhism, 30–2
tiger exorcism, *see* do dzongup
torma (dough figures), 131–2
    and body problem in offering rituals,
      132–7
torma che (senior torma), 145
totul (Bardo Thodol), reading of, 108–9
trade, 17
tsenga tsali (mutual-aid group), 20, 22–3, 56
tso ceremony
    in Nyungne ritual, 35, 54–5
    in offering rituals, 145, 147

in ritual calendar, 129–30
Tsodukpa monastery, 31
tulku (reincarnate lama), 134

village, 14
village people, reciprocity relationships with,
    23
von Fürer-Haimendorf, Christoph, 148

Waddell, L. Austine, 148
Warner, W. Lloyd, 1
wealth and status, 25, 76–7
wedding
    first event (demchang), 21
    and mutual-aid relationships, 56
    vs. Nyungne ritual, 56–7
well-being and food, 70–1

yang (luck), 40
yangdzi, 63, 161
    as coercion mechanism, 86–7
    and offering ritual, 141–2
    and power of food, 68–70
yang-guup ceremony, 40
Yemba (untouchable clan), 19
yitak, 66

zhindak (host), 87
zom (cow-yak crossbreeds), 16